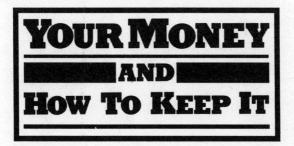

YOUR MONEY
AND
HOW TO KEEP IT

BRIAN COSTELLO

YOUR MONEY

AND

HOW TO KEEP IT

Stoddart

Published in 1985 by Stoddart Publishing Co. Limited
34 Lesmill Road
Toronto, Canada
M3B 2T6

Canandian Cataloguing in Publication Data

Costello, Brian.
  Your money and how to keep it.

Includes index.
ISBN 0-7737-5044-4

1. Finance, Personal.   2. Budgets, Personal.   I. Title.

HG179.C67 1985   332.024   C85-099025-4

Printed and bound in Canada

Mortgage Payment Comparison Chart on page 159 is reprinted
from *Hidden Profits in Your Mortgage* (Stoddart Publishing,
1985) with the permission of Alan Silverstein.

This book is dedicated to my family — Kathy and Brian. The time I spent writing took precious time away from them.

I would also like to dedicate this book to my parents whose encouragement led me to an interest in economics.

Table of Contents

Introduction

Early in 1985 we saw the introduction of a brand-new budget that completely changed the rules as far as managing our money is concerned. We used to be able to pick from a myriad of sophisticated tax shelters that mostly helped the rich — but they are being phased out. Instead, we'll now be left with only one way of saving taxes, but it's useful to almost every one of us. There are no longer any capital gains taxes. That means that we can pick and choose any investment we want, and feel confident that we'll save taxes. It can be antiques or art, land, real estate, stocks, or mutual funds. From now on the average investor/saver knows that he or she can invest some money in this great country of ours and come out ahead. It's imperative that we start to think this way, because Finance Minister Michael Wilson has, in no uncertain terms, given us only two choices. We can continue to earn interest, and pay tax on everything we earn in excess of $1,000, or we can invest in this great country of ours and pay no tax at all. The decision is ours.

In the past, one thing we had to worry about was inflation. Well, that seems to be pretty much under control right now — but who knows for how long. However, as inflation levels fell, so too did the rate of return we could earn by saving our money. And that's one thing Canadians are going to have to learn — that interest yields are only a reflection of inflation levels. That's why interest rates rise and fall as inflation levels change. But taxes are applied to the gross amount earned over and above inflation levels. This means that the combination of taxes and inflation generally have had us move backwards faster than forwards.

The new budget has added a kicker or two. No matter how much seniors feel they accomplished in fighting for indexed pensions, their fight didn't help restore indexing of our normal deductions and exemptions. The result is that Ottawa will now benefit every time we get a raise, even if that raise is only intended to offset the cost of higher inflation. So strong, in fact, is this change, that Ottawa will reap an extra $570 million in taxes in 1986 and $4.3 billion in 1990.

You know whose pockets that will come from. Even before the budget, we Canadians paid more than one-half our salaries to one taxman or another. The loss of a number of deductions, changes in the RRSP legislation, the loss of indexing, and lower interest yields will hurt virtually every taxpayer who's not prepared to change his thinking.

In Canada we've become content to simply tuck our money away in term deposits, guaranteed investment certificates, and savings accounts. But that has to change. Rather than earning interest we have to switch to earning dividends and capital gains. Thanks to the new budget, capital gains are almost tax-free dividends, thanks to the dividend tax credit. What's more, as you'll see as you work your way through *Your Money and How to Keep It*, there are numerous ways to save money despite the new taxes; in fact, there are numerous ways to earn as much money as you want totally free of tax. We'll show you how to do that as you read on. Before we proceed, though, I want to introduce you to four keys to financial success that I regularly follow.

1. Earn as much as you can or, at least, as much as you want or need.
2. Keep as much of it as you can. That doesn't mean that you shouldn't spend it as you can. But you should pay the least amount of taxes you can.
3. When you get down to the point where you have to pay tax,

try to defer it as long as you possibly can. That's the equivalent of an interest-free loan for as long as the debt is outstanding. That's a lot better than paying interest even when it's tax deductible.

4. Now that we have a new budget, it's imperative that we no longer earn interest income.

Two other things must be considered at this time. Most consumers are poor investors. We spend money when we want. As a result, we need a forced savings plan. We'll talk about that as we go along. And finally, there's no question in my mind that the new budget has made a growth industry out of the financial planning business. Every individual now needs a financial planner — somebody who can combine taxes with investments. That way you come out with the best possible combination. And, just in case you think you're doing it right, consider the words of Mark Twain: "Even if you are on the right track you'll get run over if you just sit there." When it comes to financial planning, there can be no greater truth.

1

A Budget May Be Your Guide to Financial Happiness

Governments use budgets to manage tax revenue, and corporations couldn't survive without them. Why, then, shouldn't the average consumer also benefit from proper use of a budget? The truth is that if consumers used and stuck to budgets, they would be much further ahead in their financial planning.

Have you ever noticed how some individuals who earn $30,000 or $40,000 per year can constantly be in financial difficulty, while others who earn much less enjoy a comfortable lifestyle?

A comfortable lifestyle is partly a result of financial planning — knowing what you have, what you want in the future, and what you have to do to get it. A proper budget can help you meet your priorities and keep you from going deeply in debt. It doesn't mean that you have to scrimp and save and keep track of every cent you spend. It simply maps out a plan to get the things that you and your family want most.

A budget is something that you will have to change many times until it finally works for your particular needs. But following a budget will make it easier for you to understand how and where to use your money properly. For a budget to be successful it must not put serious restrictions on you. It must be workable, practical, and, of utmost importance, it must be kept up-to-date. A budget that relates to salaries and expenses from previous years will be of little use in these days of high inflation.

It is not an easy thing to start budgeting. It takes effort to sit down and decide how much of your money you should be putting into food or housing, or what percentage of your income you can afford to use to pay off your debts — and it takes effort to stick to that budget.

A budget will help to show you the amount of money you will have for necessities and how much you can put away for emergencies and future use. It also will show you if you have been spending too much of your income in one area while depriving yourself of other, equally important needs.

The easiest way to get started is to look at your past performance. Take last year's total income from all sources and compare it to all your expenditures. Then you can compare your performance to the rest of Canada's. Statistics Canada reports that the average Canadian family of four, with a take-home pay of between $1,100 and $1,400 per month, allots the income in the following way:

Food   including in-house, beverages, and dining out 22–24%.

Housing   rent or mortgage payments, taxes and insurance, fuel, light, water, telephone, maintenance, household operation, appliances, and furniture 29–31%.

Clothing   clothes, footwear, maintenance, cleaning, and repairs 9–10%.

Transportation   public transportation, or automobile payments, maintenance, repairs, fuel, licence, registration insurance 16–17%.

Recreation and Education   club-membership fees, hobbies, subscriptions, schooling and lessons, books, sports, and theater, holidays, and personal allowances 6–7%.

Personal Care and Miscellaneous   medical expenses or premiums, dentist, drugs, tobacco, Christmas and occasional gifts, charitable donations, and the church 10–11%.

Security   life insurance and private pension plans 2–3%.

Savings   some of the previous categories include some savings — such as the equity in your house, cash value in a life insurance policy, or private pension plans — but it is also important to set aside an additional 2–3% or more in a bank account, Canada Savings Bonds, registered retirement savings plans, or other investments.

The problem with statistics like these is that they apply to the masses, yet your individual needs vary — some families are younger, some earn more money than others, some have better skills or better future-earning potential than others, and some have different priorities. As a result, you have to tailor-make your budget to your own needs, but you can use the national averages as a guideline.

You must set a goal, or goals, on paper that you can look at to remind yourself, any time you need reassuring, that you do have a plan. Then you must decide how you are going to reach those goals.

To help you, some of the chartered banks have published books which will take you step by step through your own personal financial planning. These books will help you keep track of your various sources of income, how much of it you get to take home, and what you should be doing with that money to save taxes and avoid unnecessary expenses. The various categories are grouped to correspond to the national averages, but space is left for you to put in your own expenditures and compare your own lifestyle to that of the average family of four. These are useful books that will not only help you set up a budget, but will also show you where you can change your financial planning to take advantage of your own situation.

A properly run budget will help you make trade-offs. Perhaps you should be buying term insurance rather than whole-life insurance because you need extra money elsewhere. Perhaps you should be using your reserve funds to pay off your car loan this year and save interest, rather than going on a vacation. With no car payments next year, you may be able to afford an extended vacation. A budget will allow you to set aside extra cash for your long-term savings plan. This cash can then be transferred into a registered retirement savings plan (RRSP). You will get extra tax rebates — money you can use now — and you will be saving for the future.

A budget will help you see when your money is needed. Most of us get paid twice a month, but some bills may come at awkward times or be more costly in some months than others. A budget can help us save service charges if we use available cash to pay car- or house-insurance premiums annually instead of monthly, or have enough accumulated cash to pay our heating bills, which are usually higher in the winter months.

Good financial planning will also help us pay in cash more often to save high-interest or installment-plan charges and will help us have the available cash to take advantage of seasonal sales.

Household linens, fabrics, sporting equipment, coats, and housewares are always cheaper in January, while automotive equipment, barbecues, and winter clothing are cheapest in the spring, and appliances, toys, and Christmas gifts are a bargain in the fall.

A budget may show you that everything you want doesn't have to be brand new — you may get just as much use and enjoyment out of some used items — and it may show you that you don't always have to buy top-of-the-line products — especially when the item is meant to have a short life.

A budget will show you how to get out of debt and stay out of debt. Money problems are by far the largest cause of marital breakdown, so it may even help keep your family together.

With close to fifty percent of all families now enjoying two incomes, a budget should be used to control the flow of cash. A popular formula has been to use the larger income for day-to-day operations, with the second income reserved for emergencies and investments. But the tide is now turning; in many families, both spouses contribute a set amount from each paycheck, or an agreed-upon percentage of their take-home pay, into a family company. The funds in that pool of money are then used to run the family, to pay all the operating costs. The remainder of each spouse's income is his or hers to keep and use as desired, and neither spouse has to account for how it is used. This type of agreement allows each partner freedom and individuality, while at the same time giving both partners incentive to increase their incomes. The funds they contribute to the family company, meanwhile, are well managed in accordance with a tight, well-constructed budget.

Once we have used a budget to find out how much money we can really save, we then have to enter into a forced savings plan to put that money to the best possible use. It can be extra money against our mortgages, a monthly purchase of Canada Savings Bonds, or a similar purchase of mutual funds. But we must put ourselves into a forced savings plan if we wish to succeed. By the way, any of the above-mentioned ideas are good but, if we go one step further and consider the new budget, we will want to opt for a forced savings plan that produces a tax-free income. That suggests paying money against out mortgage as our first preference, buying mutual funds on a monthly basis as the second, and a monthly purchase of Canada Savings Bond next (CSBs though actually often offer the easiest route because they can often be paid for through a payroll deduction plan).

Financial planning is hardly a cure-all for our financial problems, but it will help tell us where we are and show us where we're going. A budget will, if it is adhered to, save us money, taxes, and heartaches.

2

Investing in Yourself

Far too often I speak to individuals who believe that the world of investments is only for those who have a lot of money. That couldn't be more wrong. Even if you do no more than follow a plan I call investing in yourself, you at least have opened the door to getting ahead for the future.

If you are one of those consumers who don't as yet own a home and are struggling to get along on a meager income, you might want to put a plan like the following one into practice. It involves using your money to your best possible advantage. You must put away at least ten dollars per week to do it, in what I call your "investing-in-myself" account. However, at the end of the year you will find that you have tripled your money — and it's tax free, to boot.

Let's face facts. We can pretty well count on inflation pushing the price of goods higher every year. If we could just arrange to buy extra goods in advance, we would be ahead of the game. The next problem that always seems to come up is the need to buy goods at the last minute. We run out and head for the corner convenience store to stock up at midweek. These convenience stores know this is going to happen: their prices are higher than the supermarket prices, especially when you consider the prices you sometimes find at supermarket sales. Thursday night: that's the big one. People do their regular weekly shopping on Friday night or Saturday, but they run out of cat food, toilet paper, Kleenex — or a light bulb pops — always on Thursday. Off they go to the convenience store and voluntarily pay an extra thirty percent or so to buy the goods they need. That thirty percent extra out of their pockets might not be much this week, but over the years it will certainly add up — and don't forget that these are after-tax dollars. We have probably paid out thirty cents on the dollar to our employer in taxes and now we are paying an extra thirty cents on the dollar because we didn't plan in advance.

But suppose we did a little planning ahead at home. Suppose we put ten dollars per week in our "investing-in-myself" account. We can use a portion of that money to buy something we will eventually need. Our saving of thirty percent is effectively the same as earning thirty percent — without having to pay tax on it. Even Revenue Canada has not yet been able to garner up the strength or courage to tax us on money we save by constructive shopping. You don't have to spend the full ten dollars each week. All you have to do is systematically deposit it into a daily-interest savings account, where it will earn interest each day but will also be accessible. You will spend part of it to buy sale-priced items; the rest will earn interest. And the products that you stockpile will also grow in value. By the end of the year, the price of those goods will have increased substantially because of inflation. At the end of the year, when you tabulate the amount of money you have left in your account and consider the products you have consumed plus whatever is left over, you will find that you have pretty well tripled your money. Now you have something to work with. Now your money is starting to go farther and you are getting more use out of it. Now you have a tax shelter of your own, as Ottawa can't tax you on the money you are saving.

But let's take this a bit further. Suppose you find something on sale while shopping at the supermarket. You can use some of the money in your special account to purchase it. Now you are saving more than the thirty percent you were counting on: you have increased your benefits. In addition, you can collect coupons. The merchants and manufacturers who issue coupons know exactly what they are doing. They issue these coupons expecting that a set percentage of the consuming population will use them. Those who do win; those who don't subsidize those who do. If you like subsidizing your neighbors, then go right ahead and throw out your coupons. If you want to take advantage of some tax-free money, then incorporate these coupons into your "investing-in-yourself" strategy and you will come out ahead.

The problem is that these coupons are intended to get us into the store, where we are expected to spend enough money to offset the value of the coupon. If we do, the retailer comes out ahead, because we also bought his higher-priced items. Instead, we would be better off if we spent our spare time looking through the ads in the newspapers each week. We would know what was on sale where, and we would be able to take advantage of the best sales and the best coupons when we were near the respective stores. Don't forget that most of the major chain supermarkets will accept each other's coupons to get you into their stores and keep you away from other stores. In fact, Dominion Stores has a policy of giving customers who bring in a major competitor's coupon the face value of the coupon plus an additional ten percent. Try to tuck away the Wednesday and the Saturday ads, then compare them. Pick out what you plan to buy, what you should hold off on, and what you should use your special-investment account to stock up on. You will be shopping in the peace and quiet of your home without any of the pressure exerted by the stores' special displays. Stick to your shopping list when you go to the stores.

If you are already going to be about thirty percent ahead, why not see if you can make it fifty percent or so by properly using sales and coupons? In fact, you will find many items where you will be more than fifty percent ahead. However, there will be others that don't give you as great a bargain where you will narrow the average gain. And wait until you get a surprise next year. When it comes time to open a box of laundry detergent and you find that the advertised price now is twice what you paid, you will know that your plan is working — and working well.

The only drawback to this plan is that you can be tempted to buy goods that you don't really need. To make this plan work well, you have to purchase wisely. Please, no cigarettes, alcohol, chips, or Cheezies. You will only consume them as fast as you can bring them home from the store. Instead, concentrate on things like paper, soap, detergent, cleaners — all the non-perishables that you will need in the future and that you can store cheaply in your own home.

3

Does It Pay for Both Spouses to Work?

Almost fifty percent of all Canadian families have two working spouses. The tough recession of the early 1980s made if difficult for many people to get a job or hold one, but it also forced many families to consider having both partners work outside the home in order to survive. And once we were out of the recession, many more families considered having both spouses work so that they could get back on their feet, to do a little catching up after the setbacks they suffered in those years.

Putting aside the question of family values, which is outside the scope of this book, couples have to decide if it really pays to have both spouses work. This is an important question with many facets to consider. In fact, it's fairly obvious, from a financial angle, that many families should *not* have two working partners.

To begin with, the salaries of both spouses will be eroded by normal taxes. And once the second partner goes out to work, the spousal deduction as well as the transfer of the $100 federal-tax reduction may be lost. Then there are the higher transportation, clothing, child-care, and eating-out costs, as well as a raft of other things to consider.

Let's take a couple who are considering having the second spouse enter the workforce, and trying to decide whether it will be worth their while. For simplicity, we'll use what is still the more common situation: that is, a husband who has a full-time job and a wife who is considering going out to work. Naturally, there are many variations of this scenario, including the exact opposite one, but we will use the example in this way, as it will probably be of use to more couples.

As soon as the wife decides to start earning income, she runs the risk of canceling a very important tax deduction that her husband now uses to lower his taxes. That might, in the end, be worthwhile, but only if there is going to be a reasonable amount of money coming in that will offset that lost deduction. If only one partner is working right now, that partner gets the spousal deduction, which is worth $4,140. If the husband is in the thirty-five percent tax bracket (less than $20,000 in taxable income in Ontario, as an example), the loss of this deduction would mean an increase of $1,215 in the taxes he has to pay. Now, the wife can earn some income without taking away that spousal deduction, but only a maximum of $510. Once she earns more than that, she won't start paying tax on her own income until she earns $7,000 or so (the actual amount depends on the extra tax deductions that she takes advantage of), but the whole family will be paying the tax rate the husband pays on this income, as her extra income will only be offsetting a tax deduction that he automatically gets. That means that if you are going to go out to work, it just won't pay to earn a few thousand dollars. You might not pay any taxes alone, but as a family unit you will.

But even if the second partner does land a job that pays a higher salary, say $10,000, the two of you still have to do some serious thinking because there are many other expenses, in addition to taxes, to consider.

Before you even get to work, you may have to buy some new clothes, the kind that you wouldn't normally have purchased, and the kind that you may wear only to work. Lots of people don't like to wear the clothes that they wear to work when they socialize, so you are going to have to include this extra expense in your calculations. Then you have makeup, grooming, and transportation to consider.

Transportation won't be a major problem for those people who can walk to work, but few people fall into that category. It may also be possible for couples to go to work together, but if this means going out of the way at all, twice a day, you had better add a little on to the gas and oil bill as you will be spending more than you are now. Some individuals have ready access to public transportation. That might well make it easy to get to work, but it can cost as much as several dollars a day. And remember, the cost of getting to work is not tax deductible, no matter what the job, so this money goes right out of your pocket, after your boss has subtracted all your other deductions.

Now you have to think about day care if you have children. If you don't have a family, you probably don't need the money as much and your expenses are probably lower, so you may be able to make a lower income fit into this equation. However, if you have pre-school-age children, you will have to give some serious thought to the cost of day-care facilities. A parent who goes out to work is allowed to deduct up to $2,000 per year per child, to a maximum of $8,000 for the family unit. However, you may find that you are paying $2,000 to $3,000 per child per year to have somebody take care of the children while you are out at work. And then you have the cost of getting the children to the day care. If it's a little out of the way, the one car that the family has been using may no longer be sufficient. Now we get into some even larger expenses as we are going to have the cost of the car, the insurance, maintenance, gas, and oil. And even if you already have a second car to drive the children to day care, you still have the extra gas, oil, and wear and tear. And when you finally get to work, you may have to pay for parking.

At work itself you may find that you spend more money than you realize. You will be spending money at coffee break and for lunches on occasion. Close proximity to stores, if you work downtown, could lead to excess spending, and then there is the usual call for donations for weddings, retirements, and illnesses. At the same time, your boss will be deducting taxes automatically, as well as pension, unemployment insurance, life insurance, and possibly union dues and health and dental plan payments. Most of these payments you will not be able to avoid. The life insurance is good, but the health-insurance-package premium may be wasted money in that it might duplicate what your husband already gets from his employer. On the other hand, this can be an added attraction to a second spouse working. The husband may be self-employed or working in a place where no health insurance coverage is provided. The second spouse's employer may provide equal or better coverage, or the second coverage might include dental insurance, which could be especially valuable to the family.

Even at home you are going to find that your expenses will rise when you make the decision to go out to work. It's common knowledge that families where there are two working spouses use more prepared foods and visit restaurants or use take-out foods more often. You come home from a full day's work and you don't feel up to cooking a meal so you go out and spend more in a restaurant than you would for a meal at home. And when you do eat at home, you tend to use more foods that have been partially prepared. They also cost more.

It's more common for those families where there are two working spouses to have somebody come in to clean the house. And you also are more prone to buying appliances that will cut down the amount of work that you do around the house. Examples include microwave ovens, food processors, and automatic dishwashers. While they will provide convenience, they also cost money. It may well be that these items become a trade-off in that they use up the extra income that you have earned, but you wouldn't have been able to justify them if both spouses weren't working.

It's pretty obvious from these comments that, from a financial standpoint, it just doesn't pay to take a job that pays only a few thousand dollars. The extra income will only offset lost tax deductions and extra expenses. Where there are children involved, those expenses are higher so the acceptable salary level also has to be higher. However, when the salary being paid is a good one, it is definitely worth taking a second job, even if it lasts for only a few years. If the extra money is put toward your mortgage or other debts, your family can advance ahead of your peers very rapidly. You can afford more vacations, appliances, investments, and a higher standard of living.

4

Income Splitting — It May Be All We Have Left

The last federal budget did its very best to eliminate what was one of the last tax-saving ideas that was available to the average family. It's called income splitting. That attempt, though, fell short of its desired objective. As you follow this chapter you'll see how we can still use income splitting to our advantage.

Here's how income splitting used to work. The higher-income spouse would lend most of the family's investment monies to the lower-income spouse. No interest would be charged on this loan, so that all the income earned by spouse number two would be taxed at his or her lower tax rate.

It might sound simpler to simply give these funds to spouse number two. However, Revenue Canada invoked a thing called the "attribution rule." It says that when we give money to a spouse or minor, and they invest that money, that the giver has to add the income generated to his or her tax return and pay tax on it — if he or she is taxable. That's why we loan the money rather than give it. Revenue Canada was forced to treat this transaction as a business deal with the income taxed, if it was taxable, in the receiver's name. The new budget, though, has determined that no matter whether we give money to a spouse or minor, or lend it to him, we the giver must add the income to our tax return.

If we are taxable we then have to pay tax on that income. Granted, if we had already put income splitting in place before May 22, 1985, and if we had used a demand loan as recommended in earlier editions of *Your Money and How to Keep It*, then we can continue income splitting for 1985, 1986, and 1987. At the end of 1987 we should call our demand loans, making sure we recoup only the monies originally loaned out. That way the monies come back to us totally tax free, and from then on all the money that's left in our spouse's name will be able to earn income that's taxed at his or her lower tax rate. As a result, it's vitally important that we keep all income splitting in place until the end of 1987 — and earn the most possible with the money we have transferred.

By the way, prior to the budget anybody who had the opportunity to read my regular articles or pick me up on radio or TV knew that I suggested we switch our demand loans to six-year-term loans. Those who did so can continue with their existing income splitting loans until the day those loans mature. Effectively, we get an extra three years' worth of tax savings.

For those who have not been taking advantage of income splitting — and for those who have and wanted to expand their usage — it may appear that there's no chance. However, that just isn't the case. Not only is it more important for us to make the greatest possible use of income splitting, but we have almost as many ways to do it. Let's say you have $20,000 in family savings. If you keep those in your name, give or loan the savings to your spouse; it doesn't matter since you are the one who will report any taxable income. So why not make sure you lend it to your spouse? In year one a 10% yield will mean that you add $2,000 worth of investment income to your tax return. However, once you've claimed this income it now becomes your spouse's. In year two the $2,000, again, at a 10% yield, will pay $200. Now it's taxable in your spouse's name. In fact, that's where Michael Wilson's plan to stop income splitting breaks down. It's only in year one when it's stopped. The compounding of interest on interest can be made to grow in our spouse's lower tax bracket.

A second way to use income splitting involves two working spouses. If spouse number one earns $40,000 and spouse number two $20,000, it's wise for spouse number one to pay all the household bills including every expense normally incurred by spouse number two, even if you have to pay spouse number two's tax bills so that he or she gets a full $20,000 to invest. What we're trying to do is accumulate money in the lower-income spouse's name where it will be taxed at a lower rate than if it remains in the higher-income spouse's name. If we *give* money to a spouse to invest, the income earned is taxable in our own name. However, if we give a spouse money to pay his or her tax bill so that those funds can be invested, then we're okay. The income earned is taxable in the lower-income spouse's name.

Here's a third option that might appeal to some. What if you arranged for your lower-income spouse to borrow $20,000? You might have to co-sign the loan, but now the $20,000 would be in his or her name. At 12% this loan requires $200 a month to service it. If you give your spouse the $200 per month it isn't to invest, it's to pay interest. As a result the income earned by your spouse won't "attribute" back to you. It will remain in his or her own name. If the $20,000 were invested in a mutual fund that earned 15% (that's low over a reasonable length of time), all the income would grow in his or her name, and be taxed at the lower rate. What's more, depending on their income level, you may not lose that spouse as a dependent exemption since the interest would be tax deductible while much of the yield would be tax free. Now that the budget is in, I can see much more of this happening. We can each earn up to one-half million dollars' worth of tax-free capital gains in a lifetime. By practising moves like this, you'll be in a position to earn a cool million between you.

Who says income splitting is dead? It's more alive than ever. To help you with your interest-free demand loans, we've included a copy of our successful income splitting loan agreement that was in earlier versions of *Your Money and How to Keep It*.

When it comes to income splitting with a child, we have some serious problems. Taxpayers who followed our advice and opened a child trust must follow the above-mentioned three- and six-year rules as far as their loans are concerned. Under no circumstances, though, should you cancel your child trusts at this stage. You have a limited time left, so make sure that the

PROMISSORY NOTE

Amount: _____   Due   Date: <u>On Demand</u>

Date: _____   City and Province: _____

Upon   demand,   I,   _____,   covenant,   agree,   and

promise to pay to _____ the sum of $ _____. It is

agreed that there will be no interest charged on this loan unless I

default. At that time, I agree to pay _____% interest per

annum from the date of default.

_____   _____

        (Witness)

money inside the trust is invested in vehicles that will provide
an above-average yield. You can, if you want, lend money back
to yourself. You could then invest the money in a mutual fund
that would pay you a tax-free capital gain and dividends that
are virtually free of tax. The interest you pay back to the trust
would then be tax deductible to you but received virtually tax
free by your child. At the same time the yield earned by you on
this investment would be virtually tax free. An added advantage
is that the money earned through the trust by a child, while
taxable in his or her name (if he or she is taxable), can be offset
by claiming the child's tuition as a tax deduction. In effect, that's
the way we can make our child's education not only tax deductible, but also paid for by the taxman through saved taxes.

5

How Should Families with Two Working Spouses Manage Their Money?

When families have two spouses who bring in income, there is often a great deal of discussion as to how the money should be managed. It's often the case in older families that one individual, usually the husband, has handled all the money. If something happens to him, his wife is left not knowing where all the money is, what the family owns in the way of investments, how much life insurance and debts there are, and so on. The wife has never had to handle the family's finances before, but now that responsibility is thrust upon her overnight.

With that in mind, it's important that financial planning be a family affair with both partners — even the children — involved. You might choose to have one partner handle most of the budgeting and banking, but the other spouse must definitely be included.

There are really three scenarios that we can follow when handling the family's money.

The first option would be to let the larger salary cover the day-to-day expenses — the rent, food, telephone, heat, hydro, and so on. The second salary could then be used, as much as possible, for savings, financial growth, longer holidays, and special purchases. Of course, that's textbook theory; in these tough economic times it might take both salaries just to pay the day-to-day bills. If it is possible, though, some part of the second spouse's income should be put toward savings, the down payment for a house, or an emergency plan. Or, if you have a house, it should be put aside so that you can pay part of the principal of your mortgage each year, or each time the loan comes up for renegotiation.

The second approach is to pool all the money into a joint account. Try to use a daily-interest savings account: you will earn more interest on your money, as it usually goes into the account partway through the month and comes out before the month ends. In a daily-interest account, you earn some interest on your day-to-day money; in a conventional savings account, you earn none or very little. All the family's bills will be paid out of this account; whatever is left over is channeled into investments, an emergency fund, and special purchases, including vacations. When you use this system, you really open yourself to each other as every cent can be accounted for. Often one partner will manage the money, which means the other must ask for money when he or she wants some. A way around that problem is to allow both spouses an allowance that they can spend any way they wish.

This plan is an old standard that unfortunately has created problems in recent years. It works quite well when only one spouse works, but in two-income families it can lead to squabbles if one spouse puts in more than the other. However, if there are no complaints, it can still be the easiest and most efficient plan for the average family to use.

A third plan has been gathering quite a following in recent years. It involves running the family as if it were a business. When you have two working spouses, you often find that this approach is the best because it is the most businesslike and equitable. Each spouse contributes a set amount each month to a family pool of money. The spouses can contribute equal amounts, or they can put in a fixed percentage of their incomes after taxes and deductions. The amount each spouse will put in is decided when both spouses sit down and go over the family expenses. You must have a clear idea as to how much money is going to be required to keep you afloat. You have to include all the fixed expenses like insurance, mortgage payments, food, utility bills, emergency expenses, even enough for some joint savings and a vacation once in a while. What really happens is that you sit down and map out a plan that you hope will work. If you come up with a shortfall, both spouses have to supplement their contributions on the same percentage basis. If you have excess cash at the end of the year, you can use those funds to take a vacation, or you might buy an appliance, a videotape recorder, or some other item that is needed for your family. In essence, you will either use the excess funds to purchase something extra for the family corporation, you will carry the excess over to the next year as a surplus, or you will pay it back to each other on whatever basis you wish. It's like a bonus for running a profitable and budget-conscious operation.

The monies that each partner has left over can be used for whatever purpose you choose: maybe for a beer or two once in a while, a month-end poker club, some new clothes, another car, or whatever you desire.

That's the advantage to this type of operation. It gives today's new breed some independence, while at the same time allowing them to contribute fully to the family operation. When you need some money, you don't have to ask somebody else for it. If you have the desire to work harder, you can do so, realizing that if you wish to, you can keep your excess earnings. On the other hand, you also know that you can devote every cent to the family's well-being, if you want to. If you want to take your family away on an extra vacation, you can do so. If you want to buy a car, fool around in the stock market without worrying about messing up the family's financial picture, you can do it. In fact, you might even be able to do some of these things and give yourself a special feeling of helping the family. There are lots of examples where one partner doesn't know enough about the family's finances and as a result doesn't realize the value that is being provided by the other partner. If you run your family's finances this way, you will each see what the other is doing and you will appreciate the fact that there is extra money or there are extra purchases being made on behalf of the family.

The personal advantage, of course, is that you now have some control over your own money. You have the right to use your excess funds for your own desires and don't have to feel that you must ask permission to do something on your own. Even if you simply use the excess money for family purchases, you have the satisfaction of knowing that you did it on your own. And, of course, the other advantage is that this freedom to keep any money over and above what you contribute to the family gives you a certain amount of incentive to go out and work a little harder. Most of the excess income will be channeled right into your own account, which will mean even more to you.

Option number three is gaining a lot of strength in our new, more mobile society. It's not necessarily for everybody, but it is worth some consideration.

6

Credit Cards -
Aren't They Great!

Two-thirds of the Canadian adult population owns at least one of these plastic money creators, and the average cardholder has at least three of them. That adds up to at least eight million possible money makers for lenders and, in some cases, consumers. This chapter is intended to turn the tide more to the former than to the latter. Credit card companies have moved at a snail's pace when it comes to lowering the interest rates they charge on outstanding credit card balances. Interest rates in virtually every other field have crumbled in the past two years, but the good old credit card rates generally are mired at the 18 to 24% levels.

And, as if that weren't enough, the two biggest Canadian companies have added user fees to most of their cards. They say they don't make enough money on their card operations because more than 50% of the card holders pay off their balances before interest charges begin to accrue. *Those numbers should be closer to 100%.* There is absolutely no reason why consumers should pay 18% to 24% to 28% for loans when they can easily get them from the very same lender for 10% to 12% to 14%.

Here's how credit cards work. You have a choice between cards that charge a user fee and those that don't. For example, most of the VISA card operations won't charge you to get a card. But they will charge you to use it (e.g., 15 cents per use or a flat fee of from .50¢ to $1.00 per month). In addition, they charge you 18% or more per year, compounded monthly, on any outstanding balances. Master Card, on the other hand, doesn't charge you a user fee, but it does charge a higher interest rate on any outstanding balances of 21%. And then we have the gas companies that don't charge you to get a card but they nick you for 21 to 24% per year on outstanding balances, and the greed of department stores is even greater. They demand as much as 28.8% — rates that we normally would consider illegal. But there are consumers who are prepared to pay them.

So how do we swing this torture to our advantage? Well, in the first place, there's nothing wrong with credit cards if you're prepared to use them to your advantage. They can effectively create interest-free loans for one month or so if we buy goods with them and also pay the bills on time. If there's a fee charged each time you use a credit card, you can defeat this purpose by choosing a card that has no usage charges. That way you can buy as many goods as you want without worrying about paying any user fees or interest charges provided you pay your bill within the billing period. Most credit cards allow their users a period of time before they start charging interest on any outstanding balances. However, they have been doing their best to shorten that period. But even then, those who use credit cards can win by taking advantage of this shortened period.

An important word of warning though: It's now common for consumers to take advantage of cash machines to make cash withdrawals against their accounts. If you have no money in your account and take out a cash advance, that's the same as taking a personal loan — except that the interest rate charged on this loan is a lot more than you would pay if you approached the very same banker looking for a personal loan. What's more, the interest starts to accrue immediately upon taking the advance instead of accruing as soon as the check clears that you wrote to purchase the item for which you borrowed the money.

Another practise that consumers should be alerted to is the rapidly growing policy where card companies charge interest immediately on any new purchases. In the past you could get away with running a balance on your account where you were gradually paying it off. New purchases wouldn't attract interest until the new billing date, but now it's different. Now you can buy goods on your card and pay no interest until your check is due if you don't have an outstanding balance on your account. But, if you have an outstanding balance, you'll be charged interest immediately upon buying another item — all the more reason to use a consumer loan at a lower interest rate to keep no outstanding balance on your credit card. Not only do you pay a lower interest rate on your consumer loan, but you also get to buy goods without incurring interest charges until your bill is due for payment.

In talking about consumer loans, Master Card and VISA are sponsored by financial institutions here in Canada. They make their money by lending funds to borrowers. And a credit card balance is exactly that — a loan. But credit card loans bear interest at 18% to 20% to almost 30%. At the same time a personal loan costs only 10% to 12% to 13%. So why don't you save yourself some money and ask your lender for a personal loan to pay off your credit card loan? Your interest rate will fall by one-third, and you'll be able to buy more goods interest free until your billing date rolls around.

There's not question that credit cards are useful to the 50% of users that pay off their bills on time. They should make sure that they use cards where there is no user fee. That way they get interest free loans of up to 30 days' duration every time they make a purchase. For those who do not pay their loans off on time — and for those who are content to pad the financial institutions' accounts by paying a monthly per use fee — they have a lot to learn about the financial world.

Personal loans are a lot cheaper than credit card loans, so why should you pay a user fee to somebody who's going to earn interest when you make a purchase? For businesspeople, credit cards are a fantastic tool. They allow you to treat associates and clients to lunch, and to pay your gas bills and other expenses while you get use of the financial institution's money for as long as one month. What's more, any charges that accompany the use of these cards are now tax deductible and more justifiable.

7

How Safe Is Your Money in a Financial Institution?

When times get tough economically, more people start to worry about how safe their money is when it is on deposit in a financial institution. Many older people remember the crash of 1929, when banks couldn't pay back the money people had deposited in savings accounts. Younger people remember when Astra Trust, a small Ontario trust company, closed shop, taking some people's retirement money with them. And then there was an associated company, Remore Investment Corporation, where much more money was lost. And more recently Crown Trust, Seaway Trust, and Greymac Trust created many worries for consumers.

It's right to worry about the safety of your money. After all, you have worked and saved all your life to build up what you can. To lose it because you or somebody else was careless would be a terrible shame.

There's always going to be a certain amount of risk when you buy stocks, bonds, real estate, or commodities. The rate of return indicates how great the risk will be. That's why so many Canadians, conservative lot that they are, simply settle for leaving their money in a bank, trust company, or credit union. They purchase a term deposit or guaranteed-investment certificate that promises to pay them a set rate of return for whatever length of time they desire. Yet, even these supposedly secure investments are not without risk. Each financial institution in Canada is only insured for a maximum of $60,000 by the Canada Deposit Insurance Corporation. If we really had a financial crunch and these financial institutions started to crumble, the first $60,000 of our savings would be protected, but from then on our money would be lost.

The weakest institutions would go first, giving us lots of warning — and even then, you can bet that the financially secure institutions would buy up those that were in trouble, just as we saw with Unity Bank of Canada when it was struggling. The rest of the financial community doesn't want any suggestion of trouble: they know that would start a run on the banks, as everybody would want to get their money back. That would magnify any problems that actually existed.

The simple way to look at this situation is to forget about your fears. Canada has one of the most secure banking systems in the entire world. However, if you do worry about the security of your money, here's how you can increase the protection you are eligible for.

First, the Canada Deposit Insurance Corporation (CDIC) protects the first $60,000 of your savings at every institution that displays their insurance sticker. All federally incorporated financial institutions are automatically protected. The provincially incorporated ones have to apply to the CDIC, but they also may get this insurance. All protected companies must display a sticker to show that they are covered by this deposit insurance. If you don't see one, ask for proof that the particular institution is indeed covered.

The $60,000 insurance coverage is pretty simple. It covers your savings and checking accounts plus any term deposits or guaranteed investment certificates to a maximum of $60,000 per institution. It doesn't matter how many branches you deal with, your savings — up to a maximum of $60,000 per institution — are covered. However, if you have more than $60,000 in savings, and many middle-aged and older consumers do, you may feel at risk. You can get around this problem by splitting your savings between a number of institutions. That way you will have up to $60,000 worth of insurance for each institution that you deal with.

However, you don't need to deal with a raft of different institutions. Instead, you might put the first $60,000 in your name, and it's protected. You then put the second $60,000 in your spouse's name. It now is also protected. Then you deposit $60,000 into a joint account. It, too, is protected over and above all your other family funds. And then you can open joint accounts with each of your children, and even lend them money to put in their own accounts, which also will be covered. As well, registered retirement savings plans are considered separate accounts — different from your savings accounts — so your RRSP is now also covered to a maximum of $60,000 at each institution.

If you follow these steps you can put your money with the newest, smallest, most questionable trust company in the country, where you might earn the highest rate of return, and still sleep well at night, secure in the knowledge that your money is as safe as if it were tucked away in the largest, most secure financial institution in the world.

And that's exactly what you should be doing. You should always do a little shopping each time your term deposits come due for renewal. A small, aggressive trust company will almost always pay you a higher rate of return on your money than does a more established bank. And you should take advantage of it. It's those fractions of percents that will put you ahead of all your friends in the years to come.

When it comes to credit unions it's a different story. Credit unions do not belong to the CDIC, which is an arm of the federal government. However, they do belong to their own industry deposit-insurance facility, which gives them protection similar to that offered by larger financial operations. In addition, credit unions generally state that consumers can have as many registered retirement savings plans as they wish, with each one guaranteed up to $60,000. This can be an advantage, as the money in these retirement plans is not taxed until it is removed from the plan. At a credit union, you could open a new RRSP each time your savings exceeded $60,000. Then you would always be covered to the fullest.

Financial Services

Many Canadians worry about the safety of their money when it's on deposit with a financial institution, and rightly so. But that's no reason to always deal with only the biggest and the best. Every institution that meets the requirements qualifies for the full $60,000 in deposit insurance coverage. That means that you can deal with the smallest and newest institution there is with no fear about the safety of your money — provided you don't exceed the $60,000 coverage we spoke of earlier — and you should because they generally pay a higher rate of return than you'll earn at the larger companies.

The problem is that not every community has a good selection of small companies. And it doesn't pay, generally, for you to spend your money on long distance charges to shop the country, nor would you consider travelling to another community to invest your money — your expenses would eat up the difference. That's where financial consultants or stockbrokers can be very useful. They have ties with a large number of financial institutions across the country and can more easily place your money with a company than you can. What's more, they don't charge you for this service. They get a finder's fee from the company for directing your money their way, and you get a higher rate of return than you would have had had you not used their services.

Don't worry about deposit insurance when you deal with stock brokers or financial consultants. In the case of term deposits they don't actually get your money — they simply pass it on to the financial institution. They act only as a conduit, so it's the financial institution's deposit insurance that counts, not the financial consultant's. In addition, there's never, ever been a loss recorded where a stockbroker went broke or closed its doors. The industry has its own insurance fund so investors don't have to worry about losing their money through a failure.

8

Proper Use of a Savings Account

Canadians are notoriously lax when it comes to using savings accounts properly. Did you know that there are more savings accounts than there are Canadians? And that only includes the number of accounts in banks. On top of that are all the checking accounts, current accounts, trust accounts, and the massive network of similar accounts in credit unions and trust companies. We probably have too many accounts. Mind you, it's not necessarily a mistake to have several. In fact, I recommend that consumers maintain accounts at a variety of institutions so that they can take advantage of the different features offered by these competing lenders.

One reason for choosing a particular bank is location. It's very common for us to deal with the branch of an institution that is "right down the street." And, of course, that's why the bank thought it would be profitable to open a branch in that location. It's also fairly common to have an account at the credit union where we work. It might be really convenient to have our paychecks automatically deposited into our account each payday so that we don't have to spend the time doing it ourselves. Other reasons for choosing a particular bank include the interest rate paid on deposits, the lending officer at a branch who has been responsive to our needs, good parking facilities, convenient branch hours, proximity to the bus stop, and so on. There are all kinds of reasons to deal with a specific bank or branch — and some are quite valid.

But, many of us go wrong when we pick the kind of account we want. Some accounts pay you more interest than others, even though the rate quoted on that account looks like it is lower.

Everybody should have a daily-interest savings account. For years the banks encouraged us to save our money in "premium savings accounts" where the interest rate was decent. Yet interest was paid only on the money that was there for a set period of time. That was okay if you put money into a bank and left it there for a long period of time. But what if you had money coming in and going out — or what if you didn't deposit the money before that set time period began? You wouldn't earn any interest on most of your money — but the bank had your money, and was able to lend it out at a marked-up interest rate. And you can be sure they charged interest every day that loan was outstanding. Clearly that was unfair to savers.

As a result, the banks were pressured into providing daily-interest savings accounts. In these accounts, consumers earn interest on all the money in their accounts at the end of each day. The interest isn't credited to your account each day, but at least you have earned some interest on the money you had on deposit at that bank. And you should definitely have such an account for your every-day banking needs. As an example of the value of these accounts, let me show you what happens now compared to what used to happen.

Let's say you get paid twice each month and that you are like the rest of us — a fair portion of that money is paid out almost as fast as it comes in. You might have to pay your rent or mortgage, your daily living needs, the utility bills, or whatever. When the paycheck is deposited to a conventional savings account, where the interest rate is about one-half percent higher than a daily-interest account, you won't earn any interest at all for the entire month unless that paycheck is in the bank for the entire month — that is, deposited no later than the first day of the month, and left in the account at least until the end of the month. But you may not get to the bank until the second of the month. That delay will cost you interest on that money for an entire month, not just a day. And all those bills that you pay out of that account, even if they are paid on the last day of the month, will cancel any interest you might have earned on that money for all the other days in the month. When it comes to day-to-day banking, it just doesn't pay to use a conventional premium savings account.

With the introduction of computers and "on-line" banking, the banks were able to calculate all the interest owing on every account by simply pushing a button on the computer. And with that facility comes the chance for all of us to earn a little more of the interest that should be ours by opening a daily-interest account.

With such an account your paycheck will earn interest as soon as it is deposited, even if it is there for only one day. The daily-interest account will probably pay between ½% and 1% less interest than the premium account, but because you earn something for every day the money is there, rather than nothing when it isn't there, for the entire month, you will come out substantially ahead. And don't forget that this phenomenon takes place every two weeks for the entire year, or more often if you are paid weekly.

An individual with a $500 paycheck, for example, will earn 10¢ a day as long as that $500 is in his account. That might not sound like much. But when you figure that paycheck may stay there for eight days out of every fourteen before it is withdrawn to pay bills — and remember that happens twenty-six times each year — you are now talking about $22 to $23 each year. That's a tankful of gas, or all the light bulbs you will need for a year, or a quiet night out together — or any number of other expenses. And that's the way you have to look at it. Every time you save a few dollars, equate it to something you want: a little bonus, a night out, a case of beer, or a new sweater.

But there's more at stake here than a new sweater. First, this money may be tax free. We don't have to pay any tax on our investment income unless it exceeds $1,000 per year — and families can multiply that several times over if they practice income splitting. That means that your $22 might actually be the equivalent of $30 or more in work. Now you can look on it as the equivalent of one hour's work at $30 per hour. In addition, there is the extra income that will develop each month, because the mid-month pay isn't always as quickly spent as the month-end check. Maybe the mortgage payment comes at the end of the month, so that pay is used up quickly, while the mid-month pay stays in the account longer. By properly arranging your withdrawals and pay outs you can probably parlay the interest from this account into even more extra interest each year.

That's your day-to-day money management. But there are all kinds of us who leave long-term savings in a savings account. I don't think we should be leaving long-term savings in a savings account. Savings accounts seldom pay more than the inflation rate, which means that we aren't even breaking even with our money. If we earn ten percent on our money and inflation is running at ten percent we just break even. Yet if we pay one cent of tax on that money we instantly fall behind. Our longer-term savings should be invested so that we will earn a higher rate of return and will come out ahead of inflation even after we have paid our taxes.

That means things like term deposits, guaranteed-investment certificates, the short-term money markets, treasury bills, Canada Savings Bonds, the stock markets, or real estate.

However, there are quite a number of us who insist on leaving our savings in a bank account. Make sure you get the highest rate going, which means some shopping around, and make sure you make all deposits before the month begins and all withdrawals after the month has ended. That way you will at least earn interest on your money for the whole month.

That really is a way in which all of us can use the conventional savings account. If we use a daily-interest savings account for our day-to-day banking needs and then transfer our left-over savings to a conventional account at the end of each month, we will have the best of both systems. You earn day-to-day interest all month and then you earn another ½% on the excess that you are building up over the year. Once you have built up $1,000 that you intend to use for longer-term savings, you can switch that money over to a term deposit or another longer-term investment where you will be able to earn a more reasonable rate of return.

9

Don't Think a Dollar
Here or There Doesn't Count

Many people think a few cents will never be worth much. But it's that type of thinking that makes people paupers for their entire lives. Take a look around. The people who are prepared to work, who think about a penny here, a dime there, an extra dollar or two, are the ones who get ahead. And this is the country where you can do it. The real advantage to a grubstake is that it takes only a little bit of work at the outset, and from then on the benefits are reaped.

Instead of having to pay high interest rates to borrow whenever you want to buy something, you will have cash in your grubstake. You will have enough emergency cash to feel comfortable if you invest that money instead of buying something. You won't be constantly worried that you should be putting what money you have into an emergency savings plan — one that is liquid, and as a result pays a relatively low rate of return. Instead you can afford to lock some of this money away in higher-yielding investments that help your wealth grow that much faster.

Take a look at those people who come to Canada from countries where there has been political turmoil or economic upheaval. They have seen the value of their money eroded by high inflation, or even had it taken away from them. They have seen hardships that the average Canadian has never experienced. They are going to make sure that they never have to experience them again. They set out to build a little grubstake, and they put their money into things that grow faster and aren't taxed as much so that they benefit more over the long term. They seek out that extra half a percent; they think about that extra dollar. If we practised that policy more often we would be much farther ahead of the game.

What makes this theory work so well is the theory of compounding. If you invested one single dollar at age twenty and let it compound at ten percent per year for the forty-five years until you were ready to retire, you would have $72.89. That doesn't sound like much, and maybe inflation will have eroded much of its purchasing power by the time you retire. But it is $72.89 that the person who didn't put away any money won't have, so you will definitely be ahead of him. However, if you had started one year earlier, you would have amassed $80.18. Remember, it's still only one dollar that you have invested, but by starting one year earlier, you have gained ten percent more — not ten percent of the one dollar, but ten percent of $72.89. Your dollar has just been multiplied seven times in one year because of the impact of compounding. If you had put your dollar away when you were eighteen, you would have amassed $88.20. This time the increase would be more than eight dollars, all because you started your grubstake one year earlier.

The trick, then, is to save your early dollars rather than spending them, and then to use that money to increase your wealth. But it's also imperative that you seek out the best possible interest rate — even if it beats the next-best deal by only one quarter of one percent. As an example, if you were able to earn 10½% rather than 10% on a dollar you put away at age twenty, you would have amassed $89.39 at age sixty-five, an extra $16.50. Yet you didn't do any more work. You didn't, in fact, have any more money to begin with. All you did was get yourself an extra ½%. By doing that, you have 23% more money than your neighbor who didn't bother to work his money a little harder. In fact, if you could earn 11¾%, less than 2% more than we originally calculated, you would have double the money in the same period of time. You don't have to look for double the rate of return that everybody else gets — you need only get 2% or so and you will earn twice as much over a period of time. And we've been talking about one dollar: imagine how much money comes out of these figures when we use larger sums. If you took one dollar a day in your first year of work and tucked it away where it could grow tax-free and earn 10% until you were sixty-five, you would have $26,605 — all because you started with one grubstake of $365. If that money earned 10% from then on, you would earn $221 each month for the rest of your life. In about seven weeks you would have received your original investment back in interest alone, and you would earn that amount every seven weeks as long as the money continued to earn interest.

But if we simply earned 11¾% we would have double the amount of money, or $442, every month to supplement our other income, simply because we shopped around and got ourselves a little higher rate of return. And then, of course, comes the question: "Why didn't I start a year earlier?" If you had, your original $365 would have been multiplied by more than seven times. Your total would be about $2,700 larger, all because you started one year earlier.

It's also very much to your advantage to compound your money more frequently. Let's say you are going to buy a term deposit or a guaranteed-investment certificate. Many of these bonds are compounded annually. That is, the interest is calculated at the end of each year and added to the principal, and then the principal and interest earn interest together. If you could compound your money more frequently, say semi-annually, quarterly, or monthly, and still get the same rate of return, you would come out much farther ahead of the game. Naturally, the institutions know this; they offer a "trade-off." They will give you the faster rate of compounding if you are prepared to accept a slightly lower rate of return. As an example, if you were able to earn 10% interest compounded semi-annually instead of annually, you would really be earning 10¼%. If the interest was reinvested four times a year, you would actually be earning 10.38%. And if you were able to get your money compounded every month, you would really be earning almost 10½%. But there's more at stake here than the frequency of compounding. There's also inflation. The sooner you get the money, the sooner you can do something with it, even if it is just to reinvest it. The extra ½% is important, but the inflation factor also plays a role.

There are two areas where this compounding feature is most important to the average consumer. One works to his advantage; the other knocks the stuffing out of him for two and a half decades. Because the compounding feature works so much in your favor with a registered retirement savings plan, you should start one of these plans as soon as you can possibly arrange it. Because a mortgage uses compounding to work against you, you should go out of your way to pay as much money against your mortgage as you can. You save many more dollars than the ones you actually spend.

But this compounding feature can also be put to excellent use to give your children that grubstake you wish you had had when you needed money. If we invested the family-allowance check — which is really meant for the children's use — each month or at the end of the year, rather than spending it, our children would have a pretty good grubstake coming their way when they went out into the world.

Right now the "baby-bonus" check pays $31.27 per month in most provinces, or $375.24 per year. When we use this money each year, we get another type of compounding as we aren't just compounding the original sum but one that is being added to each year as the baby bonus checks come in. In addition, the monthly baby bonus, when it is deposited into a daily-interest savings account, will earn interest until the end of the year. Let's say the checks are worth a total of $390 per year. (This figure is probably low when you figure that this payment program is indexed against inflation and can generally be expected to increase each year.) Now suppose we banked those checks until the child was eighteen. We would end up with a grand total of $22,515 in the child's name. It's now growing at the rate of more than $1,350 per year (at 6%) or more (if we are earning more than 6%) and can be put to good use by the child, maybe to help defray the cost of going to university. Another option at this stage would be for him systematically to use these funds to make contributions to a registered retirement savings plan. If he earned $20,000 or so he could contribute up to $3,500 per year into an RRSP and get back roughly $1,050 per year that he otherwise would have paid to the tax man. At the same time, his little baby-bonus trust fund would still be growing. In fact, you would have given him about eight to ten years of RRSP contributions, depending on interest rates. Those monies inside his plan would compound totally free of tax until he started to use them.

The other option would be to lock the grubstake away in a trust fund that could grow until his retirement. In this case the $22,515 that had already accumulated would grow to be worth $1.4 million — just because you took the time to put the family-allowance check that comes each month to proper use. That grubstake would earn an income of about $11,500 per month — a far cry from the $31.27 you received originally.

And now you can see why the extra ¼% or ½% means something. In the example mentioned above, 10½% instead of 10% would mean an extra $400,000 in your child's RRSP. That's worth $40,000 per year for the rest of his life, simply because you got an extra ½% on $31.27 per month when he was a child.

10

Don't Give Up a Weekend's Worth of Interest

Did you ever get the feeling you were being ripped off by the banks? Really, they aren't out to get us. But there is the odd occasion that comes up that makes you feel you are being taken advantage of. Here's my favorite. I'm sure you've seen it, maybe even experienced it without realizing what was happening.

Have you ever walked into a bank, especially in a small town or in a plaza, and dealt with a teller whose wicket sported a sign that said "this teller working on tomorrow's date" or something to that effect? It might not make much difference to you if you are simply cashing a check. But suppose you are either putting money into your savings account or taking some out. Then it might make a considerable amount of difference. What's more, the difference might be forced on you as the banks' new policy of "cattle lines" might direct you to that teller who is working on tomorrow's date, or the branch where you deal might switch all of their tellers to this practice after a certain hour, let's say 3:00 p.m. Here's what happens. Let's say you take your paycheck to the bank to deposit it. You are directed to the teller who is working on tomorrow's date, so all the money you deposit is accepted by the bank today, but they don't bother paying you any interest until tomorrow. They get to use your money, but you don't get paid for it. How many times would a bank ever make a loan to you without charging you interest for every day?

Granted, it does work the other way as well. That is, the people who withdraw money from the teller who is working on the next day's date get their money but don't stop earning interest until the next day, because the computer thinks the money is still there for one more day. And that's really the rationale the banks use to justify this system. They contend that it works out about even, as some win sometimes and others lose. However, it bothers me to be on the losing side because I think the consumer loses on far too many occasions. We are intimidated by the great marble edifices that these banks are able to afford — and they can afford them because they know how to make money at our expense.

Let me show you what I mean. This little losing of interest one day at a time can add up. There are more savings accounts than there are Canadians. Each account, on average, contains several thousands of dollars. If only a fraction of that money was able to earn interest for the banks without their having to pay any interest on it, it would mean millions of dollars at the end of each year. And it does. In fact, it earns interest for more than one day on numerous occasions. As an example, let's suppose you are making a deposit on a Friday. As far as the computer is concerned, the next day is no longer one day away, but three. The computer is programmed to accept new deposits on Monday, which means that you have lost interest for Friday, Saturday, and Sunday. What's more, you might end up losing interest like this several times a year.

Now suppose the Monday is a holiday. Then your deposit hasn't earned you any interest for Friday, Saturday, Sunday, or Monday — four full days. Yet the bank has used this money to lower its float, lend out in loans, or whatever. You're the loser while the bank comes out smelling like a rose. And don't think it doesn't happen.

Here is what you should do. Every time you go into a bank to deposit money, make sure you have it credited to a teller who is working on today's date. Even if you deal with a teller whose computer terminal is dated for tomorrow, ask that your money be credited to your account on today's date. This can't always be done in small branches where every teller switches to the next date after a certain time. In this case you will have to ask the manager to have your deposit hand-posted to today's date. If they refuse to do that, you can always take your money out of your account and take it down the street to a bank that doesn't use this system, although the time involved might be greater than the benefits gained.

What you should really do is get to know the bank's system. If they begin working on tomorrow's date partway through the day, make sure you are in the branch in time to make your deposit today. At the same time, you should get used to withdrawing any money you need from a teller who is working on tomorrow's date. And if you have a check that is dated for the next day, have it cashed by that teller. You will get your money in your hands while the bank continues to pay you interest on your money. Let's face facts. The banks say that this system evens out — so let's make sure it at least works out evenly, but preferably in our favor.

Actually, there is a thing I like to call my "daily scam" that can work very much in your favor once or twice a year. Suppose you just received $5,000. Maybe you just sold your house and this was your profit, or perhaps you won the lottery, were transferring your matured Canada Savings Bonds or term deposits, or you quite simply had that much money in savings. If you went into your favorite bank and withdrew that money on tomorrow's date — the Friday before a long weekend — you would effectively be withdrawing that money on Monday — four days later, as far as the computer is concerned. Yet you would actually have the money in your hands. But it's really quite foolish to keep that money at home, where it earns no interest over the long weekend. What if you took it to another bank where the computer runs at midnight each night instead of partway through the day? The second bank would credit you with having made a $5,000 deposit. You would now be earning interest in two banks at the same time even though your money has been withdrawn and deposited into another account.

11

Shopping for a Loan

Most of us will need to borrow money at some time or another, whether it is for business purposes, for a mortgage, to purchase a new car, to buy furniture or appliances, or take a winter vacation in the warm and sunny islands. It's not really very difficult to get a loan, but applying for one does have to be done in the right way. The main thing to keep in mind is that a banker is simply another merchant — in this case, a money merchant. He takes money in through deposits and term deposits, and he lends it out at a higher rate, keeping the difference as his profit.

Just as the merchant wants to sell you that new television to make a profit, the moneylender wants to get his money out on the street. So don't be intimidated by these people. They want to do business with you. They want to lend you as much as you can afford to borrow. And they want to do it as often as they possibly can. That's the way they make *their* money. So don't ever go into a lender expecting to have trouble borrowing. You will only have difficulty if you don't present your case properly or if that particular lender doesn't deal in the type of loan business that you are looking for. However, the banker is no fool. While he wants to lend you money, he wants to do so in the belief that he won't lose it. The more loans that go bad in his branch, the more they cut into his profits and the less stable his job is. In fact, his future is based directly on the profitability of his branch. If it makes lots of money, he gets advanced up the ladder to bigger branches more rapidly and his salary is increased quicker. The trick, then, is to convince him that this loan is safe, that you know what you are doing — and that he is going to look good when he lends you this money. The branch will be earning more interest than it is paying out, this loan will be repaid on schedule, and others will be taken out in future months or years. The first thing you have to do is to develop a line of credit — and get to know your banker. The longer he knows you, the more likelihood you have of getting a loan. You can develop a line of credit by applying for credit cards whether you ever use them or not, by dealing on a credit basis with department stores, or by buying a car, an appliance, or some furniture on a time payment-plan from a merchant. They belong to a credit organization so it's simply a matter of the banker doing a credit check on you to see if you have a good rating. If you are really having difficulty establishing a line of credit, you may have to start off by getting somebody else, perhaps a parent or a spouse, to co-sign the loan application.

When you do business in the branch where you have your account, get to know the bank manager and the loan officers. Introduce yourself. Tell them that you aren't really looking for a loan, but you may be sometime in the future so you wanted to see who you would be dealing with. The next thing to do is to shop around. Canada's financial institutions are flush with money. We are big savers so we are always putting money on deposit at the banks — money that they have to lend out if they are going to make a profit. They are waiting for you to come in looking for a loan. You want to know what other institutions have to offer when it comes to taking out a loan. You want the lowest rate and the best repayment terms so you are going to want to have built up a rapport at several institutions.

When you go in to ask for a loan, make sure that you are prepared. Have a resumé ready. You can take the information off your income/outgo statement that you prepared when you sat down with your family to do your budgeting program. (See Chapter 1.) This will show the banker that you know what you are doing, that you are prepared, and that you have thought out this loan, and know how you can repay it. He's going to want to know what you have for collateral — so show him the assets that you have built up. Of course, he isn't really interested in clothes and articles that can't really be expected to raise much money if they have to be liquidated. He's interested more in solid assets that show that you have established yourself in town, that you are not going to skip out on your obligations — and that he is not going to lose on this loan.

If you have a good credit rating and sufficient assets, you can probably get a demand loan — one that you can pay off anytime you want, but one that can also be canceled by the bank if they think you aren't playing fair. The flexibility of being able to pay a loan off whenever you want without a fee is important in that it gives you the freedom to move to another institution where rates are lower or to pay off the loan if you suddenly come into some money. The drawback to this type of loan is that the interest rate changes as interest rates move up or down. If they move lower, it's really beneficial as your loan cost will also be adjusted lower. However, if there is an upward movement, you are going to have to pay more on your loan. There's one other thing that is important here. When you arrange this type of loan, it is usually referred to as "a prime plus" loan. That means that you will be charged the prime rate when you take out this loan — plus something extra. It might be one percent, two percent — you name it. It's really whatever you can negotiate. So whatever you do, make sure that you discuss what rate you should really have to pay.

If you can't arrange a demand loan — or if it looks like interest rates are going to rise — you should request a fixed-rate loan. These are often called consumer loans, and they are generally repaid over a period of time agreed upon by you and the lender. Consider the individual who is buying a new car. He looks at the balance owing after his trade-in and he decides whether he wants to gamble on lower interest rates and take a demand loan or whether he wants to lock in his rate. Although the interest on a fixed-rate loan will probably be a little higher, he will be able to pay this loan off over a set number of months at a set interest rate that won't change whether interest rates rise or fall. The drawback to this type of loan, of course, is that you just don't have the flexibility to refinance whenever interest rates move in your favor. That's why business people like a demand loan; it gives them the ability to change their status whenever they wish.

The rate is also going to be important. One financial institution may be prepared to lend consumer loans at one rate whereas others will either be more competitive or more expensive. That's why it pays to shop around before you commit yourself to anything. It also pays to try to negotiate your loan rate lower either when you take the loan out or if your circumstances improve during the life of the loan.

Let me give you an example of why it's worth your while to negotiate with your lender. I was dealing with an individual who had approached a financial institution about a loan. The lender wanted collateral which the borrower was prepared to provide. In fact, the borrower already had several times the loan amount invested in the same company's term deposits. Yet the lender didn't bother to offer a prime-rate loan to this individual. In the tough economic times that we have gone through in the last few years, there were hundreds of millions of dollars worth of risky loans outstanding at better rates than this institution was prepared to offer to a client who was double-covered in terms of collateral with term deposits from the very same lender. Once we approached the institution with the question of whether or not their term deposits were safe investments, the lender had to admit that this individual was indeed a very good risk and should be entitled to a preferred rate. But even then they didn't want to offer a prime-rate loan unless they were pushed to do so. You see, it always pays to negotiate with a lender. Treat bankers as merchants with whom you can bargain. If you went to a garage sale, you wouldn't always accept the asking price, would you? Of course not. In most cases you would negotiate. If you won, you won. If you didn't, at least you would have shown the merchant that you weren't an easy target.

12

How to Choose a Financial Consultant and a Stockbroker

They say the computer industry is a growth industry, but after the 1985 federal budget and with the changes in tax laws that are promised for the future both in the United States and Canada, there's little doubt that the financial consulting industry is by far an industry with even more growth potential. The combination of taxes and inflation plus lower yields means that *everybody must have a financial consultant.* You might think you are doing things right, but are you? Things are changing so fast that it's become a must to seek a second or third opinion to ensure that you're on the right track to financial success.

Many consumers aren't aware of the values offered by a knowledgeable financial consultant, but the following suggestions may help.

Consider that you're planning a vacation in the sunny south. You call an airline and ask for its rates. Satisfied with the arrangements, you send off your check, even though you don't know for sure that this is your best deal. Not being a professional, you are restricted to calling an airline or two to compare rates or read the travel ads in your local newspaper.

If you go to a travel agent rather than an airline, the agent can advise you on all airlines. In fact, he or she may be able to get you the very same seat on the very same airline at a reduced price. Or the agent may suggest you switch to another company to take advantage of a seat sale.

Do you pay for the travel agent's services? No. In either case the agent gets a finder's fee from the airline, and you pay nothing extra. In the worst case scenario you've paid the very same price without having to shop around or you've paid less because the agent got you a better deal.

That's the way a financial consultant works. He or she will help you choose your financial destination. Or, if you've already chosen where you want to go, a consultant will help you implement your plan at no cost (in many cases), just like the travel agent.

If you want to buy some term deposits, as an example, the consultant will shop the market to get the very highest rate available. He or she will get a finder's fee from the financial institution while you get the rate you would have earned had you purchased the term deposit by yourself, or quite possibly a higher one.

If it's time to remove money from your RRSP you can deal with the company where you have your plan and accept its rate or you can approach a financial consultant or annuity broker to shop the market for you. Again, you get the best rate available at no extra cost.

Life insurance is another example. Financial consultants can also be useful in providing life insurance facilities. In chapters 35 and 36 I talk about the value of life insurance. When it comes to implementing that plan, you don't want to be locked into a company where you can only get its product. The industry is competitive; rates change regularly. Somebody who can shop the market will save you money.

And when it comes to mutual funds and other investments, you want more than just the investment. You want and need the professional advice that is so important. That's where a financial consultant is most helpful, in combining tax changes with investment decisions to ensure that you get the best *after-tax* yield. Remember, it's now how much we earn, it's how much of it we get to keep. It's after-tax income that counts.

Many financial consultants operate under the title of financial planners. Some charge a fee for their time, others levy no charges but earn a living through the finder's fees we mentioned earlier. Either are quite useful. The decision is up to you. It's not the cost that counts — it's the results.

Another type of financial consultant is a stockbroker. In the past, brokers were generally associated with the buying and selling of stocks and bonds. But as they became more tax wise and as new products were introduced, many stockbrokers have specialized in financial planning while at the same time providing product.

If you have decided that you might like to invest in the stock markets, you are going to have to find yourself a stockbroker as there are really only two ways you can buy securities listed on the major stock exchanges. You can go to your banker and ask him to enter an order, or you can go to a stockbroker, open an account, and have the broker execute the order.

Using your banker can provide a certain amount of anonymity, if that's what you desire, as the banker effectively buys the shares for the bank's account and then has the shares transferred to, and registered in, your name. However, the banker is going to charge you a fee for this service in addition to the fee that the brokerage house levies. Unless you are buying a new issue that is being sold without commission, you are going to pay a commission to buy or sell any shares no matter what brokerage firm you use. And generally speaking, that commission will be the same no matter which firm you choose to do business with. The same is true for the banker. He is going to have to pay a commission, and then he is going to tack on an additional charge. You might as well deal with a broker yourself.

Besides, you will also get free advice from stockbrokers. They are in business to sell stocks, bonds, and other investments, so they have a team of analysts who study a long list of companies and are well equipped to advise what commodities should be bought or sold. In addition, brokers have expanded their operations in recent years from strictly selling stocks or bonds to providing the best available rates in term deposits, guaranteed-investment certificates, mortgages (for investment), short-term money markets, treasury bills, and a raft of other investments that consumers might generally approach their banker to find. In fact, I often find that a stockbroker can get you a better interest rate on a term deposit than you can get yourself. In some cases they even come up with a higher rate from the very same company you went to on your own. Stockbrokers have clout. They can offer the institution a deal whereby they raise a large parcel of money at a lower cost, and faster than the institution could do using its own network. Stockbrokers also offer Canada Savings Bonds (CSBs) each fall and often arrange to pay a higher rate of return than you can earn by buying these popular bonds at a banking institution. They pay you a higher rate of return than you can earn in a bank savings account when you put CSB purchase money on deposit with them. They also pay you one or two weeks' extra interest each fall on top of the higher rate of return on your deposits, and then they sell you the CSBs commission-free, just as the banks do. And by the way, this same commission-free policy generally applies to term deposits and guaranteed-investment certificates so don't be afraid to deal with a stockbroker because you think you will be charged a high commission. You will often get a higher rate of return and better service, and at no extra cost. However, not all brokers are good. As in any business there are bad apples in the barrel so you have to be selective.

But just because a broker has made a mistake for somebody else doesn't mean that he won't do well for you. It's up to you to make the decision to get your feet wet, learning how the markets work and asking the right questions.

The first step is to learn a bit about the stock market as investing isn't quite as simple as going in to arrange a personal loan. You will be buying a piece of a company. You will own a share of that company and will have the right to share in its profits, if there are any. If the company does poorly the value of its shares will fall. If you have to sell your shares when they are down, you will face a loss. So you want to avoid the risky companies and stick with those that have shown that they are successful.

As a company becomes more profitable it will probably share its profits with you by increasing its dividends. When that happens the value of the shares you own will generally rise as more people will want them, and they'll be prepared to pay a higher price to buy them. You could sell at these higher prices, if you wished, which would give you a profit that you could invest somewhere else. However, you might choose to hang on, recognizing that you have been earning more on paper than you would have in a bank or trust company, especially when you consider that pure interest is usually only slightly higher than the inflation rate — and eventually lower than inflation after you have paid tax on it. With dividends you benefit from something called the dividend tax credit, which effectively wipes out most of the tax you would normally pay. And with capital gains — that is, selling at a higher price than you originally paid — you only have to pay tax on half the gains. The other half is yours to keep free of tax.

The idea, though, is to make sure that you make a profit and don't suffer any major losses. I've already told you that you can often earn a higher rate of return on term deposits and guaranteed-investment certificates by dealing with a broker. And brokers virtually always pay higher interest rates on money left on deposit with them. But really the bulk of their business comes from selling stocks and bonds to or on behalf of their clients. That's the riskier part that you want to make sure is handled properly. So how do you pick a broker? The easiest and usually the most successful way is to ask a friend, relative, or close associate who already has enjoyed good dealings with one. If you check with somebody you trust who has done well in the stock market, you will probably make out well yourself. If you can't get a personal reference, call up at least three brokerage firms. Ask for the manager (so you don't have to deal with the "broker of the day"), make an appointment with him or her, and go in for a personal interview.

Before you arrive, though, decide what your investment objectives are. Then you will be able to discuss them with the branch manager and ask to be placed with someone who shares those same goals.

Age has an important bearing here. If you are young you are able to take more risks. You have more time for things to go right for you. As you grow older, though, you will want more secure situations as you will have fewer years of employment to make up for your mistakes. An older individual may want to deal with a broker at an older, more established company, one that offers a lot of new underwritings that pay a good rate of return. A younger individual may want to deal with a more aggressive broker who has the pulse on more speculative companies that might make a killing sometime in the future.

You'll want to approach three companies so that you can play one against the other to see which one will do the job for you. And you shouldn't just stay with the one broker unless he is doing a spectacular job for you. You should reassess your position each year to make sure you are doing as well as you can. Remember, it's your money and if you aren't making a profit, you should move somewhere where you will.

When you talk to the three brokers, don't let them ask all the questions. They will want to find out things about you so they can see what type of investments to suggest. But you also want to find out something about them. Ask for the typical size of their accounts, which will give you an idea as to how important you will be as a client. And ask for their investment strategy to see if it matches yours. If you want to go for the high-flying, get-rich-quick issues and the broker specializes in slow-moving, old-time issues, you know you have a problem right from the beginning.

A number of investors like to borrow money to invest. Such money goes into something called a "margin account." You will want to make sure the company that you are considering offers you a margin account. You will also want to check and compare the interest rates charged on these accounts as they influence your net return.

It's becoming more and more important that brokers know something about taxation as well as investment. It's not always what you earn at a quoted interest rate that counts, but what you pocket after dealing with the tax man. So ask your potential broker what he does to keep up with the tax laws as they relate to investing.

It's also a must that you ask in which order the company sends out its research material. If it deals with many large institutional clients, it will have a large and presumably good research department that sends out recommendations. You will want to be assured that you get early access to those recommendations. Too often the research goes to the large clients well before it gets to the guy on the street. By the time you want to buy the stock, it's already partway through its rise.

Does the firm have a seat on the world's major stock exchanges? Does it offer access to the bond and short-term money markets? Is the agent on straight commission or does he draw a salary? These are important questions to ask as you may decide that you no longer want your money invested in Canada or in Canadian companies. If the company owns a seat on the New York Stock Exchange, as an example, which simply means that it is a member there and is entitled to have a trader who can buy and sell securities, then you will be able to invest easily in the United States or in other countries. Some companies form an affiliation with a foreign broker to handle these transactions, but that might mean that they don't have as much information about the foreign companies' prospects. As a result, I find that it pays to check out what access you will have to foreign markets. Another reason, of course, is that you might want to follow your portfolio while you are basking in the sun in the southern climes. If your broker is international or has an international affiliation, you may find it easier to keep an eye on your investments.

The short-term money markets are an important part in any portfolio as they will provide you with a better-than-average yield while you are waiting to pick your stocks. Or if you decide to sell your holdings if you think the stock markets are going to fall, you can tuck your money away at rates that are higher than a savings account until you decide to buy stocks again. And bonds are important too in that they are generally looked on as a more secure way to invest. In addition, you can make very large gains when interest rates are falling. On top of that, they can be factored into a portfolio to provide a monthly income if you plan to live off your investments at any time in the future.

The last two considerations might be important for another reason. If a company is involved in the international and the bond markets, I find that they often have access to foreign currencies at a better conversion rate than the banks. In no way do they intend to compete with the banks when it comes to providing savings accounts or foreign money for vacations. However, for their clients they generally do pay a higher rate of return than you will earn at a bank, trust company, or credit union, and whenever I plan a vacation, I always check the conversion rate being offered by the brokers where I deal before I turn over my Canadian dollars at a financial institution. In some instances the money saved is substantial.

I also find that it's an asset to deal with brokers who are on straight commission or who have a small guaranteed salary, as it means that they are prepared to work harder to satisfy their clientele. There is a worry that they might want to "churn" your account, that is buy and sell too often. But don't forget that you make the final decision on what transpires. You can always say no if you feel trades are being made too frequently. In the meantime, you have a broker who is working a little harder on your behalf.

Remember, it's important to the broker that you make a profit. Under no circumstances does he want you to lose. The more you make, the happier you will be and the more often you will deal with him. If, on the other hand, you aren't making a profit, find out why. And don't be afraid to hold him responsible if you were advised to invest in a losing market. Just because investing in the stock markets is unpredictable, it doesn't mean that you shouldn't be able to go back to the broker and question why he put you into a losing issue.

When you have finally decided on the firm and the broker you want to deal with, make sure you know about all possible charges. You want all costs put on the table before you deal. That includes any safekeeping charges, the interest rate earned on funds on deposit, and any additional cost for extra services. In addition, you want assurances that you will receive the proper tax documents on time each year and immediate delivery of the proceeds of any sales either to you in person, to your bank, or into your account so that you can begin earning interest right away.

Then you have to test the broker. Ask him to recommend three stocks, watch them for a little while, and start to deal with him if they do well.

It's your money. You're hoping to combine it with a broker's expertise so that you come out ahead. That's why shopping around is important and that's why it's vitally important that you pick a broker with whom you are on the same wavelength.

Negotiable commissions are a new innovation in the Canadian securities industry. Stock-market investors can now make a deal with their broker as to how much commission they will pay. Naturally, the more business you do, the more clout you will have. That might mean that commissions will actually rise for small investors who are looking for ideas and research information from their broker. However, it also probably means that a number of companies will start to offer store-front operations — perhaps inside a bank branch — where you will be able to buy and sell stocks cheaply, provided that's all you want to do. If you're content simply to place an order rather than looking for safekeeping of your securities, for analysts' reports, or for any of the other services offered by brokers, then you will be able to deal cheaply. If you want a raft of different services and are only a small investor, you might pay more. If you have some clout, demand a lower commission. And if you aren't happy, don't hesitate to shop around.

With the introduction of negotiated commissions, we've seen the introduction of a new type of stockbroker called a discount broker. They don't offer services, but instead only buy and sell stocks or bonds at a lower commission rate than you'd pay with a full service broker. If you don't need any financial help and if you've already decided which shares you want to buy, you can open an account with one of these brokers and save yourself some fees. But don't forget that most important of all in financial planning is the information you get. Simply using a discount broker to save fees when you need financial help would be defeating the purpose.

There's no question that financial consulting is a growth industry. It no longer pays to earn straight interest as it's taxable. Instead, we have to use our money in ways that help us save tax at the same time as earning a tax-free or close to tax-free income. Remember what Mark Twain said: "Even if you're on the right track, you'll get run over if you just sit there." That statement wasn't meant for money management, but there's no better place to use it. If you think you've been managing your money properly, don't be surprised if you get run over by a speeding taxman.

13

The Banker of the Future Is Here Now

There are major changes taking place in the financial community right now. Financial consulting has been catapulted into a growth industry; new, smaller banks are opening, and the trust companies, credit unions, and caisses are expanding the services they offer. And this is only the beginning. With computers taking over the banking industry, we can expect huge changes in coming years.

One of the changes I envision is a meshing of banking services. The banks have always offered stock purchase facilities but now they are becoming actual stockbrokers. At the same time the stockbrokers are crossing lines and beginning to offer banking services, and that's only right. After all, if you have a substantial sum of money on deposit or invested through a stockbroker then why shouldn't you also be able to use those funds for personal purposes without having to go into broker's office to get it? In addition, there are other services offered by brokers that are a better deal than those available at a bank, trust company, or credit union.

For example, let's say you're planning a southern vacation. Normally, you approach your banker, or several if you're smart, to convert Canadian dollars into American. I say several because the rate for foreign money changes rapidly both from institution to institution and inside institutions on a regular basis.

But why not approach your broker as well? Stockbrokers buy and sell stocks, bonds, and other investment vehicles throughout the international markets, so they always have access to foreign currencies. And they'll almost always make those currencies available to their clients at a better rate than they would pay through a conventional lending institution.

Now, before we get too excited about this idea, let's make it very clear that brokers aren't interested in buying and selling a few hundred dollars' worth of foreign currency for or from everybody who walks in off the street. But they will do it for existing customers, and the savings can be substantial, especially when thousands of dollars are involved. Generally speaking, the broker will arrange for money at a lower rate than you will pay at a conventional lender — and will buy back your foreign currency at a better price than you'd receive elsewhere. With the difference in value between our dollar and the American buck, this is a nice way to close the gap a bit.

But the brokers are now moving even closer to providing banking services. In fact, several have now introduced checking accounts, and one even provides a credit card so that clients can run an overdraft if needed.

Walwyn Stodgell Cochran Murray Ltd., in conjunction with Citibank Canada, has introduced a "cash management account." You earn slightly more on the balances you leave on account than you would earn with an ordinary account, and you get a reduced rate when you borrow money to buy investments. In fact, stockbrokers have always been lenders. They offer margin accounts where they'll lend an investor half the purchase price of investments. But Walwyn says that it'll go further with it's cash management account. It will offer an additional 25% of the purchase price. That gives investors an opportunity to buy much more stock when things are going right. Walwyn doesn't offer a credit card with this account as yet, as it is the case with Merrill Lynch, but it shouldn't be long before it does.

Midland Doherty has a similar account.

These accounts aren't meant for the little guy yet. Generally, it's expected that you will have $25,000 invested with the brokerage firm and you have to be prepared to pay some fees for the right to write checks on your brokerage account. These fees range from $100 a year to $250, but they can be expected to fall in coming years as will the balance requirements. And don't forget that these fees are tax deductible, so the real cost is lowered by your tax savings.

There are major changes on the horizon. The banks are edging in on the brokers and the brokers are becoming closer to bankers. One day not too far down the road we'll have one-stop financial planning as financial consultants offer their tremendous talents plus banking and stocks. It can only mean more benefits for investors.

14

Canada Savings Bonds

There are several types of Government of Canada bonds. The more common bond, of course, for the average consumer is the one that goes on sale each fall. That is the Canada Savings Bond. But before I tell you about CSBs, let's take a quick look at the other types of bonds sold by our federal government. They are simply called Government of Canada Bonds and are sold by stockbrokers. The interest rate is fixed, as is the number of years that they pay that interest. After the fixed term is up, they pay no interest, but you can and should cash them in and get your money back. Throughout their lifetime there is no guarantee as to their value. If interest rates that are available in the banking community are higher than these bonds, yield-holders of these bonds will not be able to sell them and recoup their original investment. However, if the opposite is the case, that is, if interest rates are lower than the yield on these bonds, then the price at which an investor could unload Government of Canada Bonds would be higher than his original cost. As a result, he would earn not only interest, but also a capital appreciation of his original investment. As a result, these bonds are popular with knowledgeable investors and institutions — that is pension funds and mutual funds.

The more common type of government bond for the average

consumer is the Canada Savings Bond. These bonds have been issued by the federal government since their inception in the mid-1940s, and they are, without a doubt, the most popular investment ever entered into by the average consumer.

They come in two different types. The first type was issued until the fall of 1976. This type we refer to as a coupon bond. To collect your interest, you used to cut the coupons off the bonds for each corresponding period and take them to one of the financial institutions to collect your interest. We used to call that "coupon clipping" and will until the end of 1986 when all the coupon-type bonds will have matured. I use the date 1986 loosely as there has never been an issue of these bonds that has been completely cashed in. I'm sure that at the end of 1986 or even 1990 there will still be some of these bonds that haven't been cashed. Yet they won't be paying any interest at all.

The second type of CSB is now more common. These are computer-type bonds which were introduced in the fall of 1976. They are the only way that Ottawa now issues CSBs. They are controlled by a giant computer in Ottawa that either issues and mails a check each fall or automatically deposits the interest due into the account you choose. There is a third option that the computer handles. That involves automatically compounding your interest until you decide to collect it or cash in the bonds. If there is one investment Canadians like, it is Canada Savings Bonds.

The advantage to these bonds is their great flexibility. Often that is the only advantage, as on far too many occasions Canadians have bought bonds, and held on to bonds they already owned, when they could have done much, much better if they put their money elsewhere. Canada Savings Bonds don't always pay a very competitive rate of return.

In the past few years, though, they have offered not only the most flexible terms available to the average consumer, but also a very attractive yield. Of course, that phenomenon has attracted all the speculators and sophisticated investors into the campaign so Ottawa has been able to raise huge sums of money. It's also forced Ottawa to change the terms of the CSB campaign: so that they are no longer locked into the yield that is offered each fall. Now these bonds change each fall so that they better reflect the rate of return available elsewhere. That means that we have to become much more aware of what's happening in the interest-rate markets each fall so that we can make an educated decision on whether we should hold onto the bonds we already own or whether we should put any money into the new issue that is on sale.

First, let's look at why these bonds are so attractive to consumers. They are virtually the same as cash, except for the rate of return you earn on your money. They generally pay a higher rate of return than a savings account — at least they do when they are put on sale in November. As the year progresses, the rate paid on a savings account will fluctuate. If it falls, so too does the rate your money earns for you. However, the rate of return on CSBs will not fall below the quoted rate during the year. Bond rates are now adjusted each November, but you are guaranteed that the rate on all the 1982-issue bonds, for example, will never fall below 8½%, while the rate on all bonds issued before '82 that have not yet matured will not fall below 10½% during their lifetime.

However, if interest rates start to rise, you know that you can always cash in your CSBs on a minute's notice and get back every cent you used to buy them as well as the interest that is owing up until the end of the last complete month you owned them. And that's exactly what we should do. Otherwise we are simply playing into the government's hands. If we can earn more elsewhere, we should. If we don't take advantage of the opportunity to earn elsewhere, the government comes out ahead because they don't have to pay as much interest as other investments. What usually happens in this case is that the more knowledgeable investors start to move their money out of CSBs and buy short-term money-market investments. First, their money starts to earn a higher rate of return. Second, that return is compounded faster so the actual yield is even higher, and third, the investors don't really give up much in the way of flexibility as they only invest their money for thirty days at a time. You only get your interest on completed months with CSBs anyway so you are almost on an even basis as far as flexibility is concerned. However, you come out substantially ahead in the amount you earn.

Once enough investors start to follow this pattern, Ottawa gets scared and increases the rate they pay on CSBS so that all bond holders will benefit. But the smart ones are ahead of the game, as they have been earning a higher rate all along. Now, that's where many consumers get hurt when they buy CSBS. They simply lock their money away in these bonds and don't pay attention to what is going on elsewhere. Generally speaking, CSBs are better than leaving your money in a savings account — especially when interest rates are falling. However, when rates rise, even a savings account can end up being better than a CSB. So please pay more attention. There are billions of dollars of consumers' money tied up in these bonds right now. That opens the door for a lot of free interest for the federal government if we don't seek out the best possible return rate available. It might also mean that our investments and savings don't keep ahead of inflation — especially if we earn more than $1,000 per year in investment income and have to pay tax on what we earn. What better way to fall behind in the fight for security than to lend our money to Ottawa at a lower rate than that available elsewhere and then to share the rewards with another arm of the government — the tax man?

But here's the other way that we lose out with these bonds. Far too often we think they go on forever, or we lock them away and forget about them without realizing that they all have a set maturity date. They don't last forever. When the clock stops ticking on a specific series, the bonds in that series instantly stop paying any interest at all. You get all your money and all the interest that has built up to that date, of course. But from then on your money sits in the government coffers earning no interest, while it is being eroded by the ravages of inflation. There are hundreds of millions worth of bonds outstanding that no longer pay one red cent of interest. These bonds have expired and the money is being eaten away by inflation. What's more, the money could have been reinvested at a higher rate in many cases, but wasn't.

Always pay attention to the series number on your bonds. That will tell you if you own some of the millions of dollars that are no longer earning any interest at all. Check your numbers against the list in this chapter to see if you should be making a mad beeline to a financial institution to collect money for your expired bonds and get it reinvested somewhere else.

Effective November 1, 1985, every bond issue that bears the number thirty-one (31) or a lower number plus S33 should be cashed immediately as none of these bonds pays interest any longer. In fact, there are still $116,600 worth of bonds that were issued back in the 1940s when CBSs replaced war bonds as a way for Ottawa to raise money. They do not pay any interest and have not for 40 years or so. Inflation has greatly diminished the value of those bonds. Back then, $116,600 would be worth a lot of money. In fact, at only 6%, that $116,600 would have grown to be worth more than one million dollars today. At the rate that CBSs now pay, 8½% to 10½%, these bonds would have multiplied to be worth $6.9 million. It's bad enough that Ottawa hasn't had to pay these people this interest, but it's even worse that the people have mismanaged their money.

That's only one issue of bonds. Every year since the introduction of these bonds there have been people who did not bother to cash in bonds that had matured. At the end of 1984, this is the list of bonds that had not yet been redeemed. If you find any bonds bearing these numbers, get your cash quickly and invest it somewhere else.

S1	$116,600	S12	$292,500	S23	$9,944,900
S2	$48,450	S13	$262,450	S24	$13,066,900
S3	$41,900	S14	$298,750	S25	$10,570,300
S4	$59,650	S15	$297,050	S26	$8,728,000
S5	$49,650	S16	$367,200	S27	$40,776,000
S6	$85,350	S17	$1,148,000	S28	$263,240,350
S7	$73,350	S18	$685,250	S29	$45,627,850
S8	$161,200	S19	$557,200	S30	$66,776,700
S9	$108,300	S20	$710,900	S31	$472,325,300
S10	$117,050	S21	$3,569,700	S33	$2,885,177,700
S11	$116,700	S22	$2,256,200		

Special replacement series (SRS) $941,500

The total number of Canada Savings Bonds outstanding that should have been cashed in by November 1985 but haven't been equals more than $5 billion. Effective November 1, 1985 every one of these bond issues should be redeemed so that you can reinvest the money elsewhere where it will at least offset the impact of inflation.

Any bond with a number higher than 31 still pays interest except for series 33. Each and every one of these bond issues is now the new type of bond where you receive interest yearly or at maturity via a Government of Canada check. No longer do you have to worry about clipping coupons and collecting special cash or maturity bonuses. In a way that's a bit of a negative in that at least some of the older coupon-type bonds paid bonuses that were only half taxable.

Seeing as how many of the bonds that are still outstanding after their maturity date, I'm going to suggest the way we should be treating these special cash bonuses just in case you still have some of those bonds and want to cash them in.

Series 23, 25, 27, and 28 paid special cash bonuses back in 1979. You didn't have to cash the bonds to get them, but you did have to present them to a financial institution where they cut off the top left-hand corner. If your top left-hand corner is intact you collected the bonus; if not, make sure you do when you take your bonds in to cash them now.

In addition, many of the coupon bonds still in existence in 1979 and later qualified for a maturity bonus. It could only be collected if you held the bonds until the day they expired. The last of this group expired on November 1, 1985 which means you can cash any of these coupon-type bond issues any time you want to without fear of losing your special cash bonuses.

And don't forget that all these special bonuses are considered half taxable and half tax free. Divide the total in half, pocket one-half tax free, and claim the other as investment income on your tax return.

The compounding coupons do not qualify for the same tax treatment. They are, quite simply, interest — interest that's taxable once you exceed $1,000 in any one year.

In addition to the tax advantages that apply to the coupon-type bonds, there are also some small advantages to series 32, 33, 34, and 35. Because their rates of return were increased when rates were rising, Ottawa allows us to claim the originally quoted rate when we bought the bonds as interest and any additional return as half taxable, half tax free. If you own any of these bond issues, make sure you get a specific quote as to the tax consequences for each bond you own before you cash them in.

When bonds mature, consumers often find themselves in a real tax jackpot if they qualify for special bonuses or if they've been compounding the bonds. As an example, the fall of 1985 saw three separate issues of Canada Savings Bonds mature — two issues qualified for special bonuses and one was the new-type bond where compounding was allowed. Holders of each of these bond issues had several defensive moves they could take.

With all series don't forget that you don't pay any tax on the original value of the bonds. That's simply a return of your own money, so why should you pay any tax on it?

With series 28 you could cash the bonds in November and receive the original value tax free. However, the special cash bonuses would also have to be collected at the same time, half being tax free. If one wishes, the interest and compounding coupons do not have to be cashed. They can be held to a future year and cashed at that time. The benefit is that it's a form of income spreading whereby some interest is cashed in each year without pushing you into a higher bracket in one year.

The same theory applies to Series 31, but in the case of series 33 and all bonds that mature from 1986 on, there's on longer any ability to defer income this way. Effective 1986, once a bond matures all interest not already claimed on that bond must be added to your income.

But even then there are things that we can do that'll help us save taxes when we know we have some sizable extra amounts of income about to become taxable.

When you know you have a compounding investment that's going to come due in any one year, you may want to contribute extra money to a registered retirement savings plan that year to offset some of the extra income that's going to come in. That way some of the excess will be sheltered from the taxman's grasp. Those who now receive a pension get a special break in that they can rollover as much of that pension income into their RRSP as they wish. By properly planning your affairs, you may be able to maintain your income level even though it was going to rise, while at the same time not have to worry about higher tax bills. All you're really doing is receiving the investment income rather than the pension income. The pension income becomes tax free because it was rolled over into your RRSP. It will not compound tax free inside the plan or you can gradually remove it, and face only a small tax bill rather than the large one you were in store for.

Another option may be to buy a sophisticated tax shelter as long as these remain available. The tax deductions you get will offset the extra income you have coming in.

Another option, if we think well in advance, would be to switch all our other investment income into capital gains and Canadian dividend-producing investments. That way the investment income we receive the rest of the year would be virtually tax free leaving room for the extra investment income that we didn't normally receive.

For those investors who are prepared to think along the more sophisticated lines there's a sure-fire way to best this income explosion problem. When you know in advance that it's going to happen, you can always have a talk with a financial consultant and see if you can't put the following idea in place.

Let's say you have $10,000 extra coming due. You can always go out and borrow $50,000 or so. At 12% the interest charges would be $6,000 a year, which allows you to cover $6,000 worth of extra interest this year. You get a $6,000 tax deduction which effectively offsets $6,000 worth of extra income. If you use the $50,000 to buy mutual funds, good quality stocks or income-producing real estate, you'll get this tax deductibility plus a yield which might be mostly tax free. Next year that income will help to service your loan which means you now have an investment that's partly been paid for by the taxman.

Before you get too carried away with this last idea, let me give some advice. Get the help of a professional, somebody who can assess whether or not you are a candidate for this type of financial maneuver. Also, you should read carefully the material on getting money out of your RRSP and "leverage" for further insight into what we are trying to accomplish.

When it comes to buying CSBs, it's a must to compare their rate of return to what's available elsewhere in the marketplace at the same time. If you can earn more elsewhere and can afford to lock most of your money away for a longer period of time, why not do so? You will earn more interest and you can still keep some of your money in CSBs, a savings account, or other short-term investments that will give you access to emergency money if you need it.

If the interest-rate picture suggests that you should buy bonds, then don't be afraid to buy them from a stockbroker rather than simply walking into your neighborhood bank. First of all, brokers don't charge you one cent more than the other financial institutions. Too often consumers are afraid to deal with a stock-broker as they are afraid that they are going to have to pay a commission. When it comes to CSBs, however, you will pay exactly the same price as you would at a bank, but will probably come out with better service and probably a slightly higher rate of return. Brokers will usually give you a higher rate of return on your money during the period leading up to the CSB sales period than you can earn if you leave your money in another financial institution. And brokers keep paying that high interest rate until you actually have to pay for the bonds, which is usually partway into the sales campaign. In past years Ottawa has allowed savers a period of ten days to two weeks after the campaign began, during which they could earn interest on their savings and also on their bonds. The theory was that it took a certain amount of time to get your money out of your savings account without losing interest at the end of the month. However, with the advent of daily-interest savings accounts, this time period has been shortened to only one week and could conceivably be shortened further in coming years — all the more reason to deal with a broker. You can issue a check that takes several days to clear your bank, instead of having the money instantly removed from your savings account when you buy at your bank.

But there is another way to buy CSBs. When it appears that interest rates are falling, you should sit down and calculate how much income you are going to have each month, money you won't need for bills. If interest rates are really going to fall, these savings that you are going to be accumulating are going to earn less and less each month. Why not arrange with your employer, if he offers a payroll-deduction plan for the purchase of CSBs, to-deduct that amount from your paycheck each month? Now you know that you have guaranteed yourself no less than the CSBs' rate of return. If you find that interest rates turn around and start to rise, you can always cancel your forced savings plan, sell the bonds, and invest the money elsewhere. While you are buying these bonds on your payroll-deduction plan, you will have to pay interest on the outstanding balance but that interest is charged at the same rate the bonds are paying, or less, so you will do no worse than break even while locking in a high rate of return as interest rates fall, and opening the door to a number of moves if they start to rise. In effect, it's like having an insurance policy that guarantees that you can't do any worse than break even. It won't cost you a cent, but you have every opportunity to gain. And don't forget that every cent of interest you pay on this payroll-deduction plan is completely tax deductible. In fact, many people take compound bonds where the interest accumulates. They pay no interest until years down the road, but they write the interest they pay off against other income as a tax deduction now. They end up with an extra bonus.

If your employer doesn't offer a payroll-deduction plan, you can approach any of the major financial institutions. Always hold out for a low interest rate on the loan to buy the bonds. Actually, many people don't realize that they take out a loan when they buy CSBs on a payroll-deduction plan. I remember a phone call from an older woman who called to say what a brilliant idea I had when I suggested this purchase plan on one of my radio shows. A year later she called back to tell me how disappointed she was to find out that she had been paying interest on a loan all this time. Yet when I showed her how she had earned more interest on the bond than she had paid on the loan and told her that it was totally tax deductible, and at a lower rate than the banks charged their very best customers, she jumped higher than she had at any time in the last fifty years. It's just another one of those examples of earning a little extra because you managed your money properly. CSBS, as the singularly best and most popular investment for the average consumer, can offer those same possibilities if they are handled properly. However, if interest rates do not go in your favor, don't waste any time getting out of them and investing your money elsewhere.

15

RRSPs —
Take Out the Second R

I wish I had a dollar for every time somebody has told me that they don't want to put any money into a registered retirement savings plan because they are young and don't want to think about retirement. They want to spend their money now and have a good time while they are young. These people shouldn't let themselves be fooled by the advertising campaigns that always accompany these plans. It is true that Ottawa did devise the plans to encourage us to save for our retirement so that we would be less likely to demand government assistance when we got old. But we shouldn't think these plans are solely for retirement purposes. Instead, we should use them for immediate benefits, for the tax savings they provide now. We'll worry about retirement later.

Let me relate to you a story about a friend who called me up and told me that he had several salespeople trying to get him to put money into their RRSPs. Right off the bat, I'm leery about salespeople as they have to be paid somehow — and usually out of your pocket. That means that not all your money works for you, so you don't make as much in the long run. There are lots of financial institutions that will take your money and pay you a decent, competitive rate of return without charging any fees whatsoever.

This individual had $4,000 in savings in a bank. He was in the thirty-five-percent tax bracket, which means about $20,000 in taxable income in Ontario. He wanted to keep $3,000 in an emergency savings account in case he needed it sometime, which partially explains his reluctance to lock his money away in a registered retirement savings plan: he thought he would never be able to get his hands on it until he retired. This is not true! He had another $1,000 he wanted to use to buy some new stereo components. My answer to him was this: "If you do it my way, I will get you the stereo equipment you want for nothing." He was interested. I wanted him to put his $3,000 into an RRSP where the money would be invested in short-term certificates. He would earn just as much, or more, inside the plan than he would in the savings account, except that the money would grow faster because it would compound free of tax inside the plan.

Because he was in the thirty-five-percent tax bracket, Ottawa would send him back $1,050 more than he was expecting in tax rebates. He could go ahead and buy the stereo now, putting it on charge if he wanted, and the tax rebate would probably be back in time for him to pay for it. He would get his stereo, have the $1,000 in an emergency savings plan, and also have an additional $3,000 inside his RRSP, which he could get at any time he wanted. He would have to wait until the monthly short-term deposits matured, but he would never be more than thirty days away from that. He had the best of all worlds.

Needless to say, when it was explained to him that way, he lost his fear of RRSPs and has bought one every year since. In fact, the next year he called me up and said, "Guess what? The tax man bought me a stereo last year; this year he's picking up the tab for a trip to Acapulco."

You see, you don't want to think of RRSPs as a long-term investment, but instead as a way to save taxes and invest your money at the same time. When you put your money into an RRSP, you form a partnership with the tax man. You make your contribution, he chips in his portion, and the combination earns interest in your name without any tax being levied as long as the money remains inside the plan. It will grow much faster inside the plan than it would anywhere else. First of all, you won't have as much money if you have to pay tax on it, and secondly the money that you do have will earn interest that will only be taxed once you exceed $1,000 in investment income.

To further the theory that RRSPs should be looked on as short-term investment vehicles — in essence, registered savings plans instead of registered retirement savings plans — consider these uses. Suppose you are working full time, but you know that you are going to go back to school full time next year. If you put the maximum contribution into one of these plans now, you may save tax dollars at thirty or thirty-five percent, but when you quit work and go back to school, your income — and as a result your tax level — will fall substantially, maybe even to zero. Then when you collapse your RRSP, you will pay little or no tax on the money that you get back. You have helped finance your education by using an RRSP properly. You may not want to collapse the entire plan, but only take out enough to satisfy your needs. That way you can judge what your tax situation will be and also leave more money to withdraw in the coming year.

Women who are working now but know they will probably leave work in the future to start a family should also put the maximum into one of these plans as they can save tax dollars now, when they are paying them, but probably not have to pay any when they are no longer working while raising a family. It's also the perfect way to spread your income out over a number of years. Your disposable income is a little lower right now, but so are your taxes. In fact, when you get your tax rebate, it will fill in some of that gap. However, once your salary comes to a halt the disruption won't be painful: you will be able to smooth out the drop by taking money out of your RRSP. You might also be planning a sabbatical or you might thank your lucky stars that you had money in your plan when you join the ranks of the unemployed. While working, you were paying a high tax rate; while unemployed your rate is substantially lower. When you had a regular paycheck you saved substantial tax dollars by putting money into one of these plans. Now that your income is sub-stantially lower, so is the tax take. If you saved thirty-five cents on the dollar when you put money in last year and have to pay only fifteen cents on the dollar now that you are taking it out, you have not only earned ten or twelve or fourteen percent inside the plan, but you have earned an additional twenty percent on your money in saved tax dollars. If you can put the money in at a high rate and take it out at a lower one, the net difference is an extra bonus to you for using the plan properly.

Naturally Ottawa wants us to use these plans to supplement our retirement, and rightly so. That's why it is a must that anybody who is contemplating retirement should consider putting the maximum into a RRSP. Unfortunately, though, two things are bound to happen. One, we have a tendency to wait until later in our lives to do these things and, as a result, lose many of the advantages of an RRSP. We should start putting money into RRSPs as soon as we possibly can. Even a young, newly hired individual must get used to practising tax planning. Once you pay that money to the tax man, you have very little hope of ever getting it back. The next thing we do wrong is to pick the wrong plan.

There is a cardinal rule that I try to follow when it comes to contributing to a registered retirement savings plan. When you deal with a deposit-taking institution, you must always opt for a plan where there are no fees. None to get in, none to get out, and none to manage your money while it's inside the plan. That way all your money is working for you. Don't forget, also, that these institutions effectively charge you a hidden fee. When you contribute to a plan they may pay you 10%, but they lend the money back out as a mortgage two or three percentage points higher. You could have earned the two or three percent yourself instead of giving it to the institution *and you pay it every year*.

That's why I don't worry too much about the acquisition charges involved with mutual funds. You'll pay as much as nine percent upfront, but you only pay it once. And mutual funds normally outdistance a term deposit when the money is left invested for a reasonable period of time. That's not to say that you shouldn't consider a mutual fund where there are no fees, but generally I find you're better off looking at past performance rather than the lack of fees when it comes to investing money. I mean, if you save a few dollars in fees but buy a fund that's shown a several percent lower past performance, the chances are that you'll earn less every year — and that'll cost you more in the long run than you save now.

We also have to seek out the highest rate of return possible. In our chapter on the compounding of money, I show how important a quarter of a percent can be over a long period of time. That's especially true inside one of these plans, as your money is multiplying for a number of years completely tax free as long as it's inside the plan. Generally speaking, you will get the best rates interest wise combined with the lowest fees (none) at the smaller trust companies. They like these plans as they can generally count on long-term money to remain on deposit. Shop the smaller companies each year when you are going to make your contribution and don't be afraid to move the rest of your money from institution to institution. Go where the best rate can be found. That's why it is so important that you get a plan where there are no fees whatsoever.

There are occasions, though, where you may want to consider paying a fee for one of these plans, such as when you take a self-administered or self-directed plan, or purchase a mutual fund inside your RRSP. Self-directed plans allow you to manage the money inside your plan yourself. You can buy stocks listed on major Canadian stock exchanges, bonds, CSBs, term deposits, or a variety of other eligible investments including mutual funds. The advantage to this type of plan is that you can manage your own money. If you think you are smarter and can manage your money better than the banker, then go to a stockbroker or a money manager to open a self-directed RRSP. Stockbrokers have become the whiz kids at these plans as they spend all day managing money anyway. But they have also removed one of the major drawbacks to this type of plan — the costs involved. Lots of trust companies also offer these plans, but they charge some pretty healthy fees to manage them. In addition, they allow you only a small number of trades each year before they increase the tab. Stockbrokers, however, charge you only a flat rate of $100 per year to handle these accounts, allowing you as many trades as you want.

If you are a good investor or if you have a particularly good broker, you may be able to make considerably more in one of these self-directed RRSPs than you would by simply leaving your money in a fixed-rate plan with a financial institution. However, one word of caution. All the money that you take out of these plans is taxed as income. Any capital gains that you make outside the plan are tax free so you are ahead of the game when you invest outside the plan. In addition, any losses you incur outside the plan are treated as capital losses and are added to your one-half million dollars' worth of tax-free capital gains.

If you already have a considerable amount of money in your RRSP, you might be able to make it grow faster by using one of these self-directed plans. However, if you are not a knowledge-able investor, you might be better off sticking with a conven-tional deposit plan of the kind you generally find at financial institutions or switch to a high-quality mutual fund. But remember the main criteria: no fees to get in, none to get out, and none to manage your money while it is on deposit if you are using a deposit-taking institution. If you choose a mutual fund, don't worry about the fees — we'll worry about them later. The most important thing to remember about these plans is that if you are paying tax, you should consider having an RRSP. Regard-less of your age, you will be a winner if you avoid paying taxes, so do not let yourself put off purchasing one of these plans because you are young. The sooner you start the faster the money begins to grow.

As an example, let's use my thirty-year-old friend who got himself a free stereo when he used an RRSP as a short-term plan. Let's see how he might come out over the long term. If, starting at age thirty, he put $3,000 each year into one of these plans and earned a very low 9% inside the plan (you can never be sure what long-term interest rates will be, but last year they varied from 13% to 20%), he would accumulate $705,373.83 by age sixty-five. Had he started only five years earlier, at age twenty-five, he would accumulate $399,501.20 more, for a total of more than $1.1 million. At age sixty-five he would be able to purchase an annuity that would pay him more than $100,000 a year for the rest of his life. The most important thing, though, is that this man con-tributed only $15,000 more in those five extra years. Except he didn't really put in $15,000 of his own money. He put in his share, and Ottawa contributed $5,250 in tax savings. For a total invest-ment of $9,750 over five years, this individual has been able to turn a profit of almost $400,000. Now you can see why it's so very important that we start these plans at the earliest date possible.

In fact, it will even pay to put in less than the $3,000 we have been using in this example. Unfortunately, many twenty-five-year-olds who are just starting out may find that $3,000 is beyond their means so they may choose to pass until they have enough money to start a decent-sized plan. But that could be a giant mistake — a smaller plan started earlier could prove more beneficial than a bigger plan opened several years later. A $1,000-a-year plan begun at age twenty-five would grow to be worth more by age sixty-five than a $3,000-a-year plan begun at age forty. Even though the contributions are significantly smaller, the end result is higher because of the total compounding that takes place inside these shelters.

Consider again my friend who planned to spend $1,000 on his stereo. If he had started a $1,000 RRSP at age twenty-five, he would accumulate $368,292 by age sixty-five. That's based, again, on nine percent, which is a very conservative figure. However, if he was to earn fourteen percent, let's say, he would see his plan grow to be worth $1.3 million. Interest rates will play an important role, especially as the plan starts to grow quickly in the latter years. That's why it's so important to get your money into the plan as soon as you can.

Over the forty years from age twenty-five to age sixty-five, my friend will contribute $40,000 if he continues to contribute $1,000 per year. Yet, if he remains in the thirty-five-percent tax bracket, Ottawa will have returned to him a total of $14,000 ($350 x 40). That means that his total out-of-pocket contribution will have been only $26,000 — which will have multiplied to be worth $368,000 or much, much more depending on where interest rates go. At today's annuity rates, that money would pay a lifetime income, and in one year my friend would receive more than his total investment. Each year from then on he would be in a pure profit position. He had enjoyed tax breaks when he put the money in each year, and he would also get an additional tax break when he took it out. Any individual who earns pension income from a source other than the government can receive the first $1,000 tax free, so now he has another opportunity to save some additional taxes.

Just to show you how much the penalty will be if you hold off opening one of these plans, consider a few figures. A five-year delay in implementing this program — waiting until you are thirty — would mean you contribute $5,000 less. Actually that's only $3,250, as the tax man contributes his share along with you. When the plan matures, when you are sixty-five — you will have $133,000 less inside it. So $3,250 can really be a lot of money if you handle your affairs improperly.

We have a number of other things that we must consider when we put our money into these plans. If you earn substantially more than your spouse and will have a substantially higher pension, you should put your money into a spousal RRSP. You still get the very same tax deduction when you put your money in, but the money accrues in your spouse's name. When it comes time to start living off that income, your spouse can buy an annuity or a registered retirement income fund and earn the first $1,000 totally free of tax. In addition, the rest of the income your spouse earns will probably be taxed at a lower rate than it would if it remained in your name on top of your other income. It's another excellent way for us to split our family income to save tax dollars.

It used to be a nice trick for you — the high-income spouse — to deposit the maximum amount into an RRSP for your spouse and then to have your spouse collapse the plan right away and add the income to other earnings for tax purposes. You would be saving tax at a high rate; your spouse would pay tax at a low rate, if at all. So as a family you would come out ahead. But Revenue Canada caught on to that one. Now we must wait three years after putting money into a spousal RRSP before we collapse the plan, or we will have to add all the contributions we have made to any spousal RRSPs to *our* income in the year the plan is collapsed. So make sure, when you put money into a spousal plan, that you know exactly what you are doing. And if you do use a spousal RRSP, make sure you have a marriage that is on good footing. If you split and your spouse collapses the spousal RRSP, your spouse gets the money and you will be reassessed for the tax over the past three years.

Don't be afraid to have several RRSPs. As you've seen from our figures, some of these plans can grow to a pretty huge size. Financial institutions are only covered to a maximum of $60,000 by the Canada Deposit Insurance Corporation, and it may not take very long for you to exceed that limit. If you want to deal with the smaller institutions where you generally get the best deals, you will want to spread your money out for security. However, don't dwell on the security of your money too much when you are dealing with these financial institutions — we will have to be in one giant of a jackpot before the banking industry allows a major collapse without first merging any troubled institutions into a healthy one.

Naturally, not everybody bothers to contribute money to these tax-saving plans, especially not young couples who are more likely to take what savings they have and put them toward furniture or the mortgage on their house.

One question I hear all the time is: "Should I put the savings that I have into a registered retirement savings plan or should I use that money to pay down my mortgage?" It's not a question that everybody has to face as they might not have any excess money or their mortgage might not come due at the same time as they are putting money into one of these plans. Then again, their mortgage might be completely closed, which means that they can't put money against it even if they wanted to. However, that last group is a small one. Generally speaking, most consumers can arrange to put some extra cash against their mortgage if they wish to — and they should consider it — but not necessarily at the expense of their registered retirement savings plan.

Even with substantially lower interest rates, you still know that you are going to get a generous tax rebate when you make a contribution to one of these registered plans. At the same time, you are going to earn tax-free investment income inside the plan so that you would have to be paying a pretty hefty rate on your mortgage before it became an advantage to pay it off rather than putting money into an RRSP.

Here's what you can do. If you put the money you have into an RRSP each year you will get a tax rebate that you can use to pay down your mortgage. You weren't counting on the money anyway, as it had already been deducted from your payroll, but now that you do get it back you can use it to pay off your loan. As an example, consider a homeowner in the thirty-five percent tax bracket (about $20,000 in taxable income in Ontario) who puts $3,500 into his RRSP. He will get a tax rebate of $1,225 that he otherwise would not have qualified for. Let's say that at the same time he had a $70,000 mortgage taken out at fourteen percent. When that mortgage anniversary date rolls around, he could take his $1,225 registered retirement savings plan tax rebate and pay it against the mortgage, knocking down the principal amount. If he continued to do that every year he would pay his mortgage off in 14½ years instead of the normal twenty-five. At the same time he would have a tax-sheltered registered retirement savings plan worth some $204,409 if today's interest rates applied throughout the entire period. His house, which rises in value tax-free is paid for, so it continues to grow in real dollars. He also has a sizable amount of money built up inside his RRSP which, at only ten percent, will grow by more than $2,000 per month from then on even if he never makes another contribution.

There are occasions when you pay such a high rate on your mortgage that it would be better for you to pay any extra savings you have against that loan. However, if you can get into the habit of putting money into a registered retirement savings plan and then using the rebate faithfully to pay down your mortgage, you will have the best of both worlds.

16

Federal Budget Changes RRSP Rules

The spring 1985 federal budget has drastically altered RRSPs, and many of the changes, while positive at first glance, are in fact going to prove negative for taxpayers.

The most dramatic change is the escalation in the contribution limits. Beginning with 1986, the contribution limits rise $2,000 a year from the 1985 level of $5,500 until they top out in 1990 at $15,500 per individual. That sounds like a lot of tax savings, but it may not be for most of us. In the first place there's an affordability problem. Only the higher income groups will be able to afford a contribution that large. The second problem is a change in the percentage of our earned income that we can contribute to the plan. At 20% until the end of 1985 it falls to only 18% from then on. That means that a self-employed individual with $30,000 in earned income who could contribute $5,500 before the changes will only be able to contribute $5,400 beginning in 1986. Yet the budget made it sound like he or she could contribute $7,500 — a cruel trick, indeed.

Another major change involves the definition of "earned income." Prior to 1986, we could include most of our employment income plus pension income and any rental income we received after deducting expenses. Beginning in 1986, though, the pension income and rental income will no longer apply. That means that those who have retired and were putting 20% of their pension into a spousal RRSP will no longer be able to. And those who purchased rental properties so they could contribute to an RRSP will likewise be penalized. We can still roll pension income into our own RRSPs, but come 1990 even that privilege will be removed unless we simply use it to fulfil the $15,500 limit that will apply at that time. Those with larger pension incomes will definitely be penalized at that time.

Canadians who are presently enrolled in pension plans at their place of employment may be hurt even more by the changes in RRSP rules. If you're enrolled in a money purchase pension plan, you'll have to total your employer's contribution to your pension plan, your own contributions to your pension plan at work if you do contribute, and your contribution to your RRSP. The total must not exceed 18% of your earned income or $7,500 in 1986 with the numbers rising by $2,000 a year until 1990.

That's pretty straightforward. However, when it comes to defined benefit plans, which most companies use, it's a little more complicated. Initially we were going to be restricted to a maximum contribution to our RRSPs each year of only $2,000. However, Finance Minister Michael Wilson has buckled under the pressure of constant complaining and has allowed those who have defined benefit plans to operate under the old rules for 1985 and 1986. That is, we subtract from $3,500 the amount that we contribute to our company pension plan with the remainder allowed to be deposited in our RRSPs. From 1985 on we will be restricted to a maximum contribution of $2,000 to our RRSPs with the yearly maximums that we can contribute to our company pension plans increasing to $15,500 by 1990.

However, the budget hasn't taken away one of our favorite tricks. It's called overcontributing to a registered retirement savings plan. It can save you a ton of tax dollars. As you proceed through the RRSP sections of this book, you'll become well aware of the values of overcontributing to an RRSP. Not only was it not taken away by the '85 budget, it was effectively legitimized by Finance Minister Michael Wilson as he authorized the tax free removal of overcontributed funds from our RRSPs. As the numbers escalate to $15,500 a year, our overcontribution theory will grow in value.

The new budget also gave us a number of other tax-planning tactics that we can use rather than an RRSP if you don't qualify or in addition to an RRSP if you do qualify. I'll explain these in detail in future chapters.

17

An RRSP and a Pension Times Two

Under the old RRSP rules, we had an interesting way to get full contributions to a registered retirement savings plan at the same time as we took maximum advantage of a pension plan at work.

If you contributed $3,500 to your pension plan at work, you were effectively eliminated from taking a tax deduction when you contributed to your RRSP. Those with a pension were allowed to deduct only 20% of their earned income to a maximum of $3,500 less any contributions made personally to a pension at work. If you contributed a full $3,500, you'd used up your maximum limit. Of course, that didn't stop you from contributing to your RRSP anyway and treating it as an overcontribution. Indeed, that may very well be to your advantage. Or you could check into the following possibility.

Revenue Canada allows us to play catch up for past years when we didn't contribute to a pension at work. That means that if you didn't contribute to your pension one year in the past that you can effectively choose between an RRSP or a pension this year. And that's where this idea comes in.

Let's roll the clock back to the end of 1984. At that time you told your employer you no longer wanted to be part of the company pension plan. You felt you could do better on your own.

And you carried through with that idea for all of 1985. Come the end of 1985, then, you can contribute $3,500 into your RRSP (provided your earned income allows it). Ah ha! But beginning 1986 you can go back to your employer and request the right to rejoin the company pension plan and the right to contribute to that pension plan for a past year when you weren't a member. That means that you get $3,500 for 1986 plus an additional $3,500 for 1985 — a past year. When you combine the three contributions in two years you have a total of $10,500, which works out to an average of $5,250 per year, well above the standard $3,500 yearly limit. In addition, you may also enjoy the advantages of your employer matching the contributions to your RRSP which will put you even further ahead.

There are taxpayers out there, you know, who have practised this type of tax planning for years. Every second year they opt out of their company pension plan and make it up the year after. They get three years' worth of tax relief every two years.

Now, before we get too carried away with this idea we have two people to approach. One is your employer to see what you can and cannot do now that we have pension and RRSP limits that will rise every year until 1990. The second is a finacial consultant who will help escort you through this financial jungle. It may well be that you should choose another tax-planning idea; or you may be in the wrong type of pension; or you may be better off opting for a registered retirement savings plan only rather than a company pension plan. Or you might just be a candidate for substantially greater use of your pension and RRSP. With the limits rising to $15,500 by 1990 and with the ability to defer contributions to your RRSP for as long as seven years — and then catch up to the full amount — you may want to reverse the order of planning; that is, pension first, RRSP second. A financial consultant is a must in this case.

18

Offbeat Uses of RRSPs

I hear from a large number of consumers who tell me that they don't want to contribute to a registered retirement savings plan because they will only have to pay the tax back sooner or later. "What's the good of putting money into these plans now, even though I know that I will save taxes, when I will probably have to pay back a higher tax rate when I start drawing on that money?" they ask.

Good point. But don't forget that while the money is inside the plan it will be growing and compounding completely tax free. As a result, there's a very good chance that even with the tax liability, when you take it out you will be ahead of the game.

Or, maybe you'd rather arrange to remove the money with very little tax liability no matter how much money is inside the plan. Consider this example. An individual who has accumulated $100,000 inside his RRSP come retirement time would have to add the full amount to his income if he collapsed it in one fell swoop. In most provinces that means a 50% loss. He gets to keep one half of his RRSP and loses one half to the taxman. No wonder financial institutions get a positive response when they suggest a lifetime annuity where the income is gradually added to the person's income over the rest of his lifetime or a registered retirement income fund where it's spread over twenty years or so. The tax liability is lower, but you still have to give up all rights to that money.

But consider the following idea. We know that many Canadians escape our cold winters by retiring in warmer climates to the south. Generally, we vacation there in the winter months and return to Canada in the summer. But what if we reversed the coin? What if we moved to Florida, as an example, and vacationed back here in Canada each summer? We don't have to give up our citizenship, but we do have to give up our residency status in Canada and move, lock, stock, and barrel to the U.S. But when we do, we now qualify for special tax treatment on our pension plans and RRSPs. As it now stands, Canadians who live in the U.S. are taxed a flat 25% on the portion of their RRSP payments that are considered principal returns and their normal tax rate on the portion that is interest. Right off the bat, then, a Canadian in a reasonably high tax bracket would be ahead of the game if he or she were to move to Florida come retirement time.

But here's an oddball idea. What if you were to get all of the investments inside your RRSPs to mature at the same time? That's not too difficult, really, as most institutions arrange the maturity date of your term deposits inside your RRSPs for your seventy-first birthday. That way you have flexibility come age seventy-one to purchase a lifetime annuity or a RRIF (registered retirement income fund).

Once all your RRSPs are brought to maturity you could transfer all the funds to a brand new RRSP. Then move to Florida and once there cancel your RRSP. Since it's a very short-term RRSP (maybe even one day), there is very little, if any, interest built up in that plan. Now you collapse the plan in Florida and you pay only a flat 25% tax on it as it is all principal. The individual with a $100,000 RRSP in Canadian who collapsed it would pay $50,000 in tax. The individual who moved to Florida and collapsed his plan would pay only $25,000. That's a saving of $25,000, which is a pretty healthy down payment on a retirement home.

Now, before everybody races off to Florida, you should be aware of a few complications. First, you must actually leave Canada. That means selling your house or leasing it to somebody, and settling up with the taxman on the value of your estate. For many, though, it's still a good deal, especially if it is your plan to retire in the warm southern states. In addition, you have your health to consider. If you leave Canada for an extended period of time, you don't lose your Canada Penson Plan checks, but you can lose your hospital and medical insurance. As a result, you should spend some time with your accountants and lawyers before you make this decision.

It may well pay off — and does in many cases. But make sure that you aren't in for any major surprises when you do it. And, by the way, if you move to the Netherlands and use this same trick, you won't even have to pay the 25% withholding tax that applies in the U.S. — and their shoes last a lot longer.

But leaving your country is a pretty drastic (although often justifiable) step to take to save tax dollars. There are other steps that can be taken which could provide the same tax relief. When MURBs (multiple unit residential buildings) were in vogue, a consumer with a sizable RRSP could purchase one of these tax shelters and arrange enough of a tax deduction that he could remove all the money from his RRSP tax free. In fact, in the fall of 1984, this tax shelter was available: a Mississauga, Ontario MURB offered $82,455 worth of tax deductions over a five-year period. That allowed an investor with an existing RRSP to contract for this plan now which would lock in his price and pay for it over the next five years. His RRSP would continue to earn tax-free interest inside his plan, but he would make systematic withdrawals over the following five years to pay for his MURB. Whenever he removed money from his RRSP, he knew that he had to add it to his income for that year and pay tax on it. However, at the same time, he knew that he had purchased a tax shelter that offered offsetting deductions. In fact, in this case, he was able to remove $82,455 tax free from his RRSP by paying $41,259 toward the MURB. Now he had more than $41,000 back in his name completely free of tax plus an investment in a MURB which was by now probably in a profitable position. It was producing a positive rental (a monthly income to live on) and it was rising in value completely free of tax as real estate always does. In the meantime this individual was able to withdraw his money from his RRSP completely tax free. In addition, his money was still rising in value tax free, as it would inside an RRSP, but now he didn't have to worry about removing the money come age seventy-one.

Now for the bad news. MURBs are no longer widely available. They have been replaced by other similar investments called limited partnerships which include nursing homes, businesses, and hotels. Again, these are being phased out, but there's still a pretty good selection available.

In fact, by investing in a hotel you would be purchasing units that produce substantial tax deductions that could be used to offset any other form of taxable income. That includes salary, investment income, and RRSP withdrawals. It's simply a matter of crisscrossing deductions against income, and you will be able to remove money from your RRSP completely tax free.

So whatever you do, do not stay away from RRSPs because you worry about having to pay tax when it comes time to remove the money. The financial institutions advertise that you have to pay tax or buy an annuity or a Registered Retirement Income Fund. But, that's only because they want to discourage you from removing your money. In fact, there are other ways that you can remove your money tax free including purchasing a rental real estate property that doesn't generate enough rent to offset the mortgage payments and maintenance expenses. Now you simply calculate the losses by year end and remove an equivalent amount from your RRSP. The losses offset the money coming out of your retirement plan so it ends up in your hands tax free. In the meantime the real estate rises in value tax free much as it would in your RRSP.

I also hear from many consumers who cannot contribute to a registered retirement savings plan and as you can expect, they feel slighted when they hear that the contribution limits will be increased to $15,500. They can't use these plans now so they aren't excited about the prospects of other consumers getting a much larger tax deduction. But maybe they should consider the following pages.

19

Overcontributing to an RRSP

It's not unusual for consumers to overcontribute to their RRSPs by accident. They may have changed jobs and contributed more to their company pension plans than they anticipated, or their salary or employment status may have changed after they had already contributed to their RRSP. As a result, they have more deductions than they can use. So, what happens to them? Well, the answer's generally "nothing" — while recognizing that we can use overcontributing to our advantage if we do it on purpose. In fact, it can be so useful that it can completely undo all the damage caused by the 1985 federal budget.

And just in case you think this idea isn't acceptable to Revenue Canada, let me quote a small phrase from the budget papers: "Withdrawals of non-deducted excess contributions will be permitted tax free." That's a direct quote from the new budget that confirms our right to put in as much money as we want (to the quoted maximums each year) and remove it totally tax free.

So, let's see where this idea gets us. Let's use the example of an individual who can only contribute $1,000 to an RRSP, but opts instead for $5,500.

It's a must that this be done at the beginning of the year and not in the two-month period following the year when we are allowed to get in last-minute contributions. If we, as an example, contributed only $1,000 in January, we might be able to earn $100 a year or so interest. However, if we contributed $5,500, knowing full well that we weren't supposed to, we'd be able to earn $550 inside our plan, assuming we earned 10%. That's $450 extra — and it's totally tax free because it has been earned inside our RRSP. Had we earned this money outside our plan, we would have paid tax on it as soon as we exceeded $1,000 a year through investing.

Because we contributed this money in January of the calendar year rather than in the two-month period following the year, Revenue Canada won't be able to automatically advance the contribution to the next calendar year. In fact, the money will have been in our plan for 15 or 16 months before they even find out about it when we file our tax return.

When we do file, Revenue Canada will see that we contributed $5,500 (it'll be written on the tax slip from the institution), but they'll also see that we only deducted $1,000 from our income when we filed our tax return. The $4,500 extra is an overcontribution and based on the quote I produced from the budget we will not be taxed when we remove those funds from our plan.

Revenue Canada's normal policy is to ask us to remove it within one calendar year from the date they make the request. The money's been in for one full year before we file. After they get our return we'll have one full calendar year to remove the money tax free which means the end of next year. In total, then, instead of earning $450 once we will actually earn it three consecutive years — and when we compound that money for that three-year period we'll be ahead by about $2,000 tax-free dollars.

Don't forget that you were only supposed to earn about $100 a year inside your plan or $300 over the three years plus some compounding. Now you're earning $2,000 in three years. And if you continue to overcontribute every year for three consecutive years (that is, put in $5,500 a year rather than in only one year) you will start earning $2,000 extra each year from year four on. Now your RRSP is really starting to be worthwhile. Now you'll really be able to use some of the exciting ideas that I'll talk about in future chapters.

As the years pass and the contribution limits increase to

$15,500 a year, you'll actually be able to deposit a full $15,500 a year into your plan. Even though you won't get a tax deduction for the entire amount, you will be able to earn tax-free income with that money — and it'll compound tax free inside the plan until you remove it.

One very important word of caution. Never, never contribute more than the yearly limit. You'll be penalized 1% per month on the excess amount. But, that's only if you exceed the $7,500 limit in 1986 or, eventually, $15,500 in 1990.

And, finally, there exists a possibility that even the three-year removal rule that we spoke of earlier will go by the wayside, that we'll be able to leave the excess contributions in our plans as long as we wish without fear of taxation. Until we see that though, one should be careful not to lock his money away for too long a period inside the plan. You will want access every three years. But, even then, that's not a real problem. The excess contribution made in year one will have to come out at the end of year three. But don't forget that you'll also be overcontributing in year three. That contribution can go in for year three but be left liquid so it comes out as year one's withdrawal. This way only one year's worth of excess contributions has to be kept liquid. The remaining contributions can be locked away for a longer period of time, either in longer-term, higher-yielding term deposits, or in mutual funds or stocks which normally outperform other investments when given a reasonable length of time in which to work.

20

Removing Money from Your RRSP — Tax Free

People often say that it's a shame that they have to pay full fare on a mortgage or consumer loan when there's a sizable amount of money building up inside their RRSP at a lower rate at the same financial institution. Well, that's no longer the case as these plans have now become much more useful to the average consumer. First, they're useful as tax savers. Second, they allow us to compound our money tax free as long as it remains inside our plan, and third, it can now be used to provide mortgages on our own property or, for that matter, can actually be retrieved totally tax free for our personal use.

Here's a classic situation. You are in the process of moving. You have an offer on your $100,000 house, but the purchaser wants to make a $50,000 down payment and get a $50,000 vendor take-back mortgage from you. That might get you out of your house. And you might consider accepting it if you are going to retire in an apartment. However, if you are planning to move into a new house, it's a deadly deal. You assume a $50,000 mortgage which pays more than $5,000 in taxable income to you during the year, but you also have to take on a $50,000 larger mortgage when you buy a new house than you would have if you had received all cash from your old one. You are into a double jeopardy situation. You pay tax on one hand, but don't get tax deductibility on the other. Granted, you could sell the VTB mortgage on the open market, but you might take a loss. And no matter how you look at that, it's a loss if you sell it below present market value.

But suppose you had your RRSP offer a vendor take-back loan to your purchaser. You have to open a self-directed RRSP to do it, but now, on closing day, here's what happens. Your purchaser hands your lawyer a $50,000 down payment plus a $50,000 check from his mortgage lender, which is really you. That means you get the full $100,000 for your old house which you can now use as a down payment on your new house. Since you have a much larger down payment, you can either purchase a larger house with a similar mortgage or the same size of house mortgage free. At the same time, because the purchaser of your house now makes his monthly mortgage payment directly to the institution which administers your RRSP, it is received totally free of tax. You have the best of both worlds: a registered retirement savings plan which is growing tax free plus a principal residence with a much smaller mortgage or no mortgage at all. Two or three years later your VTB will come due, the purchaser will have to refinance it through a conventional lender who will pay the remaining principal right back into your RRSP, and now you will have an opportunity to put your second house on the market and start over again. The real beauty is that every three years or so you will be able to move into a new house. Each time your principal residence will have escalated in value totally tax free because it is your home while your RRSP will have grown in value. You will have continued to contribute each year, getting a sizable tax deduction while the purchaser of your house will have paid mostly interest into your RRSP. Each time you move, you will have reaped a tax-free profit on your house and increased the value inside your RRSP. If we can lend money to the purchaser of our house, it seems strange that we can't also lend money to ourselves to purchase real estate.

Well, it *is* possible. But it's a little more difficult as Revenue Canada takes the stance that a third party must be involved when we invest funds that are held inside our RRSPs. So here's how you do it. First, you open a self-directed RRSP, the same as you do if you want to fund a vendor take-back mortgage. Then you find a financial institution that will both insure your loan as a National Housing Association (NHA) mortgage and administer it. Now you have a third party between you and your RRSP. Granted, you have to pay the normal fees to arrange this mortgage — appraisal, legal, administrative — but now you are making your monthly payment to yourself so you don't mind the fact that it's mostly interest. In fact, you don't mind the interest rate or the term or the fact that the amortization schedule is working against you because you are making monthly payments to yourself instead of to a financial institution.

Look at a $50,000 12½% twenty-five year loan. You pay $533.52 per month to cover interest and principal. Yet, after two years of these payments ($12,804.48), you have paid off only $700 worth of principal. In effect, you've paid $12,104.48 in interest over two years and $700 against the outstanding principal. If you pay that to a lender, you are going to feel pretty sick when you get the accounting, but if you pay it to yourself you won't mind. In fact, after twenty-five years of payments, you will have paid $160,056 to clear that $50,000 loan. Wouldn't it be better to pay the money to yourself rather than to somebody else? And don't forget that at the same time your house will be rising in value totally free of tax.

But why stop there? Chapter 31 tells you how to make your mortgage tax deductible. Why don't we combine that information with what we've just learned to get double the benefit?

If you pay your mortgage off and own your house free and clear, you are already ahead of the game. But what if you put a mortgage on your house to purchase investments? If you do, it isn't a mortgage any longer; it becomes an investment loan and the interest that you pay on it is totally tax deductible. But what if we were to use the idea put forth above to raise that money, that is, to borrow it from our own RRSP? If we did, we would be paying tax-deductible interest into a tax-free shelter. Then we would have everything going for us. An individual in the 50% tax bracket would get back $266.76 for every mortgage payment when he filed his tax return. In a year, that's $3,201.12 which can be put to use elsewhere. In the meantime, his RRSP is growing completely free of tax. After twenty-five years, he will have paid

$160,000 in mortgage payments into his own RRSP which will have earned interest each and every year tax free, and he will have been able to write off the interest portion of every payment made as a tax deduction. Depending on his tax rate, he will have saved up to fifty percent of those payments when he filed his tax return. In fact, when you look at the tax rates in Quebec, he would have saved much, much more.

Let me give you a more specific example. Let's say you had $50,000 in your RRSP that you wanted to remove over a number of years rather than purchasing an annuity or using a registered retirement income fund.

If you used a financial consultant to arrange a $100,000 personal loan to purchase mutual funds, as an example, through a leverage program you'd create a $12,000 or so yearly tax deduction because of the tax-deductible interest you paid. That'd allow you to remove $12,000 from your RRSP. The tax deduction offsets the taxable income. If you kept that loan in place for, say, six years, you'd be able to remove all the money from your RRSP tax free. I use six years because you'll be earning income on the monies still inside your plan, so you'll need more than $50,000 worth of deductions to remove it all.

That's okay, though, because the longer a leverage program is in place the more likelihood of it working to your advantage. Remember, the only way we can make this loan tax deductible is to use the proceeds to purchase an investment that pays a regular yield and shows the prospects of eventually making a profit. That's where the mutual funds come in handy. Past performance says they will produce a yield of 15 to 20 to 30% a year when left in place long enough. Well, if we left this one in place for seven years and earned 15% per year, we'd have a total of $266,000, mostly tax free (it's a capital gain — the return of our original investment — and Canadian dividends qualify for the dividend tax credit).

Pay off your $100,000 loan and you're left with $166,000 — a tad better than what you were going to have left over if you paid tax on $50,000 worth of RRSP withdrawals going the conventional route.

You might ask, though, what banker in his right mind would lend somebody $100,000 to do this, especially somebody about to, or already in retirement? Well, almost every banker would. If you transfer your $50,000 RRSP to a lender and authorize him or her to automatically withdraw $12,000 a year for seven years, the lender will realize that this loan won't go into default for at least that long. In the meantime, the value of the mutual fund package will have been compounding so before long it will be worth more than the value of the loan. It's a good deal for the lender even though you are not allowed to pledge the RRSP as security on this loan. The right to withdraw enough to service the loan each year, though, is just as good.

A similar theory applies to a fully mortgaged rental real estate property that created losses and a stock portfolio purchase with borrowed money.

21

A Staggering New Use for Your RRSP — Thanks to Our New Budget

Some financial consultants suggest that you should never put anything other than interest-bearing investments inside your RRSP. These are retirement funds, so you don't want to expose yourself to too much risk. In addition, we now get tax-free capital gains outside our RRSPs, but not inside, and we qualify for the dividend tax credit when we buy stocks outside our RRSP — but, again, not inside. Everything we earn inside our RRSP will be taxed as income when we remove it, unless, of course, we use some of the exciting ideas that we've talked about in other chapters of *Your Money and How to Keep It*.

I disagree with this theory. My policies are to be flexible enough to use the best investment tool that's available at any particular time. Interest rates rise and fall. When they are high, I like them. When they are low, I recognize that other yields will be much more attractive. That means stocks, mutual funds, and other types of investments. If you can't change with the times you'll be hurt sooner or later.

With lower interest rates, I've been much more disposed to mutual funds as the improved economic picture and the lower financing costs will make companies more profitable which in turn will push dividends and company shares higher. Let's face facts. When interest rates are low, you can't earn as much inside your RRSP as you used to be able to. That's why we look elsewhere in order to get a higher rate of return. I don't care whether or not I get tax-free capital gains or the dividend tax credit in this case, but I do care that I get the best possible rate of return. If I earn 15% rather than 10%, and both are taxed at the same rate, I'm going to win.

But even with the controversy over what type of investment you should have inside your RRSP, there is a way, thanks to the new budget, to have both. That is, you can earn interest inside your RRSP, get double the normal tax deductions, and earn tax-free investment income outside your RRSP. While it sounds unbelievable, it's so simple that it's amazing that absolutely everybody doesn't use it.

Here's the situation. You've built up $50,000 inside your RRSP. You don't quite know where to invest this money, but you know you won't be satisfied with a low interest rate that will simply be a little bit above the inflation level.

Well, here's my super idea. If your have enough equity in your house that you can put a mortgage on it (it could be a second) you should consider opening a self-directed RRSP and lending yourself a mortgage on your own house. Many lenders don't seem to realize that this option is available, but that's reasonable in that they're in the business of lending money. If you lend it to yourself, they won't be able to.

There are some fees involved with this idea. An administration fee for your self-directed RRSP, an administration fee for the mortgage inside your plan, and mortgage insurance on your loan. However, the fees will be recovered many times over once you put this plan in place.

When we borrow money for investment purposes, we know we can claim the interest as a tax deduction. That same principal applies even though we are only borrowing the money from ourselves (out of our own RRSP). At the same time the interest we pay ourselves (into our own RRSP) will be earned tax free inside the plan. Imagine that — a tax deduction on one hand and tax-free income on the other, even though all we did was move the money from one hand (our RRSP) to the other!

In my $50,000 example, we'll pay $6,000 a year in interest if we charge ourselves 12%. The $6,000 we pay will create a tax deduction that'll produce a tax rebate as large as $3,000 in the 50% tax bracket. At the same time the $6,000 will be earned completely tax free inside our RRSP and will be allowed to compound tax free as long as we leave it there.

We make as much as $3,000 simply because we removed our money from our RRSP properly — and we'll get another $3,000 in a tax rebate as long as we leave this loan in place.

Now, to make it work we have to invest the money. We can pick anything we want provided it produces a regular income and shows promise of making a profit sometime in the future. That means you can invest it in a business venture, stocks, rental real estate or mutual funds.

We'll use mutual funds in this example. We know that they have produced annual gains of 15 to 18 to 25 and even 30% per year when left in place over the past ten years. And there's no reason why that type of past performance won't be repeated over the next decade. But that gain is partly tax-free capital gains and partly dividends which qualify for the dividend tax credit when they are Canadian — and when they are earned outside your RRSP.

So, you see what we've done now. We've earned 12% inside our RRSP, tax free. We've produced a $6,000 tax deduction that's produced a tax rebate based on our tax rate. And we've invested in a mutual fund outside our RRSP where we qualified for tax-free capital gains and virtually tax-free capital gains. Even if we invested in interest-bearing investments inside our RRSP and earned 12%, we wouldn't come close to producing this type of advantage. With my idea we get the same yield inside the plan (actually it's above the rate regularly paid by financial institutions) plus we get a free tax rebate and we earn tax-free capital gains and dividends simply because we used our RRSP effectively and efficiently rather than leaving it in the hands of a lending institution. And don't you know that the combination of the tax-free yield outside the plan plus the tax rebate will have us doubling the yield we were going to earn in many cases. For those who figured that we should only earn straight interest inside our plan this does the job. However, it also gets us an awful lot more.

I've used the number $50,000. In actual fact, though, this idea works with substantially lower numbers. I'd be reluctant to use it much below $20,000 or $25,000 because of the time, trouble, and fees, but each case can have merit. Remember, with the rising RRSP limits it won't be long before we're there anyway if we use these plans properly.

22

A Tax Shelter We Can Live In

At one time or another, every Canadian has dreamed of living in some sort of a tropical paradise. Granted, it probably happens on a cold, snowy winter day, but it's a proven fact that more Canadians are spending their retirement years in the warmer climes of the southern U.S. Favorite spots include California, Texas, Nevada, and of course, the granddaddy of them all, Florida. The weather is warmer so the cost of living is lower. You don't face big heating bills, you don't have to suffer through the winter and, of course, you meet a lot of people who have the same lifestyle.

But it can be expensive to have two residences, especially as your income normally falls when you are retired. As a result, many people sell their houses and move into rental units so that they can buy in Florida. Or they do the opposite. They hang onto their paid-for house and rent space in Florida in the winter months. Either way, they end up paying more than necessary. If they wait until retirement time, the Florida house will surely cost more because real estate seldom falls in value. And if they rent in Florida, their cost will rise yearly because their landlord will want a better income. On top of it all, they are always at the mercy of inflationary pressures. The higher the level of inflation, the faster the increase in their cost of vacationing in the sun. So there's another way. What if we buy in Florida when we are young — in anticipation of using this property as our retirement home. We buy it at today's price. As a result, inflation will be working in our favor. Instead of paying more for this property some years down the road, we will already own it so the increases in value will be ours. In addition, because we are going to have to pay tax on this property eventually now that the new Foreign Investment in Real Property Tax Act is in force in the U.S., we might as well make this into an investment property right from the start.

With that in mind, all Canadians who have even the remotest thoughts of owning property down south should buy now before prices rise any farther and rent the property as they would any rental property they owned in their own community. Then all the expenses related to owning that property would be tax deductible — and, if a loss developed, it would be deductible against their ordinary income.

Let's say you wanted to buy a $70,000 property. You would get a two- or three-bedroom house with an in-ground enclosed pool that you could easily rent to Canadians who wanted to spend their winter months in a warm climate. In fact, when you think about it, you will also get a place to use when it's vacant. That will save you paying the ever-increasing rates charged by hotels and motels.

The income you receive from this property is taxable in Canada — when you start to make a profit. However, before that happens, you are going to have some losses. Depending on the size of your down payment and the amount of time the property is rented, you will normally enjoy several years when your expenditures exceed your profit. That loss can be used, just as if it were a contribution to a registered retirement savings plan, to offset the income that you earn at your full-time job. You now end up with an extra tax rebate that you can use for your own vacation, to pay down the mortgage on your own house, or to lower the outstanding loan on your Florida property. The most enjoyable, of course, would be to help finance the trip. The most practical would be to use it to pay down your home mortgage as it normally isn't tax deductible. Now you are using a tax deduction to help pay off your own non-tax-deductible expenses. The final option is to pay the rebate against the Florida loan. One cardinal rule that you should always try to follow is to pay off non-tax-deductible loans and keep tax-deductible ones in place. That way the taxman lowers your real cost of interest because he rebates part of the interest you pay.

One final point. When you own this property in the south, it's a business. It's managed for you so that you don't have to worry about it. That costs you, but you don't mind because it's also tax deductible and because the last thing you want to do is have any aggravation with this investment. It's liable to be your retirement home in the future so all you want is good feelings about it. But you will have to do some work on the property. In fact, you will have to go down to Florida several times a year to maintain it. The shrubs will have to be trimmed, the temperature of the pool tested, the lights changed, you may even want to paint once in a while. That, of course, means "business trips" and not vacations. As we all know, business trips are tax deductible. In this case, though, it's not quite that cut and dried. Revenue Canada has no trouble allowing tax deductions for legitimate business travel. And they also have no problem including traveling expenses for consumers who own rental properties. However, it's the word *properties* that's important. No matter where you own several properties, you are allowed travel expenses. But, when you own only one property, there can be problems. In the past, many taxpayers have been allowed up to $1,000 per year in travel expenses, if they were legitimate, even though they owned only one Florida property. The trick is to be reasonable. If you are, it's possible that you may also get up to $1,000 worth of travel to maintain and repair your property each year. Of course, the way to ensure that extra tax relief is to buy two or more properties. Then, of course, you would have no problem at all. And that can be easily taken care of by buying two properties with a partner. Now you each have to take care of one property, but because more than one property is involved, you get no hassles on the deductibility of travel expenses.

An additional advantage was created with the introduction of the 1985 federal budget. In the past when we owned a rental property and used the expenses of ownership as tax deductions, we were forced to pay capital gains taxes when we moved into it. Revenue Canada considered that we sold the property to ourselves. Once a business, it now became a personal use property — and as a result, we had to pay tax on the gain even though the property didn't really change hands.

But the new budget changed all that. Now when we buy a future retirement property we should claim every deduction we can — and then when we move into it we can do so completely tax free as there is no longer any capital gains taxes in Canada. Yes, we may be open to some in the United States, but we should get a tax credit here in Canada for foreign taxes paid. That'll end up saving us taxes here in Canada while at the same time as renters are paying for our retirement property south of the border.

This new tax treatment has proven so attractive that American developers tell me their phones are ringing off the hook. In fact, one Burlington Ontario developer, who specializes in Florida properties (Port Charlotte (Florida) Home Builders) has been so deluged with requests that he has been grouping investors together in partnerships that buy a number of properties at a time. Think about it. If ten individuals got together and purchased ten different properties at the same time, they would then be able to build one house a year, jointly, rather than being strapped with building one each. The land is locked in in the first year so you don't have to worry about price escalation; the houses are built using borrowed money so the interest expenses are tax deductible, as are all the maintenance expenses — heat, hydro etc. — and even some travel bills. Once all ten houses are built, they can be pledged as collateral to build another ten with each partner getting one of them, or they can all be sold without tax as capital gains taxes need be paid, or each partner could take one and retire in a house that was paid for by the tax man and renters. It's a super idea that can do double duty for many consumers, especially those with a little extra cash who are looking for some tax relief.

There's one other bonus here that may prove especially attractive. While we can't use the money inside our RRSPs to buy foreign properties, we can use these funds to place a mortgage on our principal residence, as mentioned in earlier chapters.

Once we do that we have the money out of our RRSP — and once we do that we can then use it for whatever purpose we wish. If we invest it, the interest we pay is tax deductible, and that includes investing it in a mortgage on a Florida property. That means that we can actually lend ourselves our own money inside our RRSP and use it to buy a retirement home in Forida. When we do we'll get tax deductions plus, now, a tax-free capital gain.

What a way to use our money — wow!

23

What If You Don't Qualify for an RRSP?

As good as they are, it's a shame that more consumers can't take advantage of registered retirement savings plans. The limits are rising as high as $15,500 a year in 1990, but the number of people who can use these tax-saving plans is falling. The definition of "earned income" has been altered so that pensioners won't be able to roll all their pension income into their RRSPs beginning in 1990, and from 1986 on real estate rental income and pension income will no longer qualify as earned income. That means that those who have purchased rental properties to produce income that could be sheltered in an RRSP will now pay more tax. And those who have been contributing 20% of their pension income to their spouse's RRSP will no longer be able to.

Fortunately, though, there are things we can do that will create as many tax deductions, or even more, than we were going to get when we were able to contribute to a registered retirement savings plan. In the first place, you could take advantage of other tax shelters like limited partnerships, hotels, nursing homes, flow-through tax credits, movies, oil drilling funds or any other tax shelters that are available from time to time. While not as easy to work with as a registered retirement savings plan, and while they generally expose us to more risk, these more sophisticated tax shelters can indeed prove rewarding in that they save us tax and expose us to investments that may pay off with tax-free capital gains down the road.

And then we have a fantastic concept that in the past was used mostly by high-income taxpayers, but now that we have a new government and a new tax policy, I'm sure that it will become one of the most widely used tax saving devices there is. It's called leverage and here's how it works.

If we borrow money to buy investments, the interest we pay is tax deductible — and now that we have a new budget there are no longer any taxes on capital gains (to a half-million dollar maximum in a lifetime). If we combine these two goodies we can effectively create some sizable tax deductions at the same time as we earn tax-free income. Let's say we borrow $50,000 to purchase stocks, marketable bonds, or mutual funds. At a 12% rate we'll pay $6,000 per year in interest — interest that's tax deductible against any forms of income we receive. If we've purchased a mutual fund, part of the yield we receive will be a capital gain, which is now tax free, and part will be dividends. If they are Canadian dividends they'll qualify for the dividend tax credit which will wipe out most or all of the tax we were supposed to pay on the dividends. Effectively what we've done here is create a tax deduction at the same time as we produce tax-free capital gains and dividends. With a registered retirement savings plan we get a tax deduction when we contribute money and we earn tax-free income as long as it's earned inside the RRSP. But that's exactly what we've just done with this idea. We have the equivalent to a registered retirement savings plan — except that we have much more flexibility, don't have to worry as much about being taxed when we remove the money, and are not restricted by the maximums we face when we use RRSPs. We can shelter as much income as we want using leverage. In fact, one individual told me that he's been able to wipe out all the tax on $350,000 in income by using leverage.

A taxpayer could also consider the purchase of rental income real estate with very little money down. If a property is very heavily mortgaged, it's likely the rental income wouldn't cover the carrying costs and expenses. As a result the property would operate at a loss and rental real estate losses are deductible against our ordinary income.

As an example: If the property taxes, maintenance, heat, hydro, insurance, interest on the loans used to buy this property and any other business expenses exceed the rental income by $600 per month, you have a $7,200 tax deduction come the end of the year. That's the same as contributing $7,200 to your RRSP. The absolute maximum for RRSPs is $5,500 so, in this example, you have a larger tax deduction than you would with an RRSP.

Next year the rents will probably be higher, the mortgage will be slightly lower, and, as a result, the tax deduction won't be quite as large. And, within a few years, the building will pay for itself so you will have to start all over again. But you will own a building that is rising in value tax free until you sell it.

Now, some consumers are bound to say, "But I'm losing in this real estate deal because I am paying out more than I am getting back." That's a good point, but you've forgotten something. This building is also rising in value. If a $200,000 building rises in value by 10% per year, it gains $20,000 on paper. That $20,000 paper gain is well above the $7,200 tax deduction that you received in the above example. If it rises by 5% (simply offsetting inflation), it's $10,000. In fact, if it only rises by 3.6%, you've offset your total loss even though the tax man has paid back part of that loss.

And, don't forget the idea we put forth in chapter 19 — over-contributing to your RRSP. If you don't qualify to use one of the plans I've just discussed, it might still pay for you to contribute. While you won't get any tax deductions for your contributions, the money will at least compound tax free inside your plan. It's almost as good as having a registered retirement savings plan.

Yes, it's nice to be able to use one of these plans, but if you don't qualify there are alternatives.

24

What's Your Best Choice as an Investment?

What's your best choice as an investment? Now, there's a major league question that everybody seems to have an answer for. Unfortunately, though, there's never any set answer because the perfect investment for one individual will be the worst choice going for another, and the perfect investment this year may not be of any use next year.

What we do know, though, is that we can no longer simply leave our money on deposit in a savings account. We'll be lucky if we keep ahead of inflation and, if we're taxable on the income we receive, we'll fall well behind inflation.

First of all, we have term deposits and guaranteed investment certificates — the popular investment vehicles offered by financial institutions. When rates are high and expected to fall, these can be useful. However, when rates are low they don't offer much in the way of future expectations because we're compelled to lock our money away for a set period of time, usually from one to five years. As a result we have no flexibility to move with the times. In addition, we have a taxing problem as the new budget has endorsed equity and real estate-type investments by eliminating capital gains taxes on the first half-million dollars' worth of capital gains, but it will tax in full any interest we earn above and beyond the first $1,000 a year. Even though term deposits and GICs pay higher rates of return than savings accounts, you can still lose money when you combine inflation rates with the taxes you pay on your investment income. In fact, I'll show you numbers shortly that'll confirm just how easy it is to be lulled into losing ground when you use these savings vehicles.

Maybe your best choice would be a mortgage. After all, that's what the banks, trust companies, and credit unions use our term deposit monies for. They pay us one rate, mark it up, and lend the money out to somebody else as a loan or mortgage. Why don't we just bypass the middleman and lend our money to somebody ourselves? That way we will get a higher rate of return and have an investment we can sell if we wish because mortgages are saleable on the open market.

Real estate will be a natural choice for many. You know what they say: "They aren't making any more of it." Generally, real estate can be counted on to rise in value over a reasonable period of time — and that's the way we should always look at investments — over a reasonable period of time. If we want short-term investments we can use the short-term interest markets or treasury bills. If we want to speculate we have gold, the commodities and options markets, but when we invest our money we should look for something where we can be comfortable for a reasonable period of time.

The stock markets look like they'll offer an attractive alternative for a few years. North American governments have shown that they are now much more open to the corporate sector. Governments were taking over both countries, drowning out business, but that's all changed now. As a result, good quality stocks should prove rewarding over the next decade or so, especially when you add in tax-free capital gains and the dividend tax credit.

And then we have mutual funds. More small investors are switching to them because they offer a great deal of flexibility, they can be cashed in any business day, and they pay a regular income. In the past that could be a negative in that higher-income individuals didn't want a regular income because it was taxable and could only be compounded for three years maximum. But now that capital gains taxes are gone, investors are more disposed to mutual funds as the regular payout of gains made by the mutual fund can be received tax free. That makes it easier to borrow to buy mutual funds as they can eventually pay for themselves.

The combination of yield plus taxes plus past performance and future expectations have to be blended to create the best investment. As an example, Stats Canada tells us that the average five-year term deposit purchased in the late 1970s and early 1980s paid about 10.85%. But, at the same time, inflation averaged 9.95%. That means that we didn't earn 10.85% at all; we earned only nine-tenths of one percent after inflation's impact is included. But good old Revenue Canada doesn't give a darn about inflation. No sirree, it taxes us on the entire amount (after the first $1,000). The individual in the 35% tax bracket, then, will pay almost 4% of this income to the taxman which means that he or she gets to keep only a little over 7% after tax. But inflation ran at 9.95% which means that this investor actually lost almost 3% after the combination of taxes and inflation. On average, then, those people who purchased term deposits and guaranteed investment certificates over the past ten years lost about 3% per year. You fell behind in the money game, even though you felt snug and secure in the belief that your money was safe in the financial institution. It was, too, as it was protected up to $60,000 by the Canada Deposit Insurance Corporation. But that's only if the institution closes its doors. You may, in fact, have wished it did, as then at least you could have switched into a more profitable investment. In the meantime, the institutions love term deposits and GICs because they work very much in their favor. They pay us one rate, which is tax deductible to them, and then they lend the money out to somebody else, making sure they protect themselves against inflation. Then they get to use loan loss provisions and other deductions to save taxes. In the meantime the combination of inflation and taxation has put us behind.

So what other choices do we have? Well, McLeod Young Weir, a national stock brokerage firm, says that the TSE 300 Composite Index averaged a 12.97% annual rate of return over the past ten years. Sure, prices rise and fall from time to time, but the gains combined with the losses produced an average rate of return each year for a decade of almost 13%. But now that the tax rules have been changed, that gain would be virtually tax free as it's part capital gains and part Canadian dividends.

Yes, inflation rates would still take their toll but you now have a 3% gain after inflation versus a nine-tenths of 1%, and a gain of almost 3% after taxes compared to a 3% loss using term deposits. So, yes, if we're prepared to hang onto our investments long enough, the stock market when used properly is almost assured of producing a positive performance.

The problem, though, is that we can't buy the TSE 300 Composite Index, although we can buy options contracts, commodities contracts, and now a mutual fund that parallels this indicator.

So, what do we use instead? Well, my preference has been good quality mutual funds. Historically, they've done even better than the TSE 300 Composite Index. The theory is that a good portfolio manager can pick and choose the sectors of the market that he or she thinks will do best at any one time. That way they get better gains. In addition, you don't buy or sell the stocks involved in the TSE Composite Index; you just monitor them. With a mutual fund the portfolio manager can buy and sell on a regular basis.

In fact, if we look at a list of selected mutual funds over a ten-year period ending in mid-1985, we can see that funds can, indeed, outperform the major stock market indices. United Funds retirement plans have been earning an average of 20% or more for the past seven years; Cundill Value Fund has averaged 24.9% every year for ten years; Taurus Fund shows 25%; Templeton Growth 22.4%; AGF Japan Fund 18.1%; and Industrial Growth Fund — probably Canada's best-known mutual fund — more than 18% per year.

Now you can see why I say that mutual funds can, indeed, be a viable alternative to term deposits and other interest-bearing investments.

In the fall of 1985, Series 28 Canada Savings Bonds matured. There were $268 million worth outstanding at the time plus bonuses and compounding coupons. But those bonds were purchased twelve years previous. If we're prepared to hang onto term deposits for five and ten years at a crack or Canada Savings Bonds for twelve years, surely we can buy stocks or mutual funds and put them away for ten or twelve years. Forget about the daily rising and falling of the stock markets. Over the long run history says good quality, secure investments will definitely rise in value.

In fact, here's one of the biggest mistakes made by Canadian investors and savers. They buy some shares of a company. The stock market slips back a bit, so they panic and sell — at a loss. Yet, if there was nothing wrong with the company, if the markets were moving lower in unison, maybe they would have been better off buying more shares at the new lower price. One hundred shares at $10 a share means a $1,000 investment. But, if the price falls to $5 per share, why not buy another $1,000 worth? That means you get 200 shares and lower your average price to $6.67 per share. Now, when the markets recover you'll be in the black sooner and will have a chance at making a profit that much sooner.

This is similar to one of the all-time successful investment theories. It's called "dollar cost averaging." It involves buying the same investment every month. You can choose either the same number of units each month or the same dollar value. For example, if you invested $100 a month for ten years with prices steadily rising you'd amass about $17,250 after ten years. If stock prices zigzagged every second year, but still ended up doubling as they did in the above example, you'd have more than $22,000. The reason is that some shares were purchased at lower prices, but because all the shares ended back at $10, the lower priced shares gained more. In a third example, if we saw prices fall for five consecutive years to only $1 per share but rise in the following five years to, once gain, $10 per share, you'd have almost $25,000. Again, it's the extra buying power that you get when prices are lower.

Dollar cost averaging almost always wins. It's the perfect tool for those consumers who are looking for a forced savings plan as they get to invest a similar amount each month and they profit down the road.

Another example of a good investment idea is the purchase of Canada Savings Bonds. You have to remember that these popular bonds are more savings vehicles than they are invest- ments, but they do work when used properly. For example, I like them as forced savings plans, especially when your employer offers payroll deduction purchase plans in the fall. The money disappears from your paycheck before you get to spend it; the interest rate you earn is generally higher than you'd earn in a savings account; and you have the ability to cash in your bonds any time you need money.

As an emergency plan, CSBs can also prove rewarding. You can keep a few thousand dollars' worth on hand in case you need fast access to money. However, now that interest is taxable while capital gains are tax free, I think we're better off investing our money in real estate, stocks, and mutual funds. The combination of tax-free capital gains plus the dividend tax credit makes stocks or mutual funds especially attractive.

25

You Can Earn Up to $43,445 without Paying Any Tax at All

Far too often we have a tendency to forget taxes when it comes to thinking about the amount of money that we earn. And we shouldn't. We have to get ourselves into the habit of thinking in after-tax terms. Earning twenty percent on our investment money might sound wonderful, but once we consider what we pay on that, we might decide we're better off earning only twelve percent — if that's twelve percent after taxes.

That's one of the reasons why we have to get accustomed to thinking along the lines of buying assets — shares in listed companies, real estate, antiques — because interest that we earn will be taxed in full, while dividends or capital gains will be taxed at a much lower rate. For starters, let's forget the first $1,000 worth of investment income as it is totally free of tax. It doesn't make a great deal of difference in this case, so let's assume that you have already earned more than that amount. Once you exceed $1,000, you ought to start thinking in terms of after-tax dollars — not pre-tax. As an example: a high-tax-bracket investor might pay fifty cents tax on every dollar of investment income if it is interest, whereas he would pay only twenty-five cents on the dollar if the gain were through dividends or capital gains. As a result, one investor would be twice as far ahead as another because he chose to buy assets rather than simply earn interest income. In fact, for the lower-tax-bracket income, it might even mean wiping out taxes that are payable on other types of income. We really only have three ways to earn money with our money. One is to earn interest, the next is to earn capital gains, and the third is to receive dividend income. (Simply put, dividend income is a sharing in the profits of a company in which you have invested.) The income on the last two can look lower compared to interest income, but once taxes are considered, they can be worth substantially more — and that's what counts most in the long run.

To clarify this, let's consider the case of an Ontario investor who earns $1,100 in investment income. We'll forget about the first $1,000 — it is tax free — and concentrate instead on the next $100. Because he earns about $40,000, he will pay forty-five dollars in tax on that $100 if it is interest income, zero if it is a capital gain, sixteen dollars if he earns it through dividends. And with capital gains and dividend-type investing, you also have the possibility of hanging on longer so that the value of your investment rises even more. As you can see, then, the prime consideration when yield is looked at is the after-tax gain — not what you think you are earning before you settle up with the tax man.

In fact, once you slip below $18,000 or so in taxable income, you actually get a rebate on the taxes that you would have otherwise paid ordinary income, if you earn dividend income from Canadian corporations. That's why it is so important that you start investing in Canadian dividend-paying stocks early in your life. First, you save taxes against other income so that you end up ahead of your peers. Then you have an excellent chance that the dividends will grow faster than interest rates as the years go by, which will mean even more tax savings because of the dividend tax credit. Then you have the cutback in income that usually takes place when we retire. The dividend tax credit might even wipe out the tax that you would normally be called upon to pay on not only your investment income but also some of your pension income. Let me show you how this special dividend tax credit works. For comparison purposes let's say you had a choice of earning 10% interest income or a similar amount through purchasing 8½% preferred shares.

Interest

Income	$100.00
Taxable Income	$100.00
Federal Tax @ 25%	$25.00
Prov. Tax @ 48%	$12.00
Total Tax	$37.00
Net After-Tax Income	$63.00
After-Tax Yield	6.3%

While a 10% yield might not sound too bad, once you have settled with the tax man you are left with only 6.3% which hardly even protects you against inflation. As a result, you end the year with very little, if any, gain.

Of course, if you don't earn more than $1,000 worth of investment income, you get to keep the full 10%. In these examples, though, I've assumed you have already earned $1,000. Now that we know that we are only going to earn 6.3% after-tax in interest, let's consider the individual who earns Canadian dividends.

Dividends

Dividend Income	$85.00
Gross Up (50% of dividend)	$42.50
Taxable Income	$127.50
Federal Tax @ 25%	$31.88
Dividend Tax Credit @ 34%	$28.90
Net Federal Tax	$2.98
Prov. Tax @ 48%	$1.43
Total Tax Payable	$4.41
Net After-Tax Income	$80.59
After-Tax Yield	8.1%

As you can see, the pre-tax yield on the dividends doesn't look as high as the pre-tax yield on the term deposit or guaranteed investment certificate. However, because of the dividend tax credit, you actually come out about 2% ahead after-tax. When the two yields are compared, the increased yield is really about 30%.

Naturally, tax brackets and province of residence can affect the final result, but a general rule of thumb suggests that you need to earn one and a half times the rate paid in dividends to come out even, if you stick with interest income. In fact, in only Alberta and British Columbia does the multiplier dip below one and a half times — and then only fractionally.

	$18,130 to $23,310	$23,311 to $36,260	$36,261 to $62,160	$62,161 & Up
Taxable Income Bracket				
British Columbia	1.50	1.50	1.50	1.50
Alberta	1.48	1.48	1.48	1.48
Saskatchewan	1.52	1.52	1.52	1.53
Manitoba	1.54	1.54	1.54	1.54
Ontario	1.50	1.51	1.51	1.51
Quebec*	1.56	1.56	1.57	1.59
New Brunswick	1.56	1.56	1.57	1.58
Nova Scotia	1.55	1.55	1.56	1.57
Prince Edward Island	1.53	1.53	1.53	1.54
Newfoundland	1.57	1.57	1.58	1.60

*In Quebec's case these numbers are approximate as tax rates can vary.

Consider this example. If you could earn 9% on common or preferred shares, you would need a yield of at least 13.3% through term deposits or other interest-bearing investments. If you could earn a dividend yield of 10%, you would require interest income yielding 14.8%.

If you use the following chart, you will be able to compare most yields on dividend income in your particular province to the yield that you would have to earn if you stuck with interest income. Simply pick your province and slide across the chart until you find a yield close to that on your term deposits. At the top of the chart you will see the equivalent yield that you would need to earn if you were investing in dividends instead. The required yields are substantially lower. As an example, a New Brunswick taxpayer who was earning fourteen percent on a term deposit would only have to earn nine percent through dividends.

Dividend Rate	7%	8%	9%	10%	11%	12%	13%	14%
British Columbia	10.4	11.8	13.3	14.8	16.3	17.8	19.2	20.7
Alberta	10.4	11.8	13.3	14.8	16.3	17.8	19.2	20.7
Saskatchewan	10.7	12.2	13.7	15.2	16.7	18.3	19.8	21.3
Manitoba	10.8	12.3	13.9	15.4	17.0	18.5	20.0	21.6
Ontario	10.6	12.2	13.7	15.2	16.7	18.2	19.8	21.3
Quebec	10.9	12.5	14.0	15.6	17.2	18.7	20.3	21.8
New Brunswick	11.0	12.5	14.2	15.8	17.3	18.8	20.4	22.0
Nova Scotia	10.9	12.5	14.1	15.7	17.2	18.8	20.4	22.0
Prince Edward Is.	10.7	12.3	13.8	15.3	16.9	18.4	20.0	21.5
Newfoundland	11.2	12.8	14.4	16.0	17.6	19.2	20.8	22.4

In these examples we have been assuming that the individual has already earned $1,000 in investment income. However, in this example, let's consider an individual who has no income other than from investments. That might be a senior citizen who has no pension or, more importantly, it might be a spouse or a child with whom we are income splitting. That is, we keep all the work-related income in our name, and we lend all the available investment monies to our spouse or children interest-free. They use this money to buy dividend-paying stocks. So, let's see how much we can earn now, without paying any tax at all.

Total Income (All Dividends)	$43,445
Gross Up	21,723
Taxable Dividend Income	$65,168
Less Personal Deductions	4,140
Less $1,000 Investment Income Deduction	1,000
Net Taxable Income	$60,027
Federal Income Tax	14,771
Less Dividend Tax Credit (34% of Dividends)	14,771
Net Federal Tax	$0
Provincial Tax	0
Total Tax	$0
Net After-Tax Income	$43,445

That's right! If the money were used to earn dividend income rather than interest, the taxes would be completely wiped out by the dividend tax credit. You would keep every cent of your investment income. In fact, this may be the perfect way to income split, to invest an insurance settlement, or for seniors to invest their money without worrying too much about taxes. If they earned the same amount through interest income, they would pay about $20,000 in federal and provincial taxes. The savings then are more than $1,500 per month.

Naturally there are a few other things to consider. Is the dividend yield well below that paid through interest? Are the companies good-quality low-risk issues, and can you sleep well at night knowing that your money is in the stock market instead of term deposits or GICs? The way I look at it, $20,000 per year can buy a lot of satisfaction. And when you consider that owning stocks has historically been a good hedge against inflation with increased earnings by the companies usually meaning higher dividend payouts plus the advantage of paying only half the normal tax if you sell these stocks at a profit, it seems to me that you would be better off owning stocks rather than simply lending your money to somebody else.

26

The Executive Forced Savings Plan

I have a super way for lots of individuals to save money, beat inflation, and also come out with some extra tax deductions, all at the same time. I call it my "executive forced savings plan." Don't let the word *executive* scare you away. This is a savings plan that can work for virtually anybody who has any kind of a future — and people who don't think they have a future should be doing something other than reading this book, as this publication is intended solely to help you do better in the coming years.

People who want to save more than they are now, people who think they have a raise coming in the future, people who are fed up with paying taxes should pay close attention. The executive plan is an every-day individual's way to combine all those philosophies into one.

Let's say you are putting the maximum into an RRSP right now. Yet you have more earnings than you need, so you invest the surplus. Once you exceed $1,000 worth of investment income, you start paying tax on that income. You are almost spinning your wheels: now that you are paying tax on your investment income, you are probably falling behind in the beat-inflation game.

What if you were to take that pool of invested money and take advantage of today's low real estate prices? If you used the money as a down payment on a piece of real estate where the rent would pay for the mortgage, taxes, and expenses, your down payment would purchase a property that would probably rise in value at about the same rate as inflation — or faster — but more importantly the down payment would only be a small portion of the total price, so you would be able to take advantage of a thing called "leverage." If you pay for half of an investment, and that investment earns ten percent per year, you have really earned twenty percent, as you only paid for half the total value. Or suppose you had only put down twenty-five percent of the purchase price and the property appreciated in value by ten percent in a year. You would really have been earning forty percent on your money. And you get two other bonuses. You get to write off all the costs associated with the running of this business that you have invested in, and if you find that it loses in the year, you can write that loss off against other income you have earned elsewhere. At the same time, this property may be rising in value, but you don't have to pay one red cent of tax on its value until you actually sell — and even then you get to treat the profits as a capital gain. This means that you keep half the gains in your pocket, tax free, while you add the other half to your income and pay tax at that rate. In short, if past history repeats itself, you come out a winner in many different ways.

But let's take this a step further. Let's say that your down payment is small, and that the financing charges and the other costs of operation make your investment run at a loss. You can carry that loss over as a deduction against other income. You have an investment that will save you taxes as it is a deduction. And it acts as a good hedge against inflation, as real estate has been proven to be one of the very best, and also offers some potential for future gain, which is a mighty important reason for investing in this type of real estate, even if it appears at the outset that it's a poor choice because it isn't paying for itself. Create a loss, get an extra tax deduction, and use that money each spring to pay the mortgage on your house, which isn't tax deductible. One investment is creating income that will help pay off another loan. You are ahead of the game again.

Let's take a few minutes to look at this investment in more

specific terms. Perhaps you should think of this as a registered retirement savings plan where there are no limits to what you can contribute each year. Your only restriction is the amount you can afford each year. As the years pass you can increase the size of your contributions to this plan, as your mortgage will be decreasing and your earlier properties will be carrying themselves because of rent increases.

Let's say you are earning $500 — or even $100 — per month more than you need to live on. Your are probably putting that money into some sort of investment program (CSBs, term deposits, stocks, bonds, even a savings account) where you will have to pay tax on the profits that result. The interest is fully taxable once you go over $1,000 per year, and the capital gains that result are only half yours. The other half is shared with the tax man.

If, instead, you bought a duplex, triplex, or fourplex, let's say, you could do all those things better and get some extra tax deductions along the way.

You would look for a property that had existing financing at a reasonable rate, but that wouldn't quite be covered by the rental income after your down payment is taken into consideration. In reality, you might have the money to increase the down payment to a level where the property would have turned a profit, but you are better off to force it to lose. You can put the rest of your money somewhere else. In fact, you might like this idea so much that you use the rest of this money to buy a bigger building or several smaller ones that all show a loss.

In the example we are using, you have decided that you have an extra $500 per month that you can get along without. You find a building you like where you will have to add $500 per month to the rental income to bring the total income up to the total outflow. This includes mortgage payments, utilities, taxes, insurance, maintenance — all the out-of-pocket expenses. You might feel a little more secure with a smaller or less expensive piece of property where the rent covers the cost of operation, but if you do that you won't have protected yourself as much for future growth; you will probably be offsetting inflation but you won't be taking advantage of it. By buying the larger house, you will make provisions for future rent increases that will, within a number of years, close the gap between the building's cost of operation and its income, or cash flow.

But, at the same time, you will have been creating a tax loss, even though the building is rising in value — a compounded yearly rise, in fact, with no tax applicable until you actually sell. That $500 per month is a tax loss to you. You've bought yourself a building that is a losing proposition — on paper, at least. You are entitled to carry that loss over to your other forms of income and get back taxes that you have already paid to Revenue Canada. You haven't sold the building at a loss so you still have all kinds of time to recoup your investment losses as the building appreciates in value. But right now you are able to use the profit-loss statement on this building to save you taxes on your other income. And that's exactly what you are trying to do. You are trying to defer the tax tab until sometime many years down the road. You can also use a thing called depreciation, whereby you lower the value of the building each year, figuring that the bricks and mortar won't last forever. You won't need this in the early years as the inflow-outflow discrepancy will be creating a direct loss for you. And, in any event, when you do use depreciation you are not allowed to carry the loss over to your other income. However, depreciation will come in handy down the road when this little tax shelter of yours starts to turn a profit. Then you can use depreciation to offset that income for years to come, so that you start to recover your earlier paper losses.

Now you can look at some of the benefits you have gained. First, you have bought a piece of real estate — one of the best, if not the best, tax shelter and hedge against inflation. Second, you have forced your real estate to lose on paper so that you write off the loss and save taxes on other income. Third, you have chosen the size of the investment plan that you want so that it comfortably fits into your available excess income. Fourth, that income, if invested elsewhere, would have generated a profit that would be taxable now. As a result you might not even come out ahead of inflation levels, and you definitely would not be able to compound it as rapidly as you are now in an investment where there will be no tax payable at all until you actually sell. Fifth, you have embarked on a leveraged investment. You might only have ten percent of the cost of this investment covered by your own money. That means that every time the property appreciates by one dollar, it's the same as ten dollars to you. And sixth, you have parlayed an investment that saves you taxes now into one that will only be taxed at half today's rate down the road. You see, the tax loss that you create right now is a dollar-for-dollar tax loss. Yet, when you turn around and sell this property at a profit, you will be able to treat the gain as a capital gain. That means the gain will be yours tax free. You've won again. You not only have saved tax on other income, but you have been able to keep compounding your investment for many years without paying tax.

This investment won't lose forever, either. It may take five years before it "skates onside" and pays for itself. That all depends on how fast rents increase and how stable interest rates remain, as you may have to refinance at some time down the road. Once the real estate starts paying for itself, you will probably want to embark on a new venture that will save you more tax dollars.

The next part of this plan is an important one. Because the mortgage on your house is generally not tax deductible, you should take all the extra money you get from your tax rebate and use it each spring to pay your mortgage. In the example we have been using, there will be an extra tax deduction of $6,000. (See what I mean about real estate being bigger and better than a registered retirement savings plan?) For the individual in the thirty-five-percent tax bracket, that could mean an extra tax rebate of $2,100. For an individual in the combined federal-provincial tax bracket of fifty percent, it could mean an extra check from Revenue Canada for $3,000. This money should now be put directly against your mortgage, as you will save yourself years of not-tax-deductible interest. In fact, in many cases a dollar paid against a home mortgage can save you as much as four dollars in interest. That's why it generally pays to put as much extra cash against your mortgage as possible. You are a double winner in this respect: you are saving yourself interest and your are paying off your mortgage with Ottawa's dollars, not your own. And remember, this saving that you are going to make is going to be a tax-free one, as your house increases in value totally free of tax as long as it is your principal residence. You are now parlaying government money into a tax-free gain for yourself. What could be a better investment, especially if you are tired of paying taxes to a long list of tax collectors? One investment is creating tax dollars while it compounds higher without tax until it is sold — and those tax dollars are being used to slash years off your mortgage. Now you've got the government just where you want it.

The way you will get the most mileage out of this savings plan is to take into consideration the raises that you have coming in future years. Too many of us simply take the raises we get and spend them. Yet we were getting along just fine on our earlier salary. When you get a raise, you should initiate this type of forced savings plan. That way you will have put one year's raise to use, providing for a chunk of money in future years with an extra tax shelter right now that will help you pay off your mortgage. If you simply take the raise, pay tax on it, and spend the rest, or even put it against your mortgage, you won't be nearly as far ahead. So take the opportunity you have when you get a raise and use it to your best advantage.

Here's something else to consider — and I find more and more middle-income people doing it all the time. They are very risk-conscious, don't want to take very many chances — and above all do not want to lose any money. However, in the long run they end up losing as they are guaranteed to end up paying the tax man. There's no risk involved here — it's a sure thing.

I find more people banding together, going into partnerships, syndicates that buy investments. That's how mutual funds became attractive. Instead of putting all your eggs in one basket you spread them around a bit. You might not make as much, although it's entirely possible that you will end up making even more in the long run, and you have fewer worries about losing your money as it's spread around. Neighbors who are friends, business associates, doctors — or a lawyer, a carpenter, a plumber, and a real estate salesman might get together. Each provides his own expertise to enhance their chances of making a good profit. There's another advantage to a partnership arrangement. The workload is spread out among several people. Maybe one individual takes a special interest in some of the things that are required that will prove to be positive down the road. Or maybe the partners work different hours so that one is always available if there is anything that needs to be done.

A forced savings plan can be used for any type of investment. It doesn't have to be real estate. In fact, for some, real estate may not seem very appealing. Instead, a mutual fund, an automatic payroll deduction into a company share-purchase plan, payroll deductions for Canada Savings Bonds, or even life insurance in a very few cases might be more attractive. By the way, life insurance is my last choice on the list and I think it should also be your last option. If you really can't save any money then you might want to opt for a life-insurance contract where the money is automatically deducted from your bank account. It will disappear before you get a chance to spend it. But, quite frankly, there are so many other options that you can choose from where you can earn a better rate of return and have greater flexibility that you should attempt to look elsewhere for your forced savings plan before settling on life insurance.

One of the ones that I settled on, as you can tell, is rental property. Not only are you directing some money into an investment, but you are getting substantial tax write-offs along the way. The investment is being used to create a paper loss — and against the property itself. You see, this is a business transaction so you are going to qualify to write off virtually all your business expenses against the income that is generated from this property. In addition, once all the income has been offset, you will be able to carry the rest of the losses forward and use them to save taxes on your ordinary income.

That includes the mortgage, of course. All the interest you pay on any loans to help you buy income-producing properties is tax deductible. That includes taking out a mortgage on your house so that you can buy another piece of property that you intend to rent out. It's not the collateral that counts, especially, but the use to which you put that money. In this case you would be using it to buy rental property, so as a result it would be a tax-deductible loan. You can also deduct the cost of finding a mortgage. Some people pay an agent a special commission to locate a good one for them — in essence drawing on his expertise, or access to money.

This cost is tax deductible, although the cost of buying the property itself is not. That commission and any commissions involved in selling the property are deducted from the value you receive when you sell. As a result, you pay tax on only half the net gain on your investment.

All property taxes are naturally deductible, as are any monies that you pay for heat, hydro, water, or any other utilities. You might require that your tenants pay their own utilities, but you may still have to pay for incidentals, including carrying these expenses while changing tenants.

When it comes to changing tenants you may have to advertise in the newspaper, or you might enlist the aid of a real estate or rental agent to find you good tenants. These costs are also tax deductible from rental income. You may even want to pay a tenant to move so that you can renovate and attract a higher-paying one. That payment will also be tax deductible.

You might not like the idea of paying an accountant to handle your affairs, but you should — and when you do, his bill will be a legitimate deduction, as will legal bills when they are necessary to keep your business operating properly. You might want to use a lawyer to oversee your leases, or you may need to enlist the aid of one if it is ever necessary to evict a tenant. In fact, if you have a tenant who is tardy in his rental payments, you might be interested in having him deal directly with your lawyer. Those costs will be tax deductible. However, the legal bills that you incur when you buy and sell your building will not be tax deductible.

It's easy to understand why property insurance would be another tax deduction. You need to protect your property in case of fire and damage, and you need to cover yourself for liability in case anything unfortunate happens to the building, the tenants, or any visitors to the premises. But you may also, in some circumstances, be able to deduct the cost of life insurance. Some lenders may demand that your loans be covered with life insurance. You might, in fact, be wise to take out some extra coverage so that if anything happens to you, your family will now have a paid-for, viable investment that will bring in a regular income. The decision, on your part, to take out this coverage won't make it a tax deduction. However, the demand by your lender to have his loan covered may make it a tax-deductible cost. But, even then, it isn't a fait accompli, as Revenue Canada looks at this one closely.

Naturally, repairs to your building will be a tax deduction, but not necessarily major repairs or renovations. The tax department looks on day-to-day repairs, like light bulbs, leaks, rickety steps, and a long list of every-day occurrences, as acceptable. However, when it comes down to installing a new furnace, it might be a different story. Major expenses that are designed to extend the life of the property are often treated as the purchase of a new asset, and as a result become depreciable over a long period of time rather than in one year. This is one of those gray areas where working with an accountant will more than pay for the cost involved. If it's a big building, you may end up hiring a superintendent or somebody to oversee part of the operation or do some of the work. Those costs are naturally tax deductible, but if you think about it, so, too, would they be if they were paid to your spouse or your children. That means that this is the perfect opportunity to increase the size of your tax deduction by paying your family members to do much of this work. The money comes out of your income, which is being taxed at a high rate, and is transferred to family members, who are taxed at a substantially lower rate. Again you win, your family wins (maybe tax free), and the only person to take a bath is the tax man.

Of course, the chances of you buying the house next door are slim, though not impossible. If you don't buy the house next door, you will have to drive over to pick up the rent checks or to make general repairs — or even simply to keep an eye on the place. If you walk, I suppose you could deduct shoe leather, but it's more than likely that you will drive. That makes your car and the operating costs tax deductible. Naturally, you won't get a full deduction unless you have quite a few buildings and can show that you use this vehicle all the time for business and not for pleasure. But, even when you are only a one-building owner, you should be able to deduct a portion of the cost of owning that vehicle, including gas, oil, insurance, car washes, maintenance, and depreciation.

Naturally, you are going to want to keep abreast of what's happening in the world of business. That means subscriptions to business papers and other related publications. Their cost will also be a tax deduction to you, as the publications are intended to help you make decisions regarding the well-being of your investments.

There's one added advantage to this idea if you have some money tucked away in your registered retirement savings plan. We know from earlier chapters that it's acceptable for our RRSPs to invest in mortgages, including mortgages on properties we own ourselves. With that in mind, why not lend ourselves a mortgage so we can buy this overfinanced rental property? The interest, we already know, is tax deductible, because this is an investment loan. But we're only paying the interest to ourselves. That doesn't matter one little bit.

So what happens? Well, we get a tax deduction on one hand and we earn the interest tax free inside our RRSP. Not a bad deal, especially when you consider that the tenants are paying for the property — and the property is going to rise in value tax free now that capital gains taxes have been eliminated.

For those with excess income that's being taxed this is a nice way to create a tax deduction and to earn some tax-free income along the way, both inside our RRSP and outside through the appreciation in value of the building.

27

Saving for Your
Child's Education

The newest federal budget has created a new type of thinking when it comes to saving for our childrens' educations. In the past we had to worry about paying tax on the compounding income being earned in the children's names and we still do — if we stick with interest-bearing investments. But now that there's no longer any capital gains taxes on the first half-million dollars' worth of capital gains, maybe we'd be better off opting for things like land, stocks, and mutual funds in our children's names. With much lower interest rates than in the past it's going to be hard to earn very much in their names anyway. Why not take a "stab" at something that might grow in value much faster than straight interest — and would be tax free.

The way most Canadians save money for a child's education is to put a little away each month in their own name. They may buy stocks, bonds or Canada Savings Bonds, hoping these will rise in value fast enough or earn enough income so that there's a large enough pool of money to pay for the child's tuition and other education expenses. Once we earn more than $1,000 worth of investment income we have to start sharing with the taxman — and, if we want to earn enough to pay for an education, we can probably count on that happening.

We used to be able to offset part of that by income splitting; that is, by lending money, interest free, to our spouse so that he or she could also earn up to $1,000 tax-free investment income. And we still can if we had proper income splitting in place prior to May 23, 1985, the day the budget was introduced. For those who had not put income splitting in place there's now more likelihood of paying tax than ever before.

And we used to be able to buy long-term compounding investments where no tax would apply until the investment was actually cashed. That, also is no longer possible in that we can only buy interest-bearing investments that compound without tax for a three-year maximum.

Naturally, these restrictions mean very little to the consumer who doesn't earn $1,000 a year in investment income. But the financial institutions are flush with our savings. Canadians, on the whole, are very big savers. And it doesn't take long for that fund to start paying more than $1,000 a year in interest.

Fortunately, there are alternatives to investing in order to meet education costs — including a brand new idea.

The first to consider is an education savings plan or a child trust. The registered education savings plan is the more common, while child trusts are growing in popularity, especially for those with larger pools of money.

There are several RESPs available in Canada. One is the Canadian Scholarship Trust Foundation; another is the University Scholarships of Canada. Each allows the consumer to contribute a small monthly amount (depending on your child's age) into a large pool of money. You don't get any tax relief for your contribution, but you do gain several advantages.

One is that the money is combined with another $200 million or so and can earn a higher rate of return because of its size. In addition, the money is now out of your name and into that of a tax-free foundation.

Instead of you paying tax on any amount over $1,000 per year, the foundation gets to reinvest the funds each year tax free until your child decides to go to university or college. At that point, the money you have contributed will be paid to the child, and his or her share of the interest will come to him or her in future years.

However, in most cases the child will be in a lower tax bracket than you and will have the full-time student deduction, plus his or her tuition, to offset income. Conceivably, then, the child could earn this money tax free.

A child trust — or an "inter vivos" trust, as it is called — is for those who have accumulated a large amount of money. The trust earns the interest each year rather than the parent. If it is paid out to the child, it is taxed in his or her name — and the child can earn approximately $5,000 a year before being taxed.

In essence, parents with $35,000 to $50,000 in accumulated capital can shelter the income generated by that capital from Revenue Canada. In fact, the numbers can be much larger when more than one child is involved. And, of course, the reason these trusts are so popular with the rich is because they can transfer money out of their names where it would be taxed at 50%.

While these trusts almost seem to be too good to be true because of their tax-saving abilities, Revenue Canada thought that way as well. As a result, they have been stopped as per the last federal budget. But, however, not for those who followed my advice in previous books and articles where I suggested you open one of these plans. For those who did, you now have at least until the end of 1987 and longer to enjoy tax savings while you save for your child's education.

Again, those who have never used a trust probably won't bother now, unless they fit into a certain category. For example, if your children are quite young we'll give you some ideas very shortly. But, if you have fifteen-year-olds or older there can still be a reason for a trust. Once a child turns eighteen there's no longer anything called the "attribution rule." It states that the interest earned on any money given to a child must be attributed back to the person who gave him or her the money. But, once the child turns eighteen, he or she is now an adult, and can claim the interest earned on this money.

Recognizing this, we could put everything we own into a child trust when the child is fifteen, buy compounding investments that don't mature for three years, and force Revenue Canada to tax the child — not you the parent — on this investment income. The tax savings may be enough to pay for an entire education depending, of course, on the amount of money you have to invest.

Even then, using a trust may be unnecessary. If you simply give your child $50,000, let's say, and he or she invests it where you suggest, making sure that you choose an investment that won't mature for at least three years, the full three years' worth of interest will come due in the same year. Provided the child is eighteen or older, you won't have to pay the tax — and you will have saved three years' worth of trustee fees.

Those with existing trusts may also be able to take advantage of this theory. If you lent money to a trust via a demand loan, you must call that loan at the end of 1987. If you used a term loan with a set number of years you have until the day that loan expires to call it. But, if either of those dates comes around the time your child turns fifteen, you could then remove the original money from the trust and reinvest it in a three-year investment that would mature after the child turns eighteen. The interest earned in the early years would be taxed in the child's name if, indeed, he or she were taxable, while the last three years would also be taxed at their lower rate rather than the rate you would pay in your name.

Another way to best the attribution rule is to put money in a child's name and buy investments that produce no yield or only a very small one. Unlike the case where we give money to a spouse, there's no attribution rule when a child earns a capital gain. In other words, all the capital gains would be taxed at the child's tax rate while any other income would be taxed at the giver's tax level.

One way to accomplish this would be to buy good quality — but low yielding — stocks in the child's name that show prospects of rising in value; mutual funds that produce mostly capital gains; or raw land or a piece of real estate that wasn't producing a positive yield. That way the capital gain would be treated as part of the child's half-million dollar lifetime limit rather than your own.

It's not uncommon for families to use the forced savings advantages of education savings plans and Canada Savings Bonds when it comes to saving money for a child's education.

But there's another forced savings plan that may work just as well, or even better, now that we have a new budget full of new tax rules.

Mutual fund companies often offer a monthly purchase plan whereby you buy the same or a similar fund every month for a long period of time. As prices rise and fall, as they invariably do, you buy the same value worth, but a different number of shares. In addition, the shares your child owns pay dividends and produce capital gains. If the money you use to implement this plan is yours, the income portion will be taxable in your name. However, if you use the family allowance check to pay for this monthly purchase, Revenue Canada will treat all the income earned using this idea as taxable in the child's name and not your own. What's more, when interest rates are low, mutual funds and stocks usually pay a much better rate of return than interest-bearing investments. This may be the best way for you to save for your child's education. Simply contract with a financial consultant to purchase mutual funds for your child every month using the family allowance check.

There's yet one more sophisticated idea that could prove to be by far the best.

Today's interest rates are low. We know that when they are low, other investments rise in value faster than normal. In addition, we know that the child is going to qualify for the family allowance.

Let's say you approach a lender and arrange a $3,000 loan in your child's name. Naturally, the lender won't deal with the child unless you co-sign the loan, but you're prepared to do that. Use the $3,000 to purchase a good quality, well-managed mutual fund in your child's name. Past performance shows there's a pretty reasonable expectation of earning at least 15% a year over a long period of time using a mutual fund so we, at least, have the expectation of earning something well above the normal 5% to 6% that we'd earn in a savings account. In fact, if we contribute the family allowance check to a savings account each month we'll probably earn only about $10 to $12 in interest each year. But, if we use this idea we have a chance to earn four or five times that amount or more each year. And don't forget that compounding will take the totals much higher over a long period of time.

If we pay a 9% acquisition fee to acquire a good quality mutual fund we'll have $2,730 left to invest for our child. The baby bonus check, at $375 per year in 1985 and rising each year thereafter, will pay the interest plus a little bit of principal each year, so eventually the loan will be fully paid off. But, the investment will always remain in place.

If the investment pays 15% a year on average, and if we hold it for 18 years until the child is ready for university or college, it will be worth $33,785, pretty well tax free, because it's partially a capital gain and partly dividends that your child has been claiming each year as they were earned. And surely $33,000 or so is a lot better than $10 to $12 a year, even though it too will compound over the years. But don't forget that as it does that there's a better chance of it becoming taxable as it's all interest.

The 15% rate of return we've used is naturally debatable because there's never any future guarantees with investments. However, past performance of mutual funds like Industrial Growth, United Funds, Trimark, and Cundill Value Fund all show yields in excess of 18% to 20% over a ten-year period. Each extra percent earned in this example increases our yield substantially while our loan cost remains the very same; 16%, as an example, means $39,483; 20% escalates to $72,682 in our child's name — and surely that'll help them with their education, give them a substantial stepping stone into the real world, a downpayment on a house, or some seed money for a business venture.

28

Pensioners Don't Have to Lead a Taxing Life at All

Remember the 1985 Conservative budget? Michael Wilson was going to cancel indexing of seniors' pensions. But the outcry was so strong that he was forced to back away. Seniors were paranoid that they would see their standard of living fall by 3% every year, so they deluged their MPs with demands for change — and it worked.

But, you know something? Pensioners don't really have to worry about indexing. Those who are in the lower-income brackets where they get supplementary benefits were going to be protected by full indexing and the rich who didn't need the money wouldn't have even felt the loss of indexing which means the only group who were going to be hurt was the middle-income pensioners who have a little extra money. And now their problems are solved.

There is a way that every pensioner who has a little money invested can effectively beat the taxman and the problem of indexing. It's a nifty trick that changes taxable income into tax-free income. And, if you aren't taxable, you won't give a hoot and a holler about where tax rates go.

It's fairly common for seniors to sell their house when they retire. They want to travel a bit and they're tired of maintaining their property. So they sell and move into a condo. They invest the money and use the income to supplement their pensions. Or another similar story has them inheriting money or getting a golden handshake at retirement time. What it adds up to is a pool of cash that they can invest.

Where Canadians have generally made their mistake is to invest this money in safe and secure term deposits or Canada Savings Bonds. Yes, their money is safe and secure, but the problem is that it will produce taxable interest income. The combination of inflation plus taxation has created a negative real rate of return in the past and there's no reason to think that it won't in the future. More important, though, is that they are at the mercy of the taxman.

Here's a simplified example. Let's say you sold your house for $100,000 and you invested that money in a 10% interest-bearing investment. You'd earn $10,000 a year interest which you'll find very useful as a supplement to your pension income. But don't forget about the taxman's share. The first $1,000 worth of interest income is tax free, but the next $9,000 is taxable. If you're in the 35% tax bracket you'll pay $3,170 tax on that income which leaves you with only $6,850. And don't forget that along the way inflation's lopped another four or five thousand dollars off the purchasing power of your money.

If instead of buying term deposits and Canada Savings Bonds you were to purchase $100,000 worth of good-quality well-managed mutual funds, you could enter into what's called a withdrawal plan. In the first place nobody ever knows for sure what rate of return you'll earn when you buy stocks or mutual funds. We do know, though, when you buy good-quality investments that you have a track record on which to base your decisions. You'll earn dividends which usually rise in value and you'll have a chance to earn capital gains which are now tax free. If you want to take some flyers you can seek out some speculative issues, but seniors should aim for the good-quality issues that already have a good track record.

Past performance says that good-quality well-managed mutual funds can return 15% to 18% to 25% or 30% per year over a decade or so, which is well in excess of the 10% interest we've been talking about with term deposits. But let's say we only earn

10% or so with the mutual fund we choose. That means we earn the same $10,000. But don't forget that part of this is a tax-free capital gain and part is a dividend that qualifies for the dividend tax credit which effectively wipes out most or all of the tax we were going to pay.

Now we've earned the very same $10,000 but we've kept it all rather than sharing more than $3,000 with the taxman. In addition, the withdrawal plan allows us to set the monthly income we want. In fact, we can even index it or control it in any way we want because it's our own money.

Here's another popular tactic. Again, we earned 10% on this investment, but we didn't take the cash. We let it compound. Now our fund is worth $110,000, the same as our Canada Savings Bonds or term deposits. If we now sell off $10,000 worth of our shares we'll effectively receive $9,100 of our own money back totally tax free. It's only right that it be tax free as, after all, it is only the same as cashing in $9,100 worth of Canada Savings Bonds. We only have to pay tax when we make money, and not when we get our own money back. The other $900 will be a capital gain which is now totally tax free.

So, you see what you've done. You've received the very same $10,000 but you've paid no tax. If you stick with the usual term deposits or Canada Savings Bonds, you're going to pay tons of tax. This way you don't care if tax rates are 100% because you don't have to pay any.

Now, just in case you don't think the theory we've just outlined works, let me give you some specifics.

If on December 31, 1975, you sold your house and invested your $100,000 in Industrial American Fund's Monthly Indexed Withdrawal Fund, here's what would have happened. You'd have to pay $4,000 in commission, which might unfortunately dissuade some individuals, so you'd only invest $96,000 in this plan.

If you started with a $750 monthly income that was indexed to the consumer price index, as are the Canada and Quebec pension plans, you'd see a yearly increase that brought you to $1,536 per month in 1984. So you haven't been bothered by inflation because your income has been steadily rising, but cost of living increases would cut into your principal if you didn't earn enough each year to service your payments — after tax. And that's what happened with interest-type investments over that time period. For example if you put your $100,000 (no commission) in *a savings account,* you'd have only *$46,954 left by the end of 1984 because your monthly income exceeded the growth of your money.*

Of course, when you have $100,000 to invest, you should look elsewhere, so let's pick the short-term money markets which, generally speaking, produced competitive yields over that length of time. The increase in monthly payments to offset inflation left you with only $74,782 in your pool of money, so once again you're falling behind.

Ah ha, but the inflation protected monthly withdrawal plan that we entered into not only hasn't been eroded, but it has $238,206 left in it. We've received almost $122,000 in monthly payments and we still have more than $238,000 left to produce a lifetime income. But let's stretch the time period out a bit to see if we win our lose with a withdrawal plan over an even longer period of time. This time we'll choose Templeton Growth Fund and we'll pick a $1,000 per month non-indexed monthly payment for 20 full years ending, again, on December 31, 1984.

You would have received $252,000 in monthly income payments for your $100,000 deposit. And you'd still have $856,896.35 invested and earning income for you. In fact, if this fund earned only 10% a year from then on you'd earn almost $86,000 a year so you'd be able to increase your income any time you wanted. In fact, any time it earns more than 1½% you've more than covered your monthly income.

And all along you're paying less tax than if you go for interest income.

So, once again, time works in our favor — and there's no reason why it shouldn't continue to do so. If you buy stocks to make a quick profit you want to read the daily stock sheets. If you buy them to produce a yield and tax advantages forget about the day-to-day activity. Who cares whether they rise or fall from time to time? It's the long haul that counts. That's why seniors should, indeed, think along these lines rather than straight interest income. They'll come out much better off over the long run.

Winter Is the Best Time to Buy a House

While economic developments can make a difference when it comes to purchasing a house, there's no question that winter is by far the best time to buy.

Think about it for a minute. The weather is freezing cold, the winds are gusting, everything is covered with snow, everybody wants to stay inside where it's nice and warm — and those few who do go out see houses that look very unattractive because they are knee-deep in snow. Could there be a worse time to be out braving the elements looking for a house?

And that's exactly what happens. Everybody sits tight. No one even thinks about buying a house in the winter months. No one get the itch until spring when the grass turns green and the flowers start to bloom. Even the real estate salespeople take their holidays in the winter; they know that most buyers enter the marketplace as winter is breaking up and during the warmer summer months when it's easier to get around and the houses look more attractive. Real estate salespeople use December, January, and February to get their books back in order, do some prospecting, take a course or two, and spend some time in the sun spending those commissions that they earned during the busy part of the season.

In the meantime, almost as many houses are being put up for sale. The biggest reasons for selling a house still affect the marketplace no matter what the weather. They include family breakups, company transfers, deaths, and financial hardship. When the family splits, it's not uncommon for the house to go up for sale right away as neither spouse has enough money to pay for it outright. If your boss decides to transfer you to another city, you generally have no choice but to move. As a result, your house might be put on the market right away, no matter what the market is like. Most of us just can't afford to pay the cost of accommodation in two different locations. (That might not be too serious, as you will be looking for a new house in the same slow market you are selling in. The bargain you get might more than offset the disappointing price you are offered on your present house.) Unfortunately, the realities of a death in the family can come home in very quick order when you find out that there wasn't enough life insurance to cover the mortgage and provide a decent standard of living. You may have no choice but to put the house up for sale.

And we all know what can happen in a period of escalating interest rates. If your mortgage comes due for renewal at a substantially higher interest rate right when your employer is unable to give you a raise, you might have no choice but to lose that house. A forced sale by the banker will take it away from you.

All these things happen throughout the year, summer or winter. But to have them happen when there are fewer buyers interested in another house always works in favor of the buyer. It's the old law of supply and demand. The more demand the better chance that product prices will rise. The more supply just when demand for that product is slow is sure to mean falling prices. And that's what you invariably see in the cold winter months. There's more supply than there are buyers so you are in a much better position to demand a lower price, better financing terms, or a combination of both. In short, you come out ahead financially when you buy in the winter months.

However, you also come out ahead in another way. Next to financing costs, the second biggest expense involved in owning a house can be the cost of energy to run it. Each year energy prices can be expected to rise so you have to be very careful to get yourself an energy-efficient unit. What better time than the cold winter months, when the snow is on the roof and all around the foundation, to check for heat loss? Look at the roof line. If your prospective house has less snow on the roof than the other houses in the neighborhood it might well indicate that insulation is lacking. Look for icicles, which show energy loss along the roof line. Check the snow that rests next to the foundation. If there isn't any, it probably tells you that there is too much heat escaping from the basement walls. It's expensive enough to heat a home nowadays; we certainly don't want to be trying to heat the great outdoors at the same time.

When you get inside the house you can listen to the furnace. If it goes on and off often while you are there, you know that the house has drafts or furnace problems. And if the furnace is constantly switching on and off, you can be sure that there will be problems in the future.

Feel the walls. If they are cold, you might be in for a major expense when it comes to insulating them. We used to fill the walls with formaldehyde foam, but that has since created problems. You might end up with a major expense if you ever want to add insulation that can't be blown into the walls. Take a close look at the windows. Do they fit well? Are there drafts? Are there storm windows? It's a proven fact that about thirty percent of our heat loss can be eliminated by stopping the escape of heated air. And that's something that you should be trying to accomplish. However, you may find, when looking at a particular house, that it will be just too big a job compared to a similar house for sale down the street at a comparable price.

That's why winter is the very best time to get a bargain. It's a little more inconvenient to go out and look at houses, but you won't have to face any lineups — there won't be too many of you out there. You won't get as good a look at the surrounding property as in the warm summer months, but then think of the nice surprise you have waiting for you. Or look at it this way. For the money you are going to save you should be more than happy to look at some color pictures the vendor has on hand.

30

Your Mortgage — It Might Be the Best Place to Invest

Now that interest rates have fallen substantially from their record highs of 1981/82, it isn't nearly as easy to find a good place to invest our money. When savings bonds were paying 19½% and term deposits 20% or so, it was relatively easy to earn ourselves a nice fat income. Of course, we had to pay tax on that investment income once we exceeded $1,000 per year, but it sure was a lot easier to earn a decent rate of return on our savings.

While savings rates are falling, the rate we pay on our mortgage doesn't move quite as quickly. We can take a variable-rate mortgage and see our rate fall as other rates also fall. But many people didn't do that when variable-rate mortgages were initially offered, so they are locked into mortgages in which the interest rate won't change for one to five years. In that case, probably the best investment these people can find will be to pay every cent they can against their mortgage every time the anniversary date rolls around. In fact, the first thing the average consumer should do is to calculate how great the benefits are when it comes to paying extra money against the mortgage. I know some consumers who say they have a seven-percent mortgage and they wouldn't consider paying one red cent extra against that loan.

However, even in the case of a seven-percent mortgage, it might be worthwhile. I'll show you how to make that decision in this chapter, and I'll also show you just how beneficial it can be for consumers to invest in their mortgages.

The problem with mortgages is that they are drawn up in favor of the lender. We use an amortization schedule that balances interest and principal so that we pay the same monthly payment over the lifetime of the mortgage. That was okay back in the days of twenty-five-year loans, but now many mortgages exist for only five years, and the most common term is three years. Interest rates at six or seven percent also made the standard amortization schedule work reasonably well. However, interest rates of twelve to twenty percent don't do us any favors at all. All we do is pay interest, interest, interest, and very little money is applied to the loan itself. In fact, the mortgage schedule as it is now drawn up works so much against us that it takes more than twenty years before the amount of money included in our monthly payment for principal exceeds the amount directed toward interest. In essence, we pay twenty years of interest payments so that we will be able to pay our mortgage off in the last five years. I think we should accelerate that mortgage schedule so that we can make it work to our advantage, rather than the lender's.

Did you know that you will probably end up paying approximately four times the original cost of your mortgage before you have finally paid it off? On a $50,000 mortgage at twelve percent, amortized over twenty-five years, you will pay approximately $516 per month for the next quarter century. That means $6,192 per year or $154,800 over the life of the loan. What started out as a pretty reasonable mortgage has quadrupled by the time it is paid off. What's worse, almost all home mortgages are paid for with "tax-paid dollars." Our employer deducts tax from our salaries before we ever get our hands on our paychecks. When we get that check home, we pay our mortgage payment out of it. That means that an individual in the fifty-percent tax bracket may have to earn $11,032 before tax to be left with enough money to pay his mortgage each month — in other words, $12,384 in yearly salary. By the time it is paid off, he will really have paid more than $300,000 simply for his mortgage.

That makes it almost impossible to make any money in real estate, even with our houses being allowed to increase in value totally free of tax. And we haven't even included the original down payment, the legal bills, maintenance, insurances, utilities, and so on. And then there are increases in interest rates to consider. All those people who had their mortgages come due in the last couple of years are now paying substantially higher rates than they used to. They found, much to their dismay, that the payments they had been making faithfully each month for several years were all going toward the interest on their mortgage. They had made no headway at all. They were renewing a mortgage that was almost the same size as the one they had taken out a couple of years earlier. And now that they were forced to take on a high interest rate, they were making even less headway against this obligation.

If we go back to our $50,000 mortgage at twelve percent, amortized over twenty-five years, where we are paying $516 per month or $6,192 per year, we will find that after two years, or $12,384 in monthly payments, we will have only paid off about $750 worth of principal! For every $1 that has gone against the loan, $16.51 has gone for interest. Think of it this way. If a vacuum salesman arrived at your door and convinced you that you should buy a vacuum for $350, you might think it was a good deal. But if you didn't have the money with you or wanted to pay for it over a two-year period and were told that you would have to pay $12,384 in financing charges, you would throw him out the door. Well, that's exactly what you agree to when you take on a mortgage — unless you do something to turn that amortization schedule around so that it works in your favor, not the lender's.

If we stretch this problem out to five years, we will find that we have paid almost $31,000 in mortgage payments but have only paid $2,250 on the outstanding amount of our loan. And remember that $31,000 might be worth as much as $62,000 in real earnings before the tax man gets his share. We have several options when it comes to beating our mortgage. One is to pay extra against the principal when we have some extra cash — if we can bring ourselves to do it, and many can't. Another way is to shorten the amortization period so that we are automatically paying more against our mortgage each month — a kind of forced savings plan, which works wonders. And there is a weekly mortgage, which can help you pay your loan off in something close to half the normal time. For those of us who can't get a weekly mortgage, there are still ways, if we play our cards right, to force even the biggest lender in the country to give us the equivalent of a weekly mortgage.

First, let's look at paying some extra money against our loan each year when the anniversary date rolls around. Each of us, on occasion, has some savings. If we manage our money properly, we can arrange to have those savings mature at the same time as our loan comes due for renewal, or on the anniversary date. Then we can use it to pay down the outstanding balance of the loan. Lenders generally will allow you to pay extra against your loan once each year. But some older mortgages are completely closed and allow no extra payments. In fact, there are some newer loans that are also closed. However, we can always pay as much as we want against our loans when they come due to be renegotiated, say, at the end of our one, two, three, four, or five-year term. It pays for consumers to talk to their lenders so that they know exactly what they can and cannot do when it comes to paying extra against their mortgage. It's especially important now as this is probably the time when paying extra against your mortgage is the best investment available. If you know in advance what you can and cannot do, then you will have a better idea what you should be planning for. So ask your lender — especially if you find mortgage contracts and the like confusing. If you find that you are one of the many who do have some flexibility with their loan payments, you have a number of things you can do, including paying extra against your outstanding loan.

If, as an example, you have an eighteen-percent mortgage — unfortunately the rate many consumers locked themselves in at when interest rates started to fall — you could save yourself $10,558 if you simply paid $183 extra against the principal at the end of the first year. If you were able to save up $965, which is just more than one full payment for one month, you would save yourself $42,000 in interest payments on that loan. We're talking about a single, one-time payment here. You see, the sooner you can pay some extra cash against that loan, the more years of interest you are going to save. If at the end of the first year you can put some extra money against your loan, you will save yourself twenty-four years of interest on that money. If you do it after two years of payments, you save interest for twenty-three years, and so on down the line until you have paid off your loan. That means that the more you can pay against your loan in the early years, the more good you will be doing for yourself. And even though the numbers I have used relate to seventeen- and eighteen-percent mortgages, the savings are almost as exciting when rates are lower. It's the long-term impact that counts.

However, in some cases, you shouldn't put any money against your loan — if you have a low interest rate, for example. You would be better off investing your money rather than paying off your mortgage. There is a fairly simple way to decide whether you should pay your loan off. First, people who have a seven-percent mortgage probably wouldn't want to pay any extra money against the loan, as they have almost paid it off anyway. But to make that decision, you have to go through a little formula that I have devised.

You know your mortgage rate. Figure out what rate you are earning on your investments. Put each one on a sheet of paper and determine, first of all, what your overall rate of return is. As an example, if you are earning twelve percent on your total investment portfolio and your mortgage is locked in at ten percent, then you shouldn't pay any extra money against your mortgage as you are earning more than you are paying out. However, that statement might be a bit of an oversimplification in that the yield we think we are earning isn't necessarily the yield we get in our pockets. Once we go beyond $1,000 in investment income in any year, we have to start paying tax on that money so we aren't really earning the quoted rate anymore.

So let's look at the first $1,000 in investment income first. If you never earn that much, then you know that the rate of return you earn on your investments is your real rate of return. If that yield overall is below your mortgage rate, then you should cash in your investments and pay the money against your loan. You are paying out more than you are earning — in effect, you are losing on the deal. Conversely, if you are earning more on your investments than your mortgage costs, then you should keep right on investing. You will end up ahead of the game. There are two other variables that enter into the picture at this point. One is the length of time left to pay off your mortgage. Even if your mortgage rate and the rate of return on your investments come out close, it might pay to put extra money against your mortgage as you save not one year's interest, but several. The other point is psychological. Some people just can't hang onto money for very long, and others need to pay off their mortgage as soon as they can because they just can't stand to be in debt. Those people are probably ahead of the game to put as much against their loans as they possibly can. It's the perfect way to invest in themselves.

That brings up the other way in which we may be able to save a pile of money against our mortgages. If we find that we never seem to have any money to put against these loans when the anniversary date rolls around, we might want to consider this ploy. If, when our mortgage comes due for renewal, we arrange with our lender to shorten the period over which it is amortized, we will save ourselves a great deal of money. An example: if, when you take on a new mortgage, you arrange to have it amortized over twenty-four years rather than twenty-five, you will save yourself one full year's worth of mortgage payments. In the case of a $50,000 mortgage amortized over twenty-five years at twelve percent, you would be asked to pay $3.69 more per month, or about $44 more per year, but you would save yourself $6,200 in mortgage payments. And don't forget that those payments are in after-tax dollars, so it might really mean a saving of as much as $12,400.

The same theory holds for mortgage renewals. Every time your lender offers you a new set of terms, demand that the amortization period be shortened by at least one year. Then you will be paying extra against your principal and saving yourself interest on that amount for the rest of the life of the mortgage. If, in our example, you were able to afford to shorten the amortization period by five full years, you would be asked to pay an extra $295 per year — but you would save $31,000 in mortgage payments. If you got a raise and were able to afford another $75 per month right from the start of your mortgage, you would be able to wipe out ten full years of mortgage payments and save yourself $62,000 along the way. What do you think the odds are of your boss giving you a raise worth $62,000 after taxes over the next ten years? Highly unlikely, as it would means an increase worth as much as $124,000 when you consider the fact that you will eventually have to pay tax on that increase.

Weekly Mortgages
There's another way to beat your mortgage, and it's a good one provided you use it to your advantage and don't let a lender take advantage of you. It's a weekly mortgage, and it's become increasingly popular as financial institutions compete in the mortgage market. Originally, credit unions only were prepared to offer this type of mortgage but, as other institutions found themselves flush with lendable cash, they too joined the parade and offered loans that can be paid off in fifteen years as opposed to the standard twenty-five years.

In doing so, you might think that lenders give up a lot of interest. But that isn't always the case. Yes, they do face more paperwork in that a weekly mortgage involves fifty-two payments per year as opposed to twelve for a standard monthly plan. But don't forget that the institution also has your payment to reinvest sooner. As a result, it has a greater cash flow with which it can make up the difference.

It seems, though, that that wasn't quite enough for some of the lenders. They decided that this was an opportunity to exact another pound of flesh — to take more out of the borrower's pocket — hoping that he or she wouldn't know it was happening.

Here's what you want to watch out for. Standard mortgage policies state that monthly payment mortgages are compounded twice a year. You'll see in your mortgage contract that your loan interest is "adjusted" twice a year or semi-annually. That's the same as being compounded twice each year which effectively means that you are charged more interest than if your rate was adjusted only once each year.

When you take a weekly mortgage you win because you pay the equivalent of thirteen monthly payments each year. The extra payment is applied directly against your outstanding principal. As well, each week the payment chips away at the outstanding principal, which results in a daisy chain effect where you pay your loan off ten or more years ahead of schedule because so much extra is going directly against your outstanding principal (see chart).

The problem, though, it is that many lenders change the compounding rules when they offer weekly mortgages without making it perfectly clear to the borrowers. It's become popular to compound mortgages monthly rather than twice a year when a consumer has a weekly mortgage. In effect, this means that you pay interest on interest twelve times a year rather than only twice a year — and that can only work in the favor of the lender. If you had money to invest you'd definitely be ahead of the game if you were able to get monthly compounding. However, when you are borrowing, it's the same as giving the lender a special bonus.

So here's what you should do. You should, first of all, check to see if your lender offers a weekly mortgage. If the answer is "yes", ask how often the lender will compound or "adjust" the interest on your loan. If it's faster than semi-annually, you don't want their weekly mortgage. You want to exercise another one of your options. It says that you can normally increase the size of your monthly payment by 10% or pay an extra 10% lump sum against your outstanding principal. Either will suffice.

If we simply take our monthly payment and divide it by twelve, we'll arrive at a number that added to our present monthly payment will give us a close equivalent to a weekly mortgage or exactly thirteen monthly payments. And that's exactly what we are trying to do in the first place. Now we have the equivalent of thirteen monthly payments, but we've been able to continue with out normal semi-annual compounding rather than leaving ourselves open to the more expensive monthly compounding.

And here's another option. Most mortgages allow us to pay extra against our outstanding principal on the anniversary of renewal date, or both. Each year, then, you probably have the right to prepay your loan. If you opt to prepay the equivalent to one extra mortgage payment at that time, you will almost duplicate the benefits reaped from a weekly mortgage.

The drawback is that I find that many home owners refuse

MORTGAGE PAYMENT COMPARISON CHART
$50,000 Mortgage @ 13% Compounded Semi-Annually

	I Conventional mortgage monthly payment	II Annual amount paid in 52 weekly instalments	III Annual amount paid in 26 bi-weekly instalments	IV Annual amount paid in 24 semi-monthly instalments	V Monthly amount paid in 4 weekly instalments	VI Monthly amount paid in 2 bi-weekly instalments
Payments	$551.20	$127.20	$254.40	$275.60	$137.80	$275.60
Amortized life of the loan	25 years	24.32 years	24.52 years	24.55 years	16.83 years	16.90 years
Interest cost	$115,367.71	$110,843.25	$112,157.68	$112,380.21	$70,586.60	$71,094.32
Interest saved over conventional loan	NIL	$4,521.46	$3,210.03	$2,987.50	$44,781.11	$44,273.39
Extra principal paid annually	NIL	NIL	NIL	NIL	$551.20	$551.20

NOTE: The monthly amount paid in two semi-monthly instalments is exactly the same as column IV.

to use the savings they have built up during the year to put towards that thirteenth mortgage payment. They find some excuse so they don't have to make that extra payment. So they will continue to make mortgage payments for twenty-five years. It's tragic.

Variable Rate Mortgages

Variable rate mortgages have been a tremendous money saver for consumers because the interest rate has declined to a low and remained steady. As the interest rate fell, so too did the rate on your variable rate loan; it was automatically adjusted lower. That's an advantage in that you don't have to worry about continually renegotiating your rate or trying to decide whether you want a short-term loan or a longer term.

The disadvantage to a variable rate loan is that when interest rates are really competitive, variable rate loans are basically tied to the prime lending rate. At the same time short-term mortgages (six months or so) may offer a lower interest rate. That means that the advantages of a variable rate loan, as good as they are, may never catch up to a lower rate short-term loan. But that's a decision that the borrower will have to make based on what's happening at the time. It it appears that interest rates are going to rise you'll want to switch out of your variable loan into a fixed-term loan where you won't have to worry about higher rates until your next renewal date. Were you to continue with a variable rate loan, you may find your rate automatically increasing as the prime lending rate rises. However, if it appears that rates are going to move lower, you should compare the rates between a short-term, open mortgage and a variable rate loan, and opt for the lowest possible rate.

While these examples oversimplify what will happen, they do offer some direction. A real estate agent, if you are in the process of buying a house, or a financial advisor, can help you choose the type of loan you should use at any one time.

Let's face facts. Mortgages are most often paid for with after-tax dollars. That means that we might be paying double what we have to. If we don't seek out the best possible deal we're only hurting ourselves. That includes using weekly mortgages where possible, paying extra against our loans, shortening our amortization period, and making our mortgages tax deductible as often as possible.

Remember that cardinal rule of ours. It says we pay off all non-tax-deductible loans as fast as possible and replace them with tax-deductible ones if we want. That means we pay extra against our loan as often as possible and accelerate our loan payments as often as possible — as long as it works in our favor and not the lender's.

31

You Can Make Your Mortgage Tax Deductible

Canadians often look enviously at their friends in the United States who are able to deduct the interest they pay on their mortgages from their income tax. Canadian mortgages are generally paid with take-home pay. Our employer deducts tax from our earnings, and we pay our expenses, including our mortgage, out of what's left. That means that a thirteen percent mortgage really costs those people in the fifty percent tax bracket (more than $53,000 taxable income in Ontario; rates vary from province to province) twenty-six percent. Those who earn less come out slightly ahead, but when you get right down to it, they are hurt even more in real dollars by the fact that mortgages are not tax deductible. But there is a way that some Canadians can deduct every cent of interest they pay on their mortgages. When Marc Lalonde was finance minister, in his first budget in the fall of 1982 he rolled back the clock on his predecessor's decision to limit the amount of interest we can deduct on investment loans. That opened the door to making our mortgages tax deductible.

Take the individual who had a $40,000 mortgage and who has also been tucking money away in a savings plan for future use, an education savings plan for his children, or a grubstake for his retirement. His investments earn interest, which is taxable once the total return exceeds $1,000. At the same time, he is making a monthly payment on his mortgage, which is not tax deductible. In effect, he is being taxed twice. Yet if he played his cards right, he could rearrange his affairs so that his mortgage was totally tax deductible.

Here's how it's done. This individual sells all or enough of his investments to pay off his mortgage completely. He then asks his lender to loan him sufficient funds to buy back the investments he liquidated, as security for which the lender is given a mortgage on the house. All the interest he is going to pay on that loan is tax deductible, as it isn't really a loan to buy a house, but instead a loan to buy investments. And Mr. Lalonde has said that all the interest paid on investment loans is tax deductible.

To give you an indication of just how important this facility is, consider the individual with a $50,000 loan amortized at fourteen percent over twenty-five years. His monthly payment is $587 for interest and principal, most of which is interest. If this individual is in the thirty-five percent tax bracket (around $20,000 in taxable income in Ontario), he would be able to claim approximately $6,600 in extra tax deductions at the end of the year. At his tax rate, this would mean an extra tax rebate of $2,310. Right off the bat he is $2,300 ahead of his neighbors. But if he plays his cards right here, he can do even better. Normally, in the first year of a mortgage of this type you are paying a very high percentage of your monthly payment toward interest. In fact, after two years of mortgage payments in this example, your $14,000 in monthly payments have only lowered your outstanding loan by $550. If your extra tax rebate were applied against your mortgage in those two years, you would effectively save yourself more than eight years of mortgage payments in those two years alone. Each year you continued thereafter would move you closer to having eliminated your house loan in half the normal time, even though you have spent no more money.

I am sure there are readers who are saying to themselves, "I don't have that much money. I have only a few thousand dollars so I guess I am left out in the cold." That isn't necessarily the case. Let's say that your $40,000 mortgage is due for renewal and you happen to have $5,000 in Canada Savings Bonds or some other investment. You could sell your bonds and pay your mortgage down to $35,000, but instantly increase it back up to $40,000 — even while sitting at the lender's desk. It's simply a paper transaction. The $5,000 you would use to buy another investment, probably preferred or common shares where you had a reasonable chance to earn more than the interest you were paying out. And one-eighth of your mortgage payment would be tax deductible, as it was really an investment loan and not a conventional mortgage. In the example of a $40,000 mortgage amortized over twenty-five years, you would get another tax deduction of about $675, which, at a thirty-five percent tax rate, would save you, in your pocket, about $236. That money paid against your loan each year would wipe out a full year's payments each time you did it. Each time you do this in the early years of your mortgage you save approximately $5,600 in future payments, simply because you made a portion of your loan tax deductible. What's more, all this time you still have your savings invested and earning extra income, which you can use to pay against your mortgage in future years. In fact, if you play your cards right you will be able to increase your tax-deductible portion each year by following the very same procedure.

Questions naturally arise from this idea. Will the lender let me do it? Will the tax man accept it? The answer, in both cases, is yes. First, the lender. He will have more respect for you. You are using some ingenuity and you are actually becoming a better risk. He sees that you don't need his money. You can pay this loan off if you wish, but instead you have decided to continue with it to buy some investments. In addition you are going to get back extra tax dollars, which you are going to apply toward the loan while the security is appreciating in value. He will be better off if you do it this way.

As for the tax man: he is more than prepared to let you claim all the interest you pay on money borrowed to make money. However, there must be some indication that you will be able to turn a profit. To borrow at fourteen percent to earn eight percent in a savings account would be considered a sure loser and would not be acceptable. However, to borrow to buy preferred shares or common stock with a reasonable yield and a decent chance to return a capital gain would be more than acceptable.

Canadians unfortunately have a tendency to mismanage their money. The idea of borrowing money to pay loans is used every day by those fortunate enough to have money. They simply pay off their not-tax-deductible loans and continue with ones that are acceptable to the tax man. And there's one other thing that you can be sure they do. They use a good lawyer so that they know it is done right.

32

Mortgaging Your Property Taxes May Be Double Taxing

It's bad enough that we get gouged by the way the amortization schedule affects our mortgage but if you let your lender pay your property taxes, you might end up losing thousands of dollars out of your pocket. In fact, if you manage your tax account yourself and you do it properly, you could save several years of mortgage payments. That's right, by simply refusing to accept the institution's request to add the taxes to your monthly mortgage payment, you might be able to pay your loan off several years in advance. That means that if you are paying $800 per month, you might be losing close to $20,000 in cold, hard cash.

Lenders seldom tell you whether or not you have an option. Most often they simply take the liberty of adding the principal, interest, and taxes together into one "convenient" monthly payment. However, they seldom pay you any interest on this money, even though they might get to use it for many months before they have to remit it to the municipality where you live. And, as if that isn't enough, they usually like to collect a little more than is necessary so that they have a bit of a pad — presumably so that there won't be any major disruptions if a municipality hikes its taxes by a large margin. They also get to keep that money in their own account, earning interest. But seldom do we, the consumer, get to share in that interest. Depending on your tax bill and the prevailing interest rates in any one year, that could mean a loss of anywhere from $50 to $150 each year — and you can imagine what an impact that would have on your mortgage if it were paid against the outstanding balance instead of sitting dormant in the lender's account.

What's worse, if it turns out that the tax portion of your monthly payment isn't enough to cover your tax bill because of a hike in taxes, for example, the lender simply adds the shortfall onto your loan balance and now you end up paying interest on those dollars for the rest of the life of the mortgage until it is paid off in full. You are penalized if you come up short. You lose interest if you pay too much. And you may have hundreds of dollars sitting in the lender's hands earning no interest at the same time as you have a mortgage with the meter running at full speed.

Obviously, what you should do is pay your taxes yourself, separate from your mortgage payment — if your lender will let you and if you can handle it properly without falling behind. After all, that's why the lender tries to add the tax bill to the principal and interest portion. He wants to make sure that the taxes are paid. The municipality has the right to sell your house if the tax bill falls behind. The lender is taking on enough of a risk by lending you the money in the first place. The last thing he wants to do is fight with the city over a tax bill that threatens his security.

Unfortunately, some lenders won't even consider letting you handle your own taxes. But most will — depending, of course, on their individual policies. If you look at the following example, I think you will get a pretty good idea as to why you might benefit if you pay your taxes yourself rather than including them with your mortgage payment.

Let's consider the individual who has a new $75,000 mortgage which bears interest at fourteen percent amortized over twenty-five years. At the same time, he has a property tax bill of $1,200 per year. (That can generally be expected to increase each year.) On the interest and principal alone, he will have a monthly payment of $880.41. And if he is asked to pay exactly enough to cover his tax bill, he will pay another $100 each month in the first year, with the institution either requesting an increase each year or adding the shortfall to the outstanding balance. Under no circumstances should he allow that to happen, even if he has to take out a short-term loan. The increase in taxes in the early years might be the same amount as the principal portion that has been paid off. Remember, in the early years of a mortgage, you pay off almost nothing against the principal. If you allowed the taxes to be added back to your loan amount, you might wipe out everything you have accomplished by paying those twelve, mostly interest, mortgage payments.

Some institutions will ask for more than the $100 per month required in this example, especially if you are buying your house midway through the tax year. But if we consider that the $100 in this example earns no interest for that year, it would mean that the homeowner was out $60 to $75 that he might have earned if he put the money away on his own and then paid his tax bill himself. On a $75,000 fourteen percent new mortgage, it only takes an increase in your monthly payment of $4.50 to cut one full year off the life of the loan. That's right, an extra $54 per year would cut $10,564 in payments off that loan. We have already seen that we could probably earn more than that by investing our tax monies and paying our tax bill ourselves. So now we know that by letting the lender automatically pay our tax bills, we have paid him pretty handsomely, to the tune of more than $10,500 in fact. What's worse, those are tax-paid dollars which means they are worth as much as $20,000 in work-related earnings.

And the situation might even be worse. Consider the individual who has the money saved up already. Twelve hundred dollars put into a one-year term deposit at twelve percent (maybe even with the same institution) would earn $144 in interest. If the homeowner didn't earn more than $1,000 per year in interest income and as a result wasn't taxed on this income, he could put the entire amount against his mortgage balance. To shorten his loan life by two full years all he has to do is increase his payment by $9.72 per month. So he now has more than enough extra cash to do that. And what's more, as his tax bill increases, he will be investing even more money and earning even more interest so the impact against his loan might be substantially higher. Some lenders do pay interest on their tax accounts so before you waltz into your bank and demand to pay your own taxes, it will pay to check out your personal situation. Interest rates vary from year to year as do taxes. Some municipalities demand more frequent payment of their taxes. And most of all you have to be able to pay on time. Not only might you incur some interest if you are late, but the lender might demand that you go back to including your tax payment with your mortgage payment.

However, every homeowner owes it to himself to do a few calculations to see how he stands on his property tax payments. Even if he didn't use the savings to pay down his mortgage, he might get a few nights out on the town free of charge every year or a week's supply of groceries, or a tax deduction, if he simply gave the extra money to a charity rather than voluntarily giving it to his lender.

33

The Granny Mortgage

Amortization schedules work against us when it comes to taking on a mortgage. And we also have to contend with the fact that a mortgage might bear a high rate of interest — generally higher than what we or our friends or relatives can earn when we put our money on deposit at a financial institution. Effectively we lend our money to the bank, the bank marks the rate up, and lends it right back out to our relatives — maybe even back to us.

In addition, we pay tax on any interest we earn over and above the first $1,000. Yet we aren't allowed to deduct the interest we pay on our mortgage. When our dear sweet granny puts her money on deposit at a financial institution and we borrow that very same amount, we might pay three times as much interest out of our pockets as she gets to keep in hers.

Let me show you what I mean. If granny has $60,000 that she has worked and slogged to save for her retirement and she puts that money in a banker's hands, she might earn 12% interest. That means $7,200 per year in income, in addition to any other pension income that she might earn. In 1984 it might have been about $12,000, and even after taxes she would have a reasonable amount left. But now that interest rates are lower and she still has to face taxes, she can end up with a much smaller amount.

Granny might be paying anywhere from twenty to thirty-five percent in taxes, which means that she only gets to pocket between 8 and 9½% after taxes.

On the other hand, when you go to the same banker to borrow $60,000, you probably have to pay something like 14% on your loan. Actually the spread between the lender's cost of money and his lending rate can be even wider, but in our example we will use 14% as your mortgage rate. Right off the bat that's 4½% to 6% higher than your granny is earning on her money. But you still have to consider that your monthly payments are made with tax-paid dollars. If you are in the 35% tax bracket at work you are really paying about 22% before tax on your loan. Effectively, an individual in the 35% tax bracket with a $600-per-month mortgage payment has to earn $11,000 per year before he has enough left over after tax to pay his yearly mortgage obligation. Granny is pocketing something like 8% or 9% — and you are paying out 20% to 22%.

Now you can see why it is so important that families stick together in tough economic times. We pocket very little when we save with a financial institution, and yet we pay out a great big chunk when we borrow from them. Maybe we can do better by dealing with ourselves. First, we could narrow the spread. Instead of borrowing from the bank, why not try to borrow from granny at the twelve percent that she is earning on her deposits? Other than the security of the money, she comes out exactly even, while you have saved yourself two percent.

I know of many families who have gone even further and circumvented the tax man. They don't tell anybody that they are paying this money to granny, so they negotiate with her to pay her a little bit less — say closer to that eight or nine percent that she was earning after tax. A word of warning, though. Revenue Canada expects that every true-blooded Canadian will indeed pay tax on this income. Maybe some day they will crack down on all the granny mortgages and loans between family members, where money is changing hands and no tax has been accounted for. That is, if they ever find a way to do it.

Another way that you can use the granny mortgage to your advantage is to make monthly payments to granny. No interest will be involved. These payments will be straight principal. After all, granny may not be too interested in cars, televisions, stereos, and vacations as repayment for her loan. I mean, how many TVs does one person need? In that case here's what you do. Let's say that you need a $60,000 mortgage. You might be able to arrange a conventional loan through a financial institution at, say, 12%. Under this option, you'd pay $619.14 per month for the next twenty-five years assuming, of course, that interest rates didn't change. That adds up to $185,742 and because home mortgages aren't generally tax deductible, it will take a consumer in the 35% tax bracket almost $290,000 in pre-tax earnings to pay it off.

A friend or relative may give you a mortgage at a lower rate, say 10% or so, which is similar to what they would earn in a term deposit or debenture. But they'd have to pay tax on the interest and you would still be paying out after-tax dollars. Instead, you should talk to this relative about a zero-interest granny mortgage.

Here's how it works. You borrow the same $60,000 from your granny, and you pay it back at $500 per month, principal only. In ten years you will have paid this loan off in full at a total cost of $60,000, instead of $185,000. You've saved $125,000 or almost $200,000 in earnings.

But granny's bound to be a little suspicious. The friendly banker told her that he would pay back about $117,000 over the next ten years, after taxes were taken into consideration. So she won't be too interested in settling for only $60,000. But don't forget that the $60,000 that you pay her is also totally tax free. And don't fail to point out to her that she is going to receive this money monthly, instead of once a year as she would with the financial institution. That will make it easier for her to handle her money, and she will also be able to increase her yield by depositing the money into a daily savings account each month. My calculations show that if she only earned 6½% on that money over the ten-year period that she would amass another $18,000 over the life of the loan.

That narrows the gap a bit, but you're right. It hardly totals $117,000. But that's where this innovative financing idea pays off. With a conventional $60,000 mortgage, you would be required to pay $850.82 per month instead of the $500 that you will pay your granny. If you took that $350 and put it into a savings account that also earned only 6½%, you would amass some $55,500 after tax over the next ten years. If, after the mortgage was paid off and you didn't owe granny any more money, you voluntarily decided to give her a gift of $40,000, she would now be ahead of the game. It couldn't be a condition of the loan because Revenue Canada would surely treat it as an interest payment. But if you were to give her this money out of the goodness of your heart or because she was so nice to you, she would now have received her $60,000 principal back plus $18,000 after-tax interest and a $40,000 gift. That's $118,000 — one thousand dollars more than the banker was going to pay. Granny has come out ahead of the game.

Now let's look at your situation. You paid granny $60,000 in monthly payments. In addition, you gave her $40,000. But the $350 per-month savings left you with $15,000 after you made that gift. That means that you actually paid only $85,000 out of your pocket. The banker was going to charge you $185,000. So you've saved $100,000 in after-tax dollars.

While this strategy sounds awfully attractive, and it is, you should take care to set it up properly. As it is, you have two people who aren't going to like you when you use this type of loan — Revenue Canada and the lenders. But what the heck. It's your money. You're the one who has to pay the bills (including the bankers and the taxman). You want to make sure you come out ahead. So make sure you talk to your dear old granny when it comes around to mortgage time. And make sure that you return the favor to other family members after you've paid your mortgage off and you have extra cash.

34

When You Decide to Renovate, the Wrong Choice Could Be Expensive

With the cost of new housing at record-high levels, more homeowners are choosing to renovate their existing homes rather than move into more expensive houses, those in strange neighborhoods with much higher monthly mortgage payments.

There are some natural considerations before deciding whether you should renovate. One, of course, is whether the renovations will suit your needs — whether they will add sufficient comfort to your present home. But two other considerations are just as important.

First, the right addition could make your house easier to sell and return more than its cost. Because the average Canadian moves every three to four years, you must give some thought to whether the renovations you undertake will improve the salability of your house, and whether they will increase the price you command when you sell it. While many consumers may own only one house in their lifetime, the average Canadian is very mobile. You must always consider the financial aspects of any renovations you decide to make, or they may cost you more money than they are worth.

When it is simply a matter of improving your own comfort, you should consider whether it would be cheaper to go out and buy a house that offers the changes you are looking for. Renovations will disrupt your lifestyle until they are completed and may expose you to expensive pitfalls along the way.

Second, your basement may be a store of hidden costs. If you are considering renovating your basement, you may have to cut into the walls to provide more window space. That could mean reinforcing the walls and contracting for expensive landscaping. You may also find that it is necessary to replace the basement floor, add insulation, and waterproof the entire foundation from the outside. Even then a basement renovation may be the wrong choice as it is almost always easier to recover the money you have spent on a ground-level addition. Unless a basement renovation is done well, it will be detrimental to closing a sale on your house.

Unfortunately, it's not always possible to combine the money, salability, and comfort criteria when choosing how to renovate. Some renovations may make your home more comfortable to live in but not necessarily more salable, and definitely not more profitable.

One prime example is a swimming pool. You may think it is great, but many buyers will see it as a costly nuisance, which robs them of a backyard and peace of mind. Prospective buyers with young children may steer clear of any homes with swimming pools. While some purchasers actively seek out homes with pools, they are only a small segment of the home-buying market. When you make the decision to put a pool in your backyard, don't automatically expect to make money on it if and when you sell your house. In fact, in most cases you will lose part of your money.

Central air conditioners are another loser. They are great in July and August, but it is difficult to recoup your investment when you sell your home.

But there are some renovations that will not only add to your comfort, but also improve the salability of your home and increase its value on the open market.

The most important area to renovate if you wish to improve the salability and profitability of your house is the bathroom. Modernizing the bathroom or adding a second bathroom will almost always pay off, especially if your home is large. Families with children or those that entertain regularly will pay a premium for a house with two or more bathrooms. They will also steer clear of houses that have only one bathroom.

Renovating the kitchen could make potential buyers hungry. It is the next most important area to improve after the bathroom. New cupboards, lots of counter space, and bright lighting will always boost the market value of a house and make it easier to sell.

Efficiency, especially when it comes to energy use, is a key. With the cost of energy rising, and with increases expected to continue, consumers are wise to include more efficient insulation. And always pay attention, when renovating, to energy-saving devices. Openness and light are now high on the list of buyers' priorities. Skylights, sliding patio doors, and enlarged windows all increase salability tremendously. Fireplaces are virtually never a money loser as energy prices continue to rise, especially if they are located in a large family room where the family can spend their time, near the heat of the fireplace, while the rest of the house is kept at a lower, less costly temperature.

Another area worth considering is the attic. For smaller houses, renovating unused attic space for a third bedroom or a study will almost always pay dividends.

And if the house is downtown and you can make provisions for parking — say in the backyard — your investment will be returned many times over.

When renovating older buildings, be careful not to take away from their rustic charm. Many buyers will pay for the glamor and comfort of exposed beams and brick walls. But too often the character of an older building is destroyed by an overactive renovator.

Professional renovators believe that it is often best to concentrate your renovations on the inside. Major exterior work may be a necessity, but it can attract unwanted attention from burglars, city assessors, and even salespeople. Renovations to the interior will be most beneficial to you.

It's also wise to avoid renovations that make your home the most expensive in the neighborhood. More costly homes nearby will add to the value of your home, but if your home is the most expensive in the neighborhood, the other homes may drag its value down.

You can't always bank on renovations paying off, however. There are times when it simply doesn't pay to put any money into home renovations. If your home is in a terrible location where all the homes are rundown or where industrial developments are planned, thousands of dollars in home improvements may be wasted. Don't bother putting money into a house in this case; you won't get it back. It's the land that's important in this instance and not the building.

One thing you can bank on is arranging the financing. Financing is an important consideration when it comes to home-improvement projects. Small jobs can be financed out of your savings, but a large project can cost thousands of dollars. One option is to increase the size of your first mortgage by refinancing. However, this route may be a mistake if your existing mortgage is at a low interest rate. In that case a second mortgage to cover the cost of the renovations and some furniture may be your best choice. Other options available include consumer loans that can be paid back in installments over two or three years, or a demand loan may be arranged with your bank manager.

Finally, if you live in an older section of the city, you should investigate grants or loans that are available through the Canada Mortgage and Housing Residential Rehabilitation Assistance Program.

35

How Much Life Insurance
Do You Really Need?

Each and every one of us should make sure that we have lots of life insurance. It's the cornerstone of sound financial planning. However, most of us end up with either too much life insurance or too little. Because we know so little about the product and because life insurance agents know so much (compared to the consumer), we end up with whatever is recommended by the agent who knocks on our door. He may have a very convincing story, but if we don't have any idea of what we actually need, we won't know whether we are buying too much or too little.

Too many consumers think that what they get from their employer's group plan is enough. Far too many families find out too late that they didn't have enough life insurance. They end up with bills, including their mortgage, that aren't covered by life insurance. Then the remaining spouse has to find a job or work long hours to support the family. To help keep consumers from spending either too much of their income on life insurance — or too little — here is a formula that works pretty well for the average family. Sit down with all the family members, as you should do when sorting out your budget, and use this formula to find out just how much protection you should have. When an insurance agent makes an appointment to see you, listen to what he has to say. Then compare his ideas to your own family plan. There might well be some good ideas in his presentation that you can use to supplement your own ideas, but by comparing what he tells you to the calculations you have made, you can decide whether he is being straight with you.

Remember, life insurance agents make their living through commissions. Most are fine, reputable salespeople who give you the straight goods because they want your continuing business. Some, though, are not. They want to sell you as much as they possibly can so that they can earn a high commission. Using a formula will help you determine which salespeople are acting in your best interests and which aren't.

1. Work out how much your survivors will need to live each year. We're talking about food, clothing, all the necessities of life, including lodging, and any other expenses that you now incur. In fact, it's usually easiest simply to take your present family expenses. The loss of one family member won't make much difference to their overall cost of living. There is one major decision that you will have to make at this stage, though. That has to do with living accommodations. Do you want your family to continue living in their present house or would you expect them to move to a lower-priced townhouse or even an apartment? The answer will be incorporated in the formula at a later date. Past experience suggests that you should try to help them keep the present family residence. There will already be a disruption in the family when you die. Having to move to a smaller house would only add to the problems.

2. Total all the income-producing assets the family owns. We're talking about stocks, bonds, cash, RRSPs, other insurance, and the Canada pension-plan benefits. You are probably going to say you have all kinds of money tied up in clothes, appliances, and so on, but we cannot use these items in these calculations as they might only have to be replaced if they were sold — and even then, if you sell them you wouldn't get what you think they are worth. So just include those items that can actually be used as investments to generate income for your family.

3. What expenses will there be when you die? Naturally, there

will be the funeral itself. Your family may have to pay extra medical expenses that weren't covered by your group insurance plans. And there are always outstanding bills such as credit cards, loans (personal or business), and a long list of incidental bills and expenses that you won't want your family saddled with. This is also where you make that decision about your mortgage. If you have decided that you want your family to stay in your present house you have to either make provisions to pay it off in total right here or go back and add the monthly payment to your answer to 1.

4. When you subtract the total in 3 from 2, you are left with all the assets your family will have to live on. It might sound simple to say to yourself that they have lots of money. But don't forget that if they simply spend the money you have left them, it won't last long. Instead, you have to make provisions for them to invest the money so that they get a life income that is sufficient to live on.

5. Decide what rate of return you think your family members will be able to earn on this money. Some people are better investors than others so you have to take into consideration that savings accounts fluctuate as interest rates change, but on average such accounts will pay somewhere around seven to nine percent over a long period of time. Short-term paper and bonds pay a slightly higher rate of return, while mortgages and the stock markets may offer the potential for a higher rate of return. It might be wise, though, to consider a conservative figure in your calculations, say, something like nine percent.

6. Multiply this interest rate times the assets you have decided are available to produce an income (4). The answer you arrive at will be your family's future income.

7. To this total you can now add the Canada pension-plan monthly benefits. Your spouse will receive a monthly income, as will each of the dependent children.

8. When you add 6 to 7, you have to remember that the income total is before tax. Just as you now have to share your paycheck with the tax man, so, too, is your family going to have to settle up on their investment income. Now you have to get out last year's tax return and do some generalized tax calculations to determine how much money your family will be left with each year.

9. Compare that total to the figure that you arrived at back in
1. Any time the numbers balance or come out showing that your
family has more after tax than they need, you know that your
insurance protection is adequate, except for any extras that you
might want to include. However, if this formula shows that your
family won't have as much income as they need, you will have to
buy some more protection.

10. It's simple to calculate the exact amount of insurance you
need. All you have to do at this stage is take the income you find
you are short and divide it by the interest rate you earlier decided
your family could earn. The result is the amount of life insurance
you really need. When you sit down with a life insurance agent,
you will be able to compare your figures to what he suggests.
Remember, however, that the numbers you have arrived at here
are the basic needs. It might also be worth your while to consider
an education plan if you have younger children, an emergency
plan, some type of buffer to protect your family from escalating
inflation levels or some extra coverage to take care of some special
obligations like a short-term loan.

36

Term Insurance Versus Whole-Life Insurance

Once you've decided how much life insurance you really need, you should set your sights on getting it. It's especially important that young families have lots of insurance, as setting aside savings each month will eventually pay off, but not quickly enough if something unfortunate happens to you. The savings will grow — and over the years you will accumulate quite a bit of wealth. But an insurance policy will pay off after only one payment if something unfortunate happens to you.

As to the type of insurance, there are really only two choices. The first is term insurance and, as the name suggests, this type of coverage is limited to a specific length of time. Generally speaking, it is the cheapest type of coverage in that there is no return on your money unless you die. But that's the same with house insurance or your auto coverage. You pay a set yearly fee. If you die, your beneficiaries benefit. If you live through that period, you have been able to sleep well knowing that your family was well taken care of if something unfortunate happened to you. The second type of coverage is a participating policy or, to use a general term, a whole-life policy or an endowment-type plan. In this case, you pay a yearly premium (that can be parlayed into a monthly, quarterly, or half-yearly premium if you wish). A portion of the money goes toward providing life insurance while the rest is used to build up a "savings" component that will provide for a return of some or all of your money when you retire or cancel the policy sometime in the future. The drawback to term insurance is that it has a set life to it. Once you go beyond the life of that policy, you have no guarantee that you will be able to renew it or, for that matter, qualify for any coverage. However, when you contract for a whole-life policy (granted, it's at a substantially higher yearly cost), you are assured that no matter what happens in the coming years you are guaranteed full coverage as long as you make your payments on time.

I happen to believe that the best route for most people to follow is to buy term insurance at a cheap price and carry it until they find that their other assets are growing fast enough that their family doesn't need as much life insurance. An individual who has worked and invested hard to become rich has built up enough assets that his heirs will be well taken care of without very much insurance. His investments, his house, his pension, and other assets will be sufficient to satisfy his family's needs. While he was accumulating his wealth, however, you can be sure that he took good advantage of the protection offered by life insurance. He bought the best possible life insurance he could find for the smallest number of dollars. He bought life insurance for exactly what it is meant to provide — emergency protection in case of a sudden death. If I knew exactly when I was going to die, I would load up on as much of the stuff as I could get my hands on. I would even go into debt to buy it — I know that it would pay off in my family's favor. But we can't do that, so we have to go on the basis that we will die suddenly. If we are young, we have to count on that possibility. We don't know for sure that it is going to happen, but we have to be prepared in case it does.

That's where life insurance comes in and that's where term insurance specifically plays a bigger role than the once-popular whole-life or endowment policy. Term insurance is cheap, it provides the coverage we need when we need it, and it can be canceled when we no longer have any use for it. Try to think of life insurance as car or house insurance. When you buy these products, you agree to pay a premium whether you ever use the coverage — and quite often you take some time to shop around.

Well, that's the way you should look at life insurance, except you know for sure you are going to die. You want to make sure you have enough life insurance until you have built up enough assets that your family no longer needs the immediate payout that will be provided by an insurance company.

Term insurance is only temporary coverage. The cost of this insurance is only a portion of the cost of a whole-life-insurance policy, maybe about twenty-five percent, which means that you can buy an awful lot more coverage for the same amount of premium each year. But that's what you want as a younger person, especially one with a family. Generally speaking, you will find that many life insurance agents will want to sell you the more costly whole-life insurance. The companies like it because more money comes in, and the agents like it because their commissions are higher. What's more, the companies almost always win because they seldom have to pay out any more money than they collect in premiums. You see, this buildup in savings is yours if you ever collect it, but you don't really get it if you die. Then all your family gets is the death benefit.

The insurance companies also win when they sell term life insurance — have you ever heard of a life insurance company being in financial difficulty? — and they come out ahead because few of the people who buy term insurance ever collect either. If you are smart you use this type of insurance to protect you when you are young and relatively risk-free. Once your assets have started to grow, when your children move out and your mortgage is mostly paid for, you start to cut back on your coverage so the company never has to pay off. They have been happy to accept your regular premiums, have invested them to earn even more money, and now don't have to pay off — so they are doing just fine, thank you.

The things you definitely want to cover with term insurance are your mortgage, any major debts you have, an education plan for your children, and an emergency plan. These obligations can be easily covered for a reasonable price if you buy term insurance.

But don't pay much attention to life insurance agents who try to sell you their product as a savings plan. It won't pay as high a rate of return as a savings plan at a bank, a term deposit, Canada savings bonds, or other investments. The advantage that

a life insurance policy offers is that you are compelled to pay —
by the month, or even by the week. It's forced savings plan, so
you do eventually end up ahead of the game. However, you can
do better in other forced savings plans because *all* of your money
is working for you, not your contributions minus a sizable commission, which is paid upfront.

37

Bartering

Have you ever wondered why some individuals do better than others even though their salaries are similar? And have you ever looked at why some professionals seem to have either more money or more assets — or both — than their colleagues? The answer is pretty simple. Revenue Canada would love to find a way, but so far they have not learned how to tax us on the work we do for ourselves — or on the work we do for friends and relatives free of charge, maybe with the favor being returned. That's the key to survival and advancement. That's why investing in yourself works so well. You not only stretch your money much, much farther, but you also don't have to share your windfall with the tax man.

Consider small farmers. They might not earn the big salaries that some city folk do, but they get along just fine, thank you (except, of course, for all those who found that high interest rates were just too much to handle). The reason is that they learn to become self-sufficient. They grow their own vegetables, have their own supply of meat, milk, and eggs, cut their own wood from a woodlot so that they don't have to buy oil or gas for a furnace. They even drill their own wells so that they don't have to buy water. And they do as much of their own maintenance as possible.

That way they are effectively paying wholesale for everything. There are no big mark-ups, no profits going into a middle man's pocket, and most important of all, no profits that are taxed. That's why it is imperative that we learn to save more, but not the saving that is associated with tucking money away in a savings account, a term deposit, or some Canada Savings Bonds. The type of saving I'm talking about is getting an item or service that we need for a low price or even free. The more we can do for ourselves, the further ahead we will be. As an example, if we need something done to our car and we take it to a garage where we pay twenty-five dollars or more per hour for labor, that bill is worth much more than the quoted amount. Unless we can deduct the work as an expense when we file our tax return, we have to look at that bill as being worth about fifty dollars because we had to earn fifty dollars at work before we could be left with the twenty-five dollars after income taxes to pay the bill.

That's one of the reasons why farmers and professionals can live on less money than an average tax payer — or earn as much and end up with substantially more over a lifetime. Consider the carpenter, plumber, electrician, or handyman who buys a house that needs renovation rather than paying a higher price for a completed or renovated property. He now puts his talents to work and improves the value of the property while he also lives there. He uses the abilities he has to increase its value and then sells it reaping a tax-free profit. He's used as much of his own talent as possible rather than paying a marked-up price which included provisions for taxes. As a result, he now has more money to put into another property which he now improves and sells — again at a profit. Before long he has a house that is paid for rather than somebody else who has paid off only a few thousand because he is locked into a mortgage on a newer house where he is paying mostly interest with very little going toward equity.

This same theory has made people rich through attending auction sales. They buy items that need refinishing or repairing. Nobody else wants them so they get a good price. But after they have put their talents to work and these items are marketable, they make a handsome profit, either on paper as they keep them and use them for their own homes or in real dollars as they sell them and use the proceeds to buy more items. In fact, they might get an extra benefit in that they eventually start a business because of this proper use of talent and then they benefit from all the tax write-offs that accrue to professionals.

But, you know, many of these people benefit in another way. When they need something done they often trade for it. That is, they barter. The dentist who needs his roof fixed may take care of the contractor's children's teeth. The plumber who needs some new clothes trades talent for them. The electrician who needs a garage built may help the carpenter wire his cottage. In fact, if you sit down one night and think of all the things that you spend money on and think of your talents, you will be surprised at how easily barter could fit into your lifestyle. If you've ever dropped the kids off at the neighbor's one day and exchanged the favor on another, you have already gotten into barter. And if you have a car but your friend doesn't and you exchange free rides for another service, then you are already into bartering and its advantages.

You may already have items that you aren't using that you could swap for things that your friends or neighbors or business associates aren't using. You are each avoiding a "mark-up" so you each come out ahead of the game. Naturally we would all like to get into the big-money barter deals where we trade our talents and abilities for many of the things that we normally pay for. But you also have to contend with the tax man. Remember: barter is intended to save you a mark-up on goods — to swap items, goods, or services at wholesale levels rather than retail. However, to make a business of trading your business talents with others will undoubtedly attract the attention of Revenue Canada. So, by all means, practise bartering but if you do it within your business make sure you use a good accountant.

38

The Tax Advantage of Owning a Farm

How would you like to be a farmer? Not a chance. That's the answer you get after hearing about the plight of the poor farmer over the past few years. When interest rates made it almost impossible to earn a decent living, the farmers went outside to get jobs so that they could support their families and save their farms. And what did the taxman do? He reclassified these farmers as part-time farmers instead of full-time. Now all their losses couldn't be claimed as tax deductions because they weren't full-time farmers.

And just to show you how badly they're treated, we, non-farmers, can use that information to our advantage and save taxes along the way. According to Revenue Canada, these part-time farmers can write off up to $5,000 in farming losses against other non-farm income. But so can anybody who has a full-time job who dabbles in the farming business. As an example: If you work for a company full-time but buy a farm, say, to retire on in the future, you will be classed as a part-time farmer and a full-time employee. As a result, you will be able to claim the first $2,500 of your farming expenses as a tax deduction against your total income and one-half of the next $5,000. Effectively, then, you get up to $5,000 in tax deductions if you go into the part-time farming business. But not everybody wants to own a farm (although most of us would like to get hold of that $5,000 tax deduction). Even then there is a way to join the part-time farming ranks.

If you approach a farmer who has room in his milk quota, you might be able to arrange this transaction. You buy two of his best cows for $7,500. Now you have $5,000 worth of tax write-offs (the first $2,500 plus half of the next $5,000) and you own two cows. Unfortunately, most neighbors frown on you bringing a couple of cows home. And spouses can get downright hostile about it. So what you do is make a second deal with the farmer. Because he has some room in his milk quota, you let him raise the cows for you. He gets to keep the milk in exchange for the expenses related to raising the cows. And farmers tell me that's a good deal as the value of the milk can be twice the cost of raising the cows. In addition, he's happy because he's been able to take the cash payment and reduce some of his hefty bank loans. His cost of operation is lower, but he still has the same inflow of cash because he is still able to sell the milk. And you are happy because you have a sizable tax deduction, two cows, and some potential for future profit.

As a consumer, have you ever thought about "eating your profits"? That's one possibility when your cows have offspring. You will have several choices. Make another deal with the farmer to raise them as well, slaughter them for personal consumption, or ship them off to market. Whichever way you choose, you are a winner.

But suppose you are approaching retirement, and you always wanted to be a farmer. This might be the perfect way to build up your herd while you are working elsewhere. All you have to do now is buy a farm, rent it out until you retire, and then move your cows over to your own property. You are then a full-time farmer in your retirement. It's almost the perfect retirement plan. You get tax deductions worth up to $5,000 when you buy inventory; the value of your herd compounds tax free until your retirement, and then you start to live off the proceeds. And, unlike a registered retirement savings plan, you don't have to liquidate your retirement plan at age seventy-one. And you don't necessarily have to pay tax on your profits as they accrue because this will now be an operating farm with all the standard tax deductions that go along with being a full-time farmer.

As we all know, farmers have had it pretty tough in the last few years. High interest rates made it almost impossible to make a profit if your farm was mortgaged to the hilt. And then the taxman reclassified some farmers as part time when they went out and got jobs simply to save their farms.

However, for investors, farming on a part-time basis can still offer some attractive tax advantages, especially now that tax changes will allow the value of our property to rise tax free.

Another type of farming that offers substantial tax write-offs is a Christmas-tree farm. Come Christmas, we all go out looking for a Christmas tree. If you've checked prices lately, you know that they never go down. They always rise on a yearly basis. Some investors have found that they can come out ahead if they go into the Christmas-tree business. They buy a large tract of land, say one hundred acres, off the beaten track where prices are relatively low. Then they have the area reforested, possibly with government help, and they have a Christmas-tree farm. However, because one-foot-tall Christmas trees aren't in very large demand, they have to wait about eight years before they have a decent crop. But all along, they've faced the normal expenses that go with owning a business: mortgage payments, property taxes, maintenance, spraying, pruning, fencing, transportation, you name it. And all those expenses are tax deductible. But since you have no income from this farm for the next seven or eight years, you get to claim those expenses as tax deductible against your other forms of income.

In the past few years, there have been great problems for farmers. Because some have been forced to seek work outside the farm, they have faced problems with the taxman. In fact, in many cases, the farmers who were simply trying to save their farms by working elsewhere have been reassessed and forced to claim only the $5,000 worth of tax deductions that apply to part-time farmers. There are many appeals in front of the tax courts right now involving these cases, so many, in fact, that Finance Minister Marc Lalonde stated in his 1983 budget that a study would be undertaken to see how best to treat these farmers. Because of the uncertainty surrounding these farm cases, it's unlikely that you would be granted total tax deductibility against your other forms of income. However, you certainly will be allowed to use the normal formulas to claim the first $5,000 worth of tax deductions. In addition, you should claim all the losses you incur on the basis that this is a legitimate on-going farm that someday will provide the bulk of your income. You might be reassessed by Revenue Canada, but you then would be entitled to a hearing to prove that this is indeed a full-time farm. In the meantime, there may be some farmers who win their cases with the tax courts. That would then give you the right to the same treatment.

There's something else you could do. Instead of calling this a Christmas-tree farm, you might want to treat it as a business specializing in the forestry industry. Business losses are almost always deductible against your other forms of income.

Now for the really good news. Not only can we use this type of tax shelter as a way to save taxes, but we can also use it for income splitting, for saving toward a child's education, and for qualifying for a registered retirement savings plan.

Here's how it works. Remember the expenses that I talked about as being tax deductible? They include interest on your mortgage payments, maintenance, insurance, property taxes, equipment, fencing, draining, et cetera — plus salaries paid to employees. In addition, you will be allowed to claim some business use of your vehicle. But it's the salaries that really help us out.

Here we have a business that's going to lose money for the next seven or eight years. And those losses will be used to lower our tax bill where we work full time. But what if we divide the work involved with this farm among all the family members? Now we can claim those salaries as legitimate tax deductions against our income. And now we can pay our spouse and our children a salary that effectively saves us taxes on our ordinary income. That's the real advantage. Now we will be getting a tax deduction when we income split.

We earn a full-time salary at our regular job. We get the standard deductions when we file our tax returns, but now we also get to deduct the losses that we incurred when we operated this business. But many of the losses were the result of paying our spouse and children a salary. They receive the salary in their names but they also get the standard deductions. As a result, they may not pay any income taxes on the money that you get to use as a tax deduction. In the case of a spouse, a net income above $510 starts to erode the married deduction. But tax doesn't start to click in until $5,000 or $6,000. In addition, the spouse would now qualify for a registered retirement savings plan. It may not create much of a tax savings in the low-tax brackets, but it may well end up as double tax relief. If spouse number one pays spouse number two a salary, it's a tax deduction for spouse number one. If spouse number two puts some of that money into a registered retirement savings plan, that spouse's net income is lowered. Maybe it will be lowered far enough that that spouse can be a partial married deduction. If so, it's as good as a second RRSP in spouse number one's name.

The same applies to the children, except that children can earn even more income before they are lost as tax deductions. And when they are lost as dependent deductions, the loss is relatively small compared to the loss of a spouse. In 1985 a child under the age of eighteen can earn $2,720 in net income before the $710 dependent deduction is eroded. Even above that limit, it falls by only fifty cents on the dollar until it's exhausted. For children eighteen and over, the deduction is $1,420 and the child can earn $2,720 in net income before that deduction is eroded.

In the case of children, the practice of contributing to a registered retirement savings plan could also save additional tax dollars. So now we have almost the perfect tax shelter: land. We know that land virtually always rises in value to offset inflation. It has a crop which will eventually produce an income (maybe an eventual full-time income); it provides us with tax losses against our ordinary income while we are employed and earning taxable income; and it offers us the chance to income split and pay family members a salary, which is tax deductible to us and taxable at a lower rate to them, if any tax applies at all. Not only that: you won't have to buy a Christmas tree every year.

39

Smoking Can Cost You a Million

We all have some pretty interesting habits, some of them bad — I know I do. But did you know that if you gave up smoking at a young age, not only would you lead a healthier and probably longer life, but you would also enjoy a healthier one financially?

Obviously we can get along without the money we spend on tobacco, as we keep on buying those packs of cigarettes every day or week or whatever. But if you quit and invested the money instead, which isn't unreasonable as you get along without it now, you would be able to build up one giant-sized pile of money.

As an example, let's consider the individual who is twenty-five years old who smokes about a pack a day. I know the price of cigarettes varies from province to province and city to city, but we are probably looking at something like $500 per year. If that twenty-five-year-old put that $500 into a registered retirement savings plan each year instead of into a cigarette machine, and if he earned fourteen percent compounded interest inside that plan, he would have a total of $1.6 million dollars in accumulated interest and principal when he turned sixty-five. At even ten percent, that money would earn him a lifetime income from then on of $160,000 per year. Who knows what $160,000 will buy forty years down the road? But it sure as shooting will buy a lot more for you than it will for the person who doesn't have it. Even with inflation eating away at the purchasing power of money, you can still be assured that this money will grow quickly once it is deposited inside your RRSP.

Remember, though, that when you put this money into your plan each year you are going to get back some tax dollars that have already been deducted from your paycheck. If you are in the forty-percent tax bracket and you received an extra tax rebate of $200, which you put into your RRSP as well, you would now be in a position to accumulate another $638,000 inside your plan. The fact that you quit smoking has been parlayed into a grand total of more than $2.2 million. With a ten-percent annuity, we can expect to earn $220,000 per year for the rest of our lives after we turn sixty-five. Naturally we will have to pay tax on that money, but we sure will be a lot better off financially now that we have quit smoking. And we will probably live longer to take advantage of that money if we have stopped puffing on that tobacco. We've talked about the impact of inflation. We don't know what rate of inflation we will face down the road. We know that governments are trying to get it under control, but we have no idea if they will be successful for long. However, this little idea has inflation working on its side as well. Each year the price of a pack of cigarettes can be expected to rise by at least the rate of inflation. Effectively that means that your quitting smoking would give you even more money each year to contribute to your RRSP, so you would have inflation-proofed your investment right off the bat. In addition, you have the continuation of indexed taxes. Yes, the index has been cut back, but the more we get inflation under control the closer we come to full indexing again. The lower indexing will help, but if we slip into a higher tax bracket, we will actually save more tax when we put money into one of these plans.

It really wouldn't pay to deposit our smoke money into our RRSP every day, but we can let it accumulate in a daily-interest savings account until the end of the year, when we make our RRSP contribution. We will earn some interest before we start to compound the money inside the plan. If you don't earn more than $1,000 per year in investment income you won't have to share that money with the tax man. The interest won't be much, but it might total something like $50 per year. If we also contributed that to our no-smoking RRSP, we would get an additional tax rebate and we would also earn another compounded chunk of money that might accumulate, inside our plan, to an additional $150,000. Now we have about $2.4 million inside our plan that would earn us a yearly salary for life of $240,000.

And we're talking very conservative interest rates here. Who knows where the rates are headed and how violently they will fluctuate? It wasn't long ago that we were earning twenty percent per year on our savings. That might happen again. Who knows?

The next thing to stop buying is alcohol. If we gave up our case of beer a week, we could amass another $3,000,000 or so inside an RRSP. And if you didn't smoke or drink you could look forward to a sizable savings in both your automobile and your life insurance. Some life insurance companies are so disposed to those who quit smoking that they give them as much as a fifty-percent cut in premiums. And all you have to do is sign an affidavit that you don't smoke. You don't have to submit to X-rays or tests or anything. Auto companies have also been known to shave the rate for those who do not smoke or drink. Drinking is a natural problem as it can lead to many serious accidents. But smoking can, and does, have the same effect. It leads to poorer health, which can cause accidents. And there have been many accidents caused by an ash falling off the end of a cigarette onto the driver's lap. The driver looks down to brush it off, swerves into a car, and causes an accident.

I know it's a hard habit to give up — besides, you like it. However, if you give it a little thought it's much more than a health hazard. It's financial suicide.

40

What Happens If You Win the Lottery?

You were watching TV tonight and you saw your lucky number flashed on the screen. You have just won the lottery and now you are Canada's newest millionaire. Well, before you get carried away, you'd better check to make sure that the number is really yours. There's nothing more embarrassing than telling everybody about your good fortune only to have it backfire. Once you are sure your ticket is indeed a winner, you might as well call a few close friends or relatives and have a few drinks. You won't get much sleep tonight anyway. Don't get too carried away, though, as you are going to want to get on the road early in the morning to pick up that one-million-dollar check at the lottery office. It doesn't matter where you live; you don't want to delay the pickup. And it doesn't matter whether you have to take a day off work. You want that check in a bank the next day earning interest in your name.

Think of it this way. Eventually, you will have to take a day off work to pick the check up whether you drive or fly to the lottery center, so you might as well do it now. The sooner you pick that check up, the sooner it will start earning between $250 and $350 per day, depending on the rate you earn when you invest it.

Now you have it in the bank. You head home, only to find that well-wishers and people wanting money for their own worthy cause have already tracked you down. And you have to get used to that, as everybody and their cousins will come after you. They will have worthy causes, great get-rich-quick investment ideas, life insurance, and real estate portfolios — and even tears. The last thing you want to be is a sitting duck for all these people. What you should do is pack your bags and take a holiday for a few weeks. You want time to think, time to be all by yourself as you've never had money like this before. Don't begrudge yourself this holiday. Don't forget that at only eight percent in a daily-interest savings account, you are going to be earning more than $1,500 each week. That's $80,000 per year that you never had coming in before, so your lifestyle is certainly going to improve. And every percent you earn above eight percent means another $10,000 per year, or about $27.50 per day, which will pay for a few daiquiris around the pool when you are soaking up the sun.

While you're away, you will have some time to sort out your situation. You will want to write down all your debts, as you will undoubtedly want to get rid of most or all of them. You will want to get your priorities straight. For example, do you want to give some of this new-found wealth away? Do you want to move to a newer or bigger house? Do you want to quit your job and do something else? Do you want a new car instead of the old clunker that you have been driving? These are some of the questions you will want to answer in your own mind. Naturally, you will want professional help when you get back home, as even a quarter of one percent per year will mean an extra income of $2,500. You surely can afford to pay for the best help available. When you get home, discuss your ideas with the pros so that everything is done to your best advantage. In the meantime, sit back, soak up the rays, and have a good time on your new-found wealth.

One thing that you are definitely going to have to mull over is your job. Do you want to go back to that job? Would you prefer to take this opportunity to go out on your own, to go back to school, or even to buy into an existing company? There are all kinds of people out there who aren't happy in their work. You have just found the key to changing your job situation if you wish to. However, whatever you do, don't waltz into your boss's office and tell him to take a hike. You've been working there for some time now and have probably built up some benefits, some time off, some pension, maybe some convertible life insurance that would come in handy if you have a medical problem, and maybe even the right to subscribe to a low-cost medical plan. In other words, no matter how rich you now are, you want to be able to hang on to what's already yours.

The other thing to give some thought to is your house. Are you happy where you are? If so, what's the status of your mortgage? If you are going to stay where you are, you have to decide whether you are going to pay off your mortgage. Generally speaking, the answer will be yes: you should pay your mortgage off. You are definitely going to be in the fifty-percent tax bracket when you combine your investment income with your salary, if you continue to draw one, so your mortgage would have to be in the seven-percent-interest range before it would be worthwhile keeping it.

When you get back home, you are going to want to see a financial adviser or two to see what type of interest rates are available on term deposits, guaranteed investment certificates, and government and corporate bonds. Mortgages might be another option as they will give you a monthly income that you can live on if you decide to leave your job.

But don't forget the great Canadian dream — owning real estate. If you don't plan to leave your job, you should take this opportunity to use some of the money to pay off your outstanding debts, use some more to bring your yearly income up to the level you would prefer, and then put the rest into investments where the appreciation would be great over the long term but the tax liability would be low now when you are still earning your salary. That means things like real estate and dividend-paying common and preferred shares. The rent on real estate will increase your income now, but the major gains will be made in future appreciation of the property. That appreciation is only taxed at one half the normal rate, and then only when you actually sell the property many years down the road. The same goes for stocks: they qualify for capital-gains tax but they have an added attraction in that the dividend tax credit allows you to earn a high rate of return without much tax.

We all dream of winning the big million, but some of us are just going to have to be content with a cool hundred thousand. If it happens to you, don't follow the instructions I have just given, as $100,000 is hardly enough in these days of high inflation to let us quit our jobs and go into retirement. But it is enough to get us into a much better financial position than most of our friends. The first thing we do, in this case, is to pay off our mortgage. While the lucky person who won a million should be putting a chunk of his money into real estate, including a bigger house for himself and his family — our principal residence is one of the few tax-free investments we have left — the individual who wins $100,000 shouldn't necessarily buy a big new house. He has some equity in the house he now has and would probably be better paying off his mortgage, if he can, and using the rest of the money to supplement his income. It is the perfect opportunity, though, to use the income you will be able to generate to let you upgrade your position in life. If you are happy with your job, you will be able to use this income to put you ten to fifteen years ahead of your peers; if you are not happy with your job, this may be the perfect chance to take some time off for a job-training program, buy into a company where your talents would be more rewarding over the long term, or even quit your job and go to university or start a company of your own.

You have to take these windfalls in stride. The chances of you winning another lottery are even slimmer than your first win so you have to do whatever you can to conserve the capital you have just won. Use these funds to get you out of debt or to add to your income, but try not to erode the money itself. Try your very best to use its earning power to create a lifetime of income, not just one year's worth.

41

Year-End Tax Planning

With the switch in power from the long-standing Liberal government to the Conservatives, taxpayers have been forced to change their way of thinking. It's a brand-new ball game — and you can expect more changes as the years unfold.

With the change in capital gains taxes and interest deductibility, and the loss of numerous tax shelters, the year-end becomes the most important part of the year. It's extremely important that we get our houses in order as the year begins, but it's even more important that we reassess our situation as the year comes to an end. We can undo existing damage and we can create tax savings that'll keep more of our salaries in our pockets rather than sharing them with the tax man.

This chapter should be reviewed every year so that you are sure your affairs are properly in order. And make sure you note any new tax changes as the years unfold so they can be combined with the information in this chapter.

While the majority of Canadian taxpayers think the most important time of the year is April 30 when they have to settle up with the taxman, there's no question in my mind that they should really concentrate on the year end. After all, most tax shelters and other tax-saving devices have a December 31 deadline. Once we miss that deadline, we might as well add a few hundred or a few thousand dollars to the New Year's party tab. In fact, if we thought of it that way, we might do a little more tax planning. If we haven't taken care of our tax situation by the time we leave for that New Year's party, then we might as well kiss the opportunity goodbye. After that date we have only our registered retirement savings plan, some research and development shares, and for the 1985 taxation year the topping up of our registered home ownership savings plans to help us save taxes.

Before we discuss the tax shelters and tax-saving devices that are available, we should understand the theory behind the Canadian tax system. It says that the more we earn, the higher the percentage of tax we pay. It's one thing to pay more tax when you earn more income. It's something else to pay a higher *percentage* when you slip into a higher tax bracket. With a higher percentage, every dollar you earn is now taxed at a higher rate than the dollars that you earned on the way up the ladder. So damaging, in fact, is this system that a family who earned $50,000 in one spouse's name would pay some $5,000 more tax than the family where each spouse earned $25,000. The gross income would be the same, but the net result would be much smaller in the case of one breadwinner. Understanding that theory, we will want to do our very best to spread our income between family members before the year end, to defer taxes to the next and following years, and to eliminate them outright by using tax shelters and tax-saving vehicles. The following is a checklist of things that you should consider before the year comes to an end to ensure you take advantage of everything that's available.

The $1,000 Investment-Income Deduction: Every taxpayer is entitled to earn up to $1,000 in tax-free investment income, and taxpayers should do their best to arrange their affairs so that they earn close to $1,000. It may mean deferring income to future years or it may mean forcing some income to show up in this tax year. As an example: You may have decided to compound your Canada Savings Bonds, term deposits, or Guaranteed Investment Certificates to take advantage of the interest rates that were prevalent at the time you purchased these investments. If so, you may face a tax problem in the year they mature. That is, all the interest may come due three years down the road. At that time, it might exceed the $1,000 level and, as a result, be taxable. If so, you may be better off adding the earned interest to your tax return now, even though you haven't actually received it. This is called claiming your interest as "deemed received." The money is tax free now because it's under $1,000 instead of being in excess of $1,000 sometime in the future.

Term deposits and GICs don't offer much flexibility at this time. However, Canada Savings Bonds do provide us with some extra breathing room. If you own coupon-type CSBs, you can delay cashing in the coupons until the first of January if you wish. That way they'll be taxed in the next year, and the tax bill won't have to be settled until the following spring. You sacrifice two months' worth of use of that money (November and December). But you get to use it tax free for more than a year thereafter. The trade-off may well be worth it.

In the fall of 1985, 1986, and 1987, consumers who own certain issues of Canada Savings Bonds have some extra maneuverability when it comes to tax planning. If you own any of the coupon-type bonds, you should check chapter 14 to see whether they have matured and whether it's worth your while to cash them in. The final series of coupon bonds to mature did so in the fall of 1985, so after 1985 every one of these coupon-type bonds should be redeemed.

Don't forget though, that the bond itself is tax free as it's only the return of your own money. When you cash a coupon-type bond, though, you often qualify for a special maturity bonus. *It is half taxable and half tax free.* In addition to this special cash bonus, you'll have coupons attached to the side of the bond. If you've been clipping them regularly you'll know that they are taxed as interest income. If you haven't been clipping them you may have compound coupons in addition to the interest coupons. These compound coupons are also taxable as interest.

There is a way to save some tax at this time. You don't have to cash the coupons until you want to. And they aren't taxable until you do cash them. That means that we may want to hold off cashing the coupons until January of next year. That way they won't be taxable until next year, and you won't actually pay the tax until you file your return the year after that. Yes, you'll lose a couple of years' interest by not being able to reinvest the money until January, but you'll win in the long run by deferring tax for more than a year — and you may keep your tax rate lower this year.

When you practise this type of tax savings though, you should make sure you cash the bond itself. This money comes back to you tax free so you might as well get it reinvested. At the same time you'll automatically receive the maturity bonus but, remember, it's only half taxable.

There are several issues of the new computer-type CSBs where you can also get some tax relief. The issues involved are 32, 33, 34, and 35. The courts have determined that a portion of the interest you earn on these bonds is tax free. Series 33 matured in 1985 so it's not a problem after 1985 except that you should make sure you cash this bond in on time. With computer-type bonds, the interest you earn is automatically taxable each year, or every three years if you've been compounding. As a result, there's absolutely no value to holding these bonds after their maturity date.

Series 32 and 34 mature in the fall of 1986 and series 35 in 1987. The same theory applies to these bonds as to series 33 so you should always make a point of finding out exactly which portion of your bond is taxable and which is not.

From series 36 on the interest is totally taxable once you exceed $1,000 a year in investment income. As a result, you should give some thought to switching your investment strategies elsewhere. There is a way to save some of the tax on these bonds. If you know they are going to be taxable, why not do something else to create a tax deduction that'll offset this extra interest? You can rollover some of your pension to your RRSP; you can enter into a leverage program; you can buy some losing real estate; or you can purchase a tax shelter that provides some tax relief.

By the time fall comes around, it's a little late in the year to put these ideas in motion. But the cardinal rule is that we should be practising tax planning all year round.

Any time you know you're going to have extra investment income, or any type of income for that matter, you should always get a head start. You should always start putting defensive measures in place long before the money comes due.

Capital Gains and Losses: This area of financial planning was drastically altered by the 1985 federal budget. Effective the beginning of 1985, new capital losses are no longer tax deductible. Losses from past years, though, can still be carried forward as they were in the past.

There's no longer any reason to create capital losses late in the year unless you're on the verge of exceeding the tax-free capital gains limit for the year. In 1985 Ottawa allowed us to earn $20,000 in tax-free capital gains. In 1986 the numbers grow to $50,000, and in 1987 they will escalate to $100,000. Eventually there'll be an accumulated total of one-half million dollars. If, in any one year, you've created enough capital gains to exceed the limit at that time, you may want to take some losses to ease the burden of any capital gains. In addition, if you're able to reach one-half million in gains, then you'll definitely want to return to the old-fashioned capital gains/capital loss defensive moves.

For those contemplating creating some losses, you should be careful not to go over the allowable tax-free limit, especially late in the year. All you have to do is wait another couple of months and you'll be able to sell tax free. Of course, if the investment looks like it's about to fall apart, you should forget about tax planning and sell. A taxable gain is better than a non-tax-deductible loss.

Those with losses that they were carrying forward from past years should continue in the normal way. Those with capital gains from previous years who have been using the reverse rule must continue to pay tax on these gains. After all, they were earned before the tax rules changed.

Loans: If you have any loans at all, you should take the time to evaluate them. Interest paid on investment or business loans is tax deductible while interest paid on loans that are for personal use is not tax deductible. The first thing you try to do is change your stance so that you are paying off non-tax-deductible loans while you let the tax-deductible ones remain where they are. The next thing you do is evaluate your investment loans. The interest you pay on loans used to purchase Canadian investments must first be used to offset the interest you earn on those investments before you start to use the $1,000 investment income deduction. However, interest earned on foreign investments doesn't qualify for the $1,000 investment income deduction. But neither does the interest paid on loans used to purchase foreign investments have to be offset against Canadian investment income. As a result, it generally pays to borrow for foreign investments and to pay cash for Canadian ones.

In addition, any time you sell any investments you should take a close look at your loan status. If you have outstanding loans that aren't tax deductible, you should use the proceeds of your sale to pay down those loans. If you want to invest again all you have to do is borrow. If you borrowed the very same amount as you received when you sold you'd be further ahead because the interest you were going to pay was tax deductible. You've paid down a non-tax-deductible loan and replaced it with one that's deductible. As a result, your real, out-of-pocket interest will be less.

Discount Bonds: Thanks to our new budget, we have more reason to buy this type of investment. If you earn more than $1,000 worth of investment income in a year, you can be taxed on the excess. As a result, you may want to switch to discount bonds where you earn some interest (usually a lower than normal rate) plus some tax-free capital gains.

If a bond pays an interest rate that's lower than a rate available elsewhere, it usually falls in value so that the new yield is more competitive with that available elsewhere. However, when interest rates fall, this bond will become more competitive and may well rise in value. In addition, as this bond approaches the day when it matures it will also rise in value. These gains are tax free as they are capital gains. A classic example may be the person who buys a $10,000 bond that's trading at only $6,000 because of it's low interest rate. Yes, you don't earn as much each year as you would had you invested in a normal yielding bond, but you win just the same because you are earning a tax-free capital gain at the same time.

Registered Home Ownership Savings Plans: The 1985 federal budget ended these useful tax deductions. Those with contributions already into their plans prior to May 22, 1985 got their tax deductions. In addition, all monies already inside these plans could be removed completely tax free for any purpose. There was an option, though, to leave the money inside your plan until the end of 1985. If you did, the interest you earned inside the plan remained totally tax free.

Beginning January 1, 1986 though, any money still inside home ownership savings plans is considered to be outside the plan. Oh, you can still leave it invested as it was, but from January 1, 1985 all income earned by RHOSP monies is taxable once you exceed $1,000 a year in total investment income.

The drawback to the RHOSP was that most financial institutions treated this money as "day money." That is, it could be removed any time we wanted so they only paid us the lowest rate going. If you are earning a low rate of return on this money, I'd be switching it to something else — term deposits, Canada Savings Bonds, stocks, mutual funds, rental real estate. They all pay better rates of return than you'll earn in a savings account-type RHOSP.

Registered Retirement Savings Plans: While the deadline for making contributions to these plans isn't until the end of February each year, many people should consider them at other times of the year. If you have trouble saving enough money or writing a sizable check come the final deadline, you should get started on a monthly savings plan immediately. That way the money will disappear more easily, and you will end up with at least some money in one of these tax-saving plans.

In addition, some consumers will want to use a very short-term RRSP. If you know that you earned much more income this year than you will earn next year, you should contribute the maximum amount to an RRSP now with the intention of canceling it next year. You will get tax relief this year when your tax rate is high and you will add the money back onto your income next year when you are in a lower tax bracket. As it can take time for the money to become available for your use when you do this trick, you may want to get your money into your RRSP now and authorize the financial institution to remove it at the beginning of January. They will be able to get working on the paperwork right now. There's another reason to get your money into your RRSP right away. Take a look at your investment income level. Once you earn more than $1,000 in investment income, you start sharing it with the taxman. If you have already surpassed $1,000, you should get your RRSP contribution in right away as the money will now start to earn interest tax free inside your plan.

Pension Plan Contributions: It may not pay to put money into a registered retirement savings plan if you can put money into a pension plan at work and have your contributions matched by your employer. The rate of return on your pension plan may not always be as high as that earned in your RRSP, but the fact that your employer matches your contributions may be a much greater benefit in the long run.

Pension plan contributions must be in by the end of the year, not sixty days after, as is the case with RRSPs. As a result, you should make a decision on your proper course before New Year's Eve.

Pension Income: You can generally roll all of your pension income into a registered retirement savings plan. You have until the sixty-day period after the end of the year to do this. However, you should set the wheels in motion now as you will need ready cash to do it come the end of February.

And don't forget that Old Age Security, Canada Pension, and Quebec Pension Plan benefits do not qualify for the $1,000 pension-income deduction. As a result, you may want to roll this income into your RRSP as a tax deduction. Then you will be able to use it to purchase an annuity. That annuity income will be included in the $1,000 pension-income deduction. You are taking a taxable income, making it a tax deduction, and then drawing it back out tax free. You come out a winner.

Defer Income: Some taxpayers get a break in that they can talk their employers into deferring their income for a couple of weeks. If you have more income than you need to live on, you could ask your employer to hold your last one or two paychecks until January 1. Then the money would be included in next year's income and taxable a year from now. This idea works especially well when your employer withholds only a small amount of tax from your paycheck.

A similar theory involves taxpayers who are nearing retirement time. Instead of retiring right at the end of the year when your tax bracket will be high, you may arrange to have some of the income paid in the following year when your tax bracket will be lower.

Pay Deductible Expenses: This is a favorite year-end trick for businesses; consumers should practice it as well. If you have any flexibility with union dues, child care expenses, interest on tax-deductible loans, tuition, investment counsel fees, acceptable legal and accounting fees, alimony and maintenance payments, safety deposit box rental fees, moving expenses, and medical or dental bills, I would look into paying some of next year's bills before this year comes to an end. You aren't going to be able to avoid paying them, but because you will have paid them this year instead of next, you will get tax relief right away instead of waiting a year and a half to use these deductions.

Charitable Contributions: Not everybody gives money to a charity. But if you do, you can get a little extra tax relief at this time of year if you donate two years' worth of money right now — some for this year, some for next. The charity is happy because it gets money faster. You are happy because you get your tax relief faster. But watch out for next year. The charities will still come knocking. And don't forget that when a family donates money to a charity, it doesn't matter whose name is on that receipt, but it should generally be claimed in the name of the spouse with the higher income. That way the tax relief is greater.

Political Contributions: These also have to be in by the end of the year if you want tax relief on the upcoming tax return. Check chapter 43 to see the best way to structure these contributions. They can be a good way to save tax dollars.

Moving Expenses: Canadians are a very mobile group. We move, on average, once every three years. For some it's from an apartment to a house; for others it's from city to city. Some people will have to pay the complete tab out of their pockets; some will get some tax relief because they get to write off moving expenses. To do so, however, you have to meet certain requirements. One is to change your job. You don't have to change companies, but you must change your location. Next you have to move so that your new house is at least forty kilometers closer to your new place of employment than your old house. Simply moving 40 kilometers won't do the trick as you could be moving across town. But your new place of employment may still be close enough to your old residence to eliminate moving expenses as a tax deduction.

Those expenses that are acceptable to Revenue Canada and are not paid for by your employer can only be written off against income earned in your new job. As a result, you will want to do some quick calculations before the year comes to an end to see whether you should pay some moving expenses up front and, as a result, get to use them this year. Any that you cannot use this year can be carried forward to next year's tax bill.

Timing of Move: Believe it or not, the timing of your move can cost you or save you tax dollars. You file your tax return based on where you lived on December 31 of each tax year. Some provinces levy higher taxes than others so the last thing you should do is to move to a province with a higher provincial tax base just before the year ends. You would be forcing your taxes higher. For example, if you live in British Columbia and have a $30,000 taxable income, you will pay about $8,800 in taxes. Yet if you were to move to Quebec before December 31, you now would be called upon to pay $11,600 tax — an increase of $2,800 simply because you didn't plan your move properly. Conversely, the person living in Quebec would be smart to make his move before the end of the year rather than waiting until after New Year's Eve. Granted, not everybody can pick and choose the day or week that they move, but if you have some flexibility, you should talk to your employer and an accountant before your move. You could save yourself a chunk of money. Generally speaking, it pays to move from the eastern part of Canada westward before the year comes to an end whereas it's a smart move to delay a change of location until the beginning of the year if you are moving from west to east. Again, generally speaking, you can help make your decision by looking at the provincial tax rate charged in each province or territory. With the exception of Quebec, all the provinces do is take the federal tax bill and tack on an additional percentage for their coffers. As a result, the federal tab is virtually the same. It's the provincial portion that will temper our decision.

While provinces regularly change their tax rates at the time of printing, here is the present progression of provincial tax rates in this country.

Nova Scotia	56.5%
Manitoba	54.0%
Newfoundland	60.0%
New Brunswick	58.0%
Prince Edward Island	52.5%
Saskatchewan	51.0%
Ontario	48.0%
British Columbia	44.0%
Yukon	45.0%
Northwest Territories	43.0%
Alberta	43.5%

In theory, you would move out of a province near the top of the list in favor of a province near the bottom before the year end if you wanted to save taxes. Conversely, if you had to move to a province that is higher on the list, you would try to delay your move until the new year.

The $1,000 Pension-Income Deduction: Don't forget that we can all earn up to $1,000 in tax-free pension income, provided we meet certain requirements. For some that benefit can click in at an early age. For others it won't actually start until you retire. As a result, it's important that you learn more about this deduction as retirement nears. Government pensions do not qualify.* But you can make them qualify by putting them into your RRSP and then taking them out as an annuity. A good annuity broker can help you roll these monies in and out. It would be a good move to get some help before the year comes to an end.

Gifts: You will not get a tax deduction by giving money or goods to a friend, relative, spouse, or child. But you may well save

---

*An exception is made for employees of government pension plans. They are allowed to claim these pensions.

taxes because now that money won't earn interest or dividends in your name. As a result, you may slip into a lower tax bracket. When we practice income splitting (Chapter 4), that's what we are trying to accomplish. However, if you have extra cash or assets, you may be able to get some tax relief by giving all or part to a registered charity. As an example, let's consider an existing life insurance policy. If you have a policy that you no longer need, you can give it to your church or another registered charity and you will get credit for all the built-up cash surrender value plus all the accumulated dividends. Besides this, any additional premiums that you pay in years to come will be tax deductible against future income. You get tax relief right now even though you haven't really put up any new money. And the charity has a shot at a sizable payoff when you die.

Some taxpayers have assets that they don't need or want that could be valuable tax deductions. If you own antiques that would be valuable to the country or your province, you may well want to contact the Canadian Cultural Property Export Review Board. In some cases, you can give the property or antiques away and get a full tax deduction for their present value. Normally, you cannot deduct more than 20% of your total income when you donate to a charity. You can carry any excess ahead to future years, but once you exceed 20%, you are finished for any one year. Such is not the case when you give "gifts of a kind" to a government or a government agency. In fact, you may get an extra bonus.

Let's say that you purchased or inherited a Canadian piece decades ago. It's appreciated in value over the years, and now you are thinking about giving it away. You will use today's value when you claim it as a deduction and there will be no capital-gains tax on the increased value if you give it away properly. The elimination of capital-gains tax and the elimination of the 20% of total-income rule may well make it a smart idea to invest in historic or "century" houses. They rise in value tax free, you earn rental income from them over the years, and you get a full tax deduction for their present value if you give them to a government agency.

Divorce or Reconciliation: If you are thinking about a change in marital status, you should consider acting before the end of the year. As a divorced person, you have a choice between claiming the alimony, maintenance, or support that you pay in a year or the dependent deductions that normally go with your spouse and children. Remember, this is a major step, and even with recent tax changes to make it easier to write-off expenses before you get the proper court order, you should still use a good lawyer and accountant. The savings will be well in excess of their fees. Lump-sum payments and property settlements are not tax deductible so some major tax planning at this time could save money for both parties and may even offer the opportunity to use the children as equivalent-to-spousal deductions — provided you arrange your affairs properly.

Get Married: After talking about divorce and reconciliation, I should also remind you that it's a lot cheaper to get married near the end of the year than in the spring or summer months. The costs of a wedding may be the same, but the tax savings can be substantially greater — maybe enough to pay for a honeymoon. A spouse is worth a $4,140 tax deduction in 1985. For an individual in the 35% tax bracket that means an outright tax rebate or tax savings of $1,449. However, the spouse must not earn more than $510 in net income while married, or the deduction is eroded dollar for dollar until it is eliminated outright. But two words can make a lot of difference here. The words are *while married*. A spouse who works all year can still qualify, provided his or her net income while married did not exceed $510. Effectively, the "dependent" spouse calculates his or her income backwards. For the purposes of this example, let's say the dependent spouse is a woman. This spouse looks at her final paycheck of the year. If it's large enough to affect her net income while married, she takes a holiday at the end of the year and arranges for her employer to pay her the last paycheck or two before she goes on her vacation. Now she has several weeks at the end of the year where she has no income. She marries during that period and has no net income to affect her spouse's married exemption.

The weather may not be as nice around the year end, but with an extra $1,449 to spend on the wedding or the honeymoon, you will be able to have a better time. Besides, won't the honeymoon be more exciting when you know that the taxman is helping you pay for it? A question often arises at this time. If we've been able to arrange our affairs so that one spouse gets the other as a tax deduction even though that spouse earned too much to qualify, why can't each spouse claim the other as a dependent deduction? I think they should be able to because we can certainly make the numbers fit. Revenue Canada doesn't agree, though. However, I always tell couples who are marrying at the end of the year to do just that — to claim each other. The tax computers may miss it. Or they may not. The only way to have a chance at this double deduction is to claim it, be prepared for a fight, and hope that you win.

Limited Partnerships, Murbs, Oil Drilling Funds and Other Tax Shelters: While Ottawa's done its best to wind down most of the commonly used tax shelters, there are still lots of them available. They had to have been underway prior to certain deadlines, but those that were may very well offer substantial tax savings. Don't forget though, that these are more speculative tax shelters. It's hard to make any promises as to their performance although, in the the case of a limited partnership, there may well be some background to that type of investment's past performance. As an example, a hotel. There are formulae that accountants use to assess a hotel's potential performance, and they can be reasonably accurate.

Usually we see an extra supply of this type of tax shelter hit the market near the year end. The reason's simple. They are easier to sell at this time of year because investors look for additional tax relief as the year winds down. One word of caution, however. Any investment should be able to stand on its own two feet without special tax concessions. If the one you're looking at does, then it's probably okay. However, if it takes the tax concessions to make it reasonable I'd move on to another; you may find it very difficult to sell if you can't pass the tax concessions on to another buyer.

Income Split: The new budget made substantial changes to the practice of income splitting. If you had income-splitting loans in place before May 23, 1985, you have until the beginning of 1988 to wind them down. That is, if you used the standard demand loan. However, if you used a term loan where you named the date and the year when the loans were to mature, you can continue until that date. In the meantime it's well worth your while to look back at our income-splitting chapter to see if you, in fact, don't still qualify for income splitting under the new budget rules. There are still several ways to use income splitting that may well be just as useful as the rules under which we used to have great success.

Buy a Car or Other Tax-Deductible Equipment: Sales and businesspeople are allowed to deduct the cost of running their vehicles and depreciation on those pieces of equipment. It may be a car or a truck or any number of different pieces of equipment. Because you get to claim the capital-cost allowance up front, you may well want to buy some extra equipment before the year comes to an end. You invest very little money right now to save taxes for the entire year. You have to pay for that product next year, but don't forget, you have deferred taxes on a sizable amount of money for an entire year so you now have more money to work with for the rest of the year.

Forward Averaging: Revenue Canada has offered forward averaging as a means of deferring taxes to future years for those individuals employed in certain jobs and for those who earn a sizable increase in income compared to the levels of the past several years. However, forward averaging is really only of use to a small group of taxpayers. If you earn more than $50,000 in taxable income, you ought to consider the idea of forward averaging. To use this idea successfully, you have to pay the minimum tax rate up front, voluntarily, to Revenue Canada. But you are already there. You are going to pay the maximum rate anyway, so why not open the door to getting some of that money back at some time in the future? All you have to do is voluntarily elect to use forward averaging. Then, instead of waving goodbye to your tax dollars, you at least have some chance to get them back in the future, if your income level falls.

For most taxpayers, though, forward averaging is not very useful. To take advantage of it, you have to pay the maximum tax rate in your province — voluntarily — and hope that you will save taxes when you bring that money back into your income at some time in the future. You see, if you pay the maximum tax rate now, you won't have the excess tax monies in your pocket. You won't be able to invest them. Revenue Canada will at least offset the pool of money that you are accumulating against inflation by indexing its value. But don't forget that you have paid more up front than you really had to. To leave that money in Revenue Canada's hands for a lengthy period of time would mean that you paid too much up front and got back too little when inflation is considered.

However, for somebody who knows for a fact that their income is going to fall dramatically in the next year or two, forward averaging can indeed work. As an example, if you are going to retire next year, you can generally count on your income being higher this year than it will be next. As a result, you make a decision to elect forward averaging this year to offset taxes and smooth out the tax bite over this year and next. Or if you are working full time now but plan to quit work next year to go back to school, take a sabbatical, or a leave of absence, then you might well be able to take advantage of forward averaging.

However, it's my experience that you can do a better job for yourself if you practice good money management to defer taxes rather than using forward averaging. As an example: Speak to your employer about holding back some of your income until next year. Or if you put the maximum into a registered retirement savings plan for a day or two, you will lower your income for one year and transfer it to the next when you will be in a lower tax bracket. The cost this way is much lower. Or if you purchase other tax shelters that you can cash in in coming years, you will get the tax relief now but enjoy any profits made by investments in future years rather than simply accepting indexing from Revenue Canada.

Registered Pension Plan — Past Service: For some taxpayers there's an interesting way to save taxes by combining your registered pension with your RRSP — and to take advantage of making contributions to your pension at work for past years when you didn't contribute. In fact, you can double your normal pension plan contributions if you play your cards right. Until major tax changes fully take place, we are entitled to contribute to pension plans at work for years when we didn't take advantage of them and we get the tax deductions this year.

There may be a drawback in that the pension contributions are deducted from our RRSP limits. That means that we may be contributing to a pension where we have less flexibility and less control over our money than we would have had we opted for an RRSP. But there may be a major positive as well. When we contribute to a pension plan at work our employer often matches that contribution. If so, you may be much farther ahead of the game if you chose the pension route rather than the RRSP.

In fact, there is a way where we may be able to use both of these ideas at the same time. Check back to chapter 17 to get more details on the extra tax savings available through combining RRSPs and past service pension plan contributions.

An RRSP for Your Child: While we generally think of registered retirement savings plans as being useful for those in the higher income tax brackets, there is a case to be made for buying an RRSP for a child. If you already earn more than $1,000 worth of investment income, you pay tax on the excess. If your spouse and/or your children do the same, you can't take the maximum advantage of income splitting. In that case you are paying your full tax rate on any other investment income that you earn. That's where buying an RRSP for a child can come in handy.

Even if your child doesn't earn enough income to pay tax, you, as a family, may come out ahead with one of these plans. If you give money to your child and he or she spends it, you have no problem. However, if the child invests that money, the tax bill comes back to you because the child was a minor. You don't have to pay any tax on the money that you gave away, but you do have to add the interest earned by that money to your tax return.

That's where an RRSP comes in handy. If you put money into an RRSP for a child, the plan will earn the interest tax free, and it will multiply tax free as long as it earns interest inside the plan. Instead of earning it in your name and being taxed at your rate, the plan will earn interest tax free. And even when the child wants to remove money from the plan, it will be at his or her tax rate — which should be substantially lower than yours. For some consumers, this is an inexpensive answer to a child trust. Rather than paying lawyers' fees to set up a trust, they deposit funds into an RRSP, pay no fees, see the money compound tax free inside the plan, and have the child withdraw funds from the plan to pay tuition and education costs. Instead of the parent paying the full shot out of after-tax dollars, they are paid out of tax-free compounding interest which is taxed at a low rate when it is removed from the plan. It may well save a few tax dollars. However, it must also be done correctly, as Revenue Canada doesn't really like this idea.

Talk to Your Children: Too often families take their childrens' finances for granted. As an example: You know that your child had a parttime or summer job. You believe that he or she didn't earn enough to be lost as a tax deduction so you file claiming the child as a dependent, only to hear from Revenue Canada that your son or daughter earned enough to be excluded. Or you quickly ask the child if he or she earned enough to pay tax. Your child says no, so you don't bother with any tax-planning measures. Then you realize it isn't enough for the child to be tax free; you must also lower the child's net income enough that he or she is also acceptable in terms of net income.

That's why it's important that we talk to our children each year around Christmas. We want to find out how much they earned, what tax deductions they can use, how much their tuition was, and what other expenses they incurred. If we can get their net income down to an acceptable level, we may well be able to get them back as an important component of tax relief.

As an example: If your child earned about $4,000 last year, you have lost him or her as a dependent deduction — unless you do a little fancy footwork.

Other reasons to talk with our children as the year winds down are to find out whether we will be able to use the $50 per month full-time student deduction to lower our own taxable incomes, to decide how much of the tuition bill they should be using to lower their net incomes, and to remind them to use their moving expenses to lower their taxable income. Most of these ideas must be taken care of before the year comes to an end so make sure you do a little family financial planning before you go out to that New Year's Eve party.

Registered Education Savings Plan: While there is no deadline for making contributions to these plans because there is no tax deduction involved, the only time that most consumers reassess their finances is at the end of the year or at tax time. If you have a better feeling for what's happening with your finances, you may want to consider opening an RESP now instead of waiting until the end of the year. The money is lumped together with the contributions of others to create a large pool of money that can generally earn a higher rate of return than you can earn by investing it yourself.

Cash in Your RRSP: While we normally think of these plans as long-term tax savings devices, there are reasons to use them in the short term. As an example: If you've been out of work for part of this year, but you know you are going to go back to work next year, you might want to cash in your RRSP now, at your low tax rate rather than waiting until next year when you will be working full time and paying higher taxes again. Cashing in an RRSP is not something that you want to do often, but if you are planning to cash in an RRSP anyway, why not do some calculations right now to see which day would be better for you.

Something that's also worthwhile considering, of course, is the upcoming tax deadline. If you cash in your plan now, you will have to settle up with the taxman next April. All things included, if you wait until January 1, you won't have to settle up until one year from January.

Losses: Far too often, consumers stop calculating once they have done enough tax planning to wipe out their tax burden for the year. A good example is the employed individual who has a small unincorporated business on the side. In the early years these businesses often generate more losses than gains. Those losses can be used to lower the ordinary income earned through investment or employment. But just because they wiped out your entire tax bill for a year is no reason to stop calculating.

Excess losses can be carried back to any of the past three years. That means that you will now get back taxes that you have already paid. Surely you could put the money to good use. All you have to do is request that Revenue Canada apply the excess losses against whichever tax return had the highest tax rate during the last three years. Or if you feel fairly confident that you are going to earn a higher rate of return in the next few years, you can hang onto those losses and apply them against future income. Once again, you come out a winner.

42

Discounting Can Be Overly Taxing

Discounters are the companies that prepare tax returns and immediately pay the consumer any rebate that's owing — minus 15%. All people have to do is take their return to an office, have it completed, and sign a form authorizing Revenue Canada to send the rebate to the tax company.

Doesn't sound bad, does it? That 15% is cheaper than a credit card loan and it's well below the 20 to 22% mortgages some consumers suffered through at the beginning of the 1980s.

But don't forget the interest on these other loans is calculated for an entire year. We don't know how long it will take for a tax rebate to come back. If it is a year, the 15% charged by the discounters isn't bad. In fact, it's downright decent when you consider you get your return prepared as part of the deal.

But what if your rebate comes back in six months? Now we're looking at an interest rate that is effectively 30%. What's more, Revenue Canada says returns should be processed more quickly this year. If so, rebates may come back after a more reasonable wait.

Normally, Revenue Canada staff can process more than a million returns a week. With some 16 million returns due to be filed, it seems reasonable to expect your rebate after waiting only three months. If so, the tax discounter who's taking 15% is effectively charging an annual interest rate of 60%.

In fact, we used to be able to get our rebates back in six weeks or so. If that happens this year, you'd be paying the equivalent of 130% to the tax discounter. How many other financial institutions would be allowed to charge such high rates? And how many consumers would stand for it?

There's another problem with the whole rebate system. We pay too much tax in the first place. We authorize our employers to automatically deduct tax from our paychecks and remit it to Ottawa every two weeks. Thus, the feds have our money beginning in the second week of January, yet they don't have to pay us interest on any over-payment we've made until after April 30 of the following year, the deadline that determines our final tax bill. Effectively, they have our money for a year or more before we start to earn any interest on it.

We'd all be ahead of the game if we managed our affairs so that we owed tax at the end of the year. But that's not the way it works. Some two-thirds of all taxpayers end up looking for a rebate. If that's the case with you, try looking for ways to make sure the situation is different next year. And do everything you can right now to seek out an alternative to a tax discounter.

If 300,000 Canadians use discounters this year, and assuming an average tax rebate of $750, some $92 million worth of rebates will be discounted in Ontario — and $360 million across Canada.

Unfortunately, it's generally lower-income groups that use the service most often, including mothers seeking to get their child tax credit earlier than normal. Consider this example. A single mother with no income will be eligible for a rebate of something like $700. If she has simple financial numbers, she probably doesn't need any help on her tax return in the first place. But because she needs the money now, she may be tempted by a discounter and accept a quick tax settlement of $595. However, she pays more than $100 for the privilege.

Granted, she may need the money, but using a tax discounter is surely a high price to pay. She would have been better off doing the return herself, taking it to a financial institution to have it checked, and applying for a normal loan.

Consumer loans right now run at something less than 15%, so

she would pay less interest even if the rebate didn't come back for an entire year. And if she used the rebate check to pay that loan down as soon as it came in, she would end up paying much less.

For those with more complicated returns, the question of tax planning arises — and that's a year-round proposition. Some tax return companies open only during the tax season. They specialize in returns, not planning. These taxpayers would be better off dealing with somebody in the business of taking care of financial management and tax planning all year long. Generally, that means an accountant.

And now for a small moment of bragging. Because of the expansion of tax discounters, I formed an association with a group of accountants last year and offered a service to many of the Hamilton/Burlington area credit unions where we supervise the preparation of tax returns for credit union members. Members, in effect, get their tax returns done by a full-time, registered chartered accountant.

The credit union then advances them the full amount of the rebate, charging the normal interest rate for the entire year, not just a few months. You pay the annual rate of interest but only for the number of days that the loan is actually outstanding.

In the House of Commons, Judy Erola, then Minister for Consumer and Corporate Affairs, congratulated the credit unions who put this idea in place. It shows true feeling and regard for the consumer, not profiteering. You can be assured Ottawa will look on this group as leaders in changing the practice of charging exorbitant rates to financially-troubled consumers for money that is rightfully theirs. Tax discounting practices should not be allowed to continue.

43

Tax Oddities

Each year I run into a number of oddball tax items. They are questions that crop up on little things that may not seem like much individually, but which can really mount up to be worth a lot of money when they are all used to our advantage. The following is a collection of small tax ideas that may well be useful to you.

Political Contributions: If you are asked to contribute money to a political party, you can get some attractive tax relief. But this type of tax relief isn't just a tax deduction. It's an actual tax rebate. That means that you use this form of tax relief to lower your tax bill dollar for dollar, not just your taxable income. As an example: If you give $100 to an acceptable party or candidate, you will lower your tax bill by $75. If this were a tax deduction instead of a tax rebate, you would lower your taxable income by $100 and save the taxes that you would normally pay on that $100. That varies from taxpayer to taxpayer. But the rich might save $50, the middle-income group $30 to $35, and the lower-income group anywhere from $10 to $20. A tax deduction, then, works better for high-income groups than the lower levels.

But a tax rebate provides the same help to everybody. In fact, the real dollars saved will be even more important to the lower-income groups in that they are a higher percentage of their total income. (Fifty dollars means a lot more to somebody earning $20,000 than to somebody earning $100,000). When it comes to political contributions then, there is some real tax relief. But we may get even more if we play our cards right.

When you give $100 to a political party, you get a $75 tax rebate. When you give $200, you get $125 back from Ottawa. And as you give even more, the percentage rebate slides lower. For this reason, if you plan to donate $200 to a political party, you should try to split it between both spouses. The $200 gets you a $125 rebate in your own name. Split between the two of you, it's worth $75 each. As a result, the family comes out ahead with $150 instead of $125. In fact, if we wish to donate even more, we might be able to go a step farther. If we practice a bit of income splitting, we may be able to give our children $100 each to donate. Now we get two more $75 deductions if they are taxable. In fact, if you have your own company, you can now donate another $100 in the company's name and save another $75 instead of a smaller amount. In fact, let's look at this example and see how well we fare.

An individual who donates $500 to a federal political party gets a tax rebate of $275. Yet the individual who spends the same $500 over five different family members and/or corporate donations would save $375 — an extra $100 simply because you used smart money management. In addition, the value of spreading contributions grows when the numbers involved are higher. As an example, a single donation of $800 gets a tax rebate of $383.33 whereas a similar rebate spread over more family members would create a tax rebate worth $600. Of course, the cost of supporting eight family members may well off-set the tax advantage.

Not All Income Is Taxable: That statement may seem silly for two reasons. Number one is that governments are doing their level-headed best to make every dollar we earn taxable. Number two is that consumers know that they get deductions so that some income is always free of tax. But that's not what I'm talking about here. I'm referring here to the fact that some forms of income do not have to be shared with the taxman, no matter how much money is involved. Yet I talk to many consumers who, believe it or not, go right ahead and add this income to their tax returns. They voluntarily pay tax on money that should be theirs completely tax free.

As an example: You put your child's family allowance check in a savings account. Because the child is a minor, the financial institution sends the T5 information slip to the mother. *Mothers often add this income to their own even though they don't have to.* If you do, you are going to pay tax on income that should not be taxed. A child can earn more than $6,000 completely tax free so whatever you do, do not add that income to your own name and pay tax on it when it could be tax free in the child's name.

Lottery winnings are also tax free. It doesn't matter whether you win the million dollar prize or one worth ten dollars. You do not normally have to add this income to your tax return. Granted, once you invest it, you will earn taxable income. But the prize itself is tax free. In fact, if you manage your money properly, you may be able to escape taxes on most of the income that you earn after you have won the lottery. But we go into that more fully in another chapter.

The same applies to inheritances. There are minor differences in Quebec but for the rest of the country you should treat any money that you inherit as a tax free gain. The estate may have to pay tax, but once it gets to you, it should pretty well be tax free.

Gambling winnings are tax free unless Revenue Canada can prove that you are a professional gambler. Their definition of a professional is vague, but it's not really meant to include the odd bingo pot or a poker hand from time to time. In fact, if you think about the race track, you will realize the taxes are already pretty high, when you consider the odds of your winning.

Getting hurt on the job may result in an insurance or Workers' Compensation Board settlement. The latter is tax free even though your employer may send you an information slip which suggests that it is taxable. Make sure that you check with your employer to determine if any of these benefits have been included in your T4 slip. If they have, you can normally get away with claiming the entire amount as net income to determine if you qualify as a dependent but only the earned income portion as taxable income in your own name.

A salary replacement insurance contract is a different story. If you purchased the policy yourself and paid the premiums without any help from your employer, the funds you receive from these plans are tax free. However, if your employer pays the premiums, the payments that you receive must be added to your income. Strike pay is normally tax free, so do not include it in your income when you complete your tax return. Expenses paid by your employer to compensate you for out-of-pocket expenditures are normally tax free. As an example, if your boss asks you to drive across town to deliver something, he may compensate you for your gas and expenses — in fact, many employees get car and expense accounts. These are generally tax free. However, if you feel that the compensation doesn't fully pay your expenses, you can add them to your income and claim your actual out-of-pocket costs as a tax deduction. A few minutes of mathematics may pay off.

Or suppose your employer regularly sends you out to deliver items using the municipal transit system. In this case he would normally reimburse you for the fare. If you do this often enough, you may want to ask him to provide you with a transit pass. Now you can use the system at will without incurring any extra cost that month. And, you will be able to use the pass to come and go to work or anywhere in the city, on your own time. You have an added benefit and it's tax free. Other types of income that can be earned tax free include war veterans' allowances, veterans' disability allowances (including payments to dependents), spouses' allowances (not alimony payments; these are from Welfare), Guaranteed Income Supplements, income earned by Indians while on a reservation, and of course, the Child Tax Credit and any other tax rebates. However, interest paid to us by Revenue Canada on late refund payments must be added to our returns and taxed as normal interest income.

Education Costs: Some consumers have a chance to work full time, earning a full-time income, and also go to school often enough that they qualify for the $50 per month full-time student deduction. In addition, they get to claim their tuition as a tax deduction, and because they have a full-time income, they have something to write that tuition off against. If you can prove (the school must provide documentation) that you are carrying a full course load, you will be able to claim these deductions whether you actually attend class or not.

In addition, there are postgraduate students who don't have to attend class to get their credits. In that case, there is very little problem getting a double deduction. If your employer asks you to take an extra course or two, it may be almost the same as a demand. In that case you may be able to write off the cost of getting to school, the tuition, the parking, and other expenses as business deductions. Of course, your best course would be to get your employer to pick up the cost of this schooling. But if he won't, you may get some tax relief by checking out this angle.

One point that's worth mentioning. If the course has a direct bearing on your job, Revenue Canada may disallow any deduction like this one. In that case, at least make sure that you take an afternoon class. Then your employer will effectively pick up the tab as you will be studying while being paid a full-time salary.

Room and Board: When children pay their parents room and board, they cannot claim it as a tax deduction. But then it's also not considered taxable in the hands of the parents. As a result, we have a perfect opportunity to income split and get the money back tax free. If we can use income splitting to move income into our children's names, they can earn it tax free. Then we can charge them room and board to get the income back tax free. We, as a family, come out ahead. And we, as individuals, also get a break. It's a winning combination.

Prizes at Work: If you win an award at work, in a sales campaign, let's say, you should expect to pay tax on it. The campaign was really part of your job. Your employer used it to motivate you, and you can be sure that he will try to add it to your income as a taxable benefit. But even then you come out ahead of the game as nobody is taxed one hundred cents on the dollar in this country.

However, if you win a prize at work that isn't really related to your job, you should not have to add it to your income. As a result, anytime you get a gift or win something at work, you should ask your employer how to make sure that it comes to you as a tax-free benefit. It may well still be a tax deduction for him, but you get to earn it tax free.

Appendix A

Personal Exemptions: Federal

	1985
	1985
Single Individual	$ 4,140
Spouse	$ 3,650
Married Couple	$ 7,780
Erosion of Spousal Deduction Starts At	$ 520
Dependent Under 18	$ 710
Erosion Begins At	$ 2,730
Dependent 18 and Over	$ 1,430
Erosion Begins At	$ 2,720
Over Age 65 or Blind or Bedridden	$ 2,590
Child-Tax Credit	$ 384
Income Limit for Child-Tax Credit	$26,330

Appendix B

Blended Monthly Mortgage Payments

These tables show blended monthly mortgage payments for a loan of $1,000, based on interest compounded semi-annually, not in advance.

AMORTIZATION PERIODS 1 TO 35 YEARS

8 1/2%	8 5/8%	8 3/4%	8 7/8%	YEARS AMORT
87.15186	87.20774	87.26361	87.31947	1
45.38858	45.44377	45.49898	45.55419	2
31.49959	31.55548	31.61140	31.66736	3
24.57909	24.63602	24.69301	24.75004	4
20.44589	20.50399	20.56217	20.62042	5
17.70624	17.76558	17.82501	17.88452	6
15.76280	15.82341	15.88411	15.94493	7
14.31689	14.37877	14.44077	14.50289	8
13.20256	13.26572	13.32901	13.39244	9
12.32023	12.38466	12.44924	12.51397	10
11.60652	11.67221	11.73806	11.80409	11
11.01917	11.08610	11.15322	11.22052	12
10.52890	10.59707	10.66543	10.73399	13
10.11482	10.18420	10.25379	10.32359	14
9.76158	9.83215	9.90294	9.97396	15
9.45767	9.52941	9.60139	9.67359	16
9.19428	9.26717	9.34031	9.41368	17
8.96457	9.03858	9.11285	9.18736	18
8.76312	8.83823	8.91360	8.98922	19
8.58559	8.66177	8.73822	8.81493	20
8.42848	8.50571	8.58320	8.66096	21
8.28892	8.36716	8.44567	8.52446	22
8.16452	8.24375	8.32325	8.40303	23
8.05332	8.13350	8.21396	8.29471	24
7.95364	8.03475	8.11614	8.19782	25
7.86407	7.94608	8.02838	8.11096	26
7.78342	7.86630	7.94947	8.03292	27
7.71067	7.79439	7.87839	7.96268	28
7.64491	7.72944	7.81426	7.89936	29
7.58539	7.67070	7.75630	7.84218	30
7.53144	7.61750	7.70385	7.79048	31
7.48247	7.56926	7.65633	7.74367	32
7.43797	7.52546	7.61322	7.70125	33
7.39749	7.48564	7.57407	7.66276	34
7.36063	7.44943	7.53849	7.62781	35

BLENDED MONTHLY PAYMENT FACTORS FOR A LOAN OF $1,000

YEARS AMORT	8%	8 1/8%	8 1/4%	8 3/8%
1	86.92826	86.98417	87.04007	87.09597
2	45.16795	45.22309	45.27824	45.33341
3	31.27635	31.33212	31.38791	31.44374
4	24.35187	24.40860	24.46538	24.52221
5	20.21416	20.27199	20.32988	20.38785
6	17.46975	17.52874	17.58782	17.64699
7	15.52144	15.58162	15.64191	15.70230
8	14.07061	14.13200	14.19351	14.25514
9	12.95135	13.01394	13.07667	13.13955
10	12.06409	12.12789	12.19185	12.25596
11	11.34549	11.41049	11.47566	11.54101
12	10.75328	10.81947	10.88585	10.95242
13	10.25823	10.32560	10.39317	10.46093
14	9.83942	9.90795	9.97669	10.04565
15	9.48153	9.55120	9.62110	9.69123
16	9.17305	9.24385	9.31488	9.38616
17	8.90517	8.97708	9.04923	9.12164
18	8.67106	8.74405	8.81730	8.89081
19	8.46531	8.53936	8.61368	8.68827
20	8.28357	8.35867	8.43404	8.50968
21	8.12236	8.19847	8.27486	8.35153
22	7.97879	8.05589	8.13328	8.21096
23	7.85050	7.92857	8.00693	8.08558
24	7.73550	7.81451	7.89382	7.97342
25	7.63213	7.71206	7.79229	7.87281
26	7.53900	7.61981	7.70093	7.78235
27	7.45488	7.53656	7.61855	7.70084
28	7.37877	7.46129	7.54411	7.62724
29	7.30977	7.39310	7.47673	7.56067
30	7.24711	7.33122	7.41565	7.50037
31	7.19013	7.27500	7.36018	7.44566
32	7.13824	7.22384	7.30975	7.39597
33	7.09092	7.17724	7.26385	7.35077
34	7.04773	7.13473	7.22202	7.30961
35	7.00826	7.09592	7.18387	7.27211

BLENDED MONTHLY PAYMENT FACTORS FOR A LOAN OF $1,000

YEARS AMORT	9%	9 1/8%	9 1/4%	9 3/8%
1	87.37533	87.43117	87.48701	87.54284
2	45.60942	45.66466	45.71991	45.77517
3	31.72334	31.77936	31.83541	31.89149
4	24.80712	24.86426	24.92144	24.97868
5	20.67873	20.73711	20.79556	20.85408
6	17.94413	18.00381	18.06359	18.12345
7	16.00584	16.06687	16.12799	16.18922
8	14.56514	14.62750	14.68998	14.75259
9	13.45601	13.51971	13.58355	13.64753
10	12.57886	12.64389	12.70908	12.77442
11	11.87028	11.93664	12.00316	12.06985
12	11.28800	11.35566	11.42350	11.49152
13	10.80274	10.87169	10.94083	11.01016
14	10.39359	10.46380	10.53421	10.60483
15	10.04519	10.11664	10.18830	10.26017
16	9.74603	9.81869	9.89157	9.96468
17	9.48729	9.56113	9.63521	9.70952
18	9.26212	9.33712	9.41236	9.48784
19	9.06510	9.14123	9.21760	9.29423
20	8.89189	8.96912	9.04660	9.12433
21	8.73899	8.81728	8.89583	8.97463
22	8.60352	8.68284	8.76242	8.84227
23	8.48309	8.56341	8.64400	8.72485
24	8.37573	8.45702	8.53858	8.62040
25	8.27977	8.36200	8.44450	8.52726
26	8.19381	8.27694	8.36034	8.44400
27	8.11665	8.20065	8.28491	8.36945
28	8.04725	8.13209	8.21719	8.30256
29	7.98473	8.07037	8.15628	8.24245
30	7.92833	8.01474	8.10142	8.18835
31	7.87737	7.96453	8.05194	8.13961
32	7.83128	7.91915	8.00727	8.09564
33	7.78954	7.87809	7.96689	8.05594
34	7.75171	7.84091	7.93036	8.02004
35	7.71739	7.80721	7.89728	7.98757

AMORTIZATION PERIODS 1 TO 35 YEARS

9 1/2%	9 5/8%	9 3/4%	9 7/8%	YEARS AMORT
87.59867	87.65448	87.71029	87.76609	1
45.83044	45.88573	45.94103	45.99634	2
31.94760	32.00374	32.05991	32.11611	3
25.03596	25.09330	25.15068	25.20811	4
20.91267	20.97133	21.03005	21.08884	5
18.18340	18.24343	18.30355	18.36375	6
16.25055	16.31199	16.37352	16.43516	7
14.81531	14.87815	14.94111	15.00419	8
13.71164	13.77589	13.84027	13.90479	9
12.83991	12.90555	12.97134	13.03728	10
12.13670	12.20372	12.27090	12.33825	11
11.55972	11.62810	11.69665	11.76538	12
11.07968	11.14939	11.21929	11.28937	13
10.67564	10.74666	10.81788	10.88929	14
10.33226	10.40456	10.47707	10.54978	15
10.03801	10.11155	10.18532	10.25930	16
9.78406	9.85883	9.93382	10.00904	17
9.56356	9.63952	9.71570	9.79212	18
9.37109	9.44820	9.52554	9.60312	19
9.20231	9.28053	9.35899	9.43770	20
9.05369	9.13300	9.21255	9.29234	21
8.92237	9.00272	9.08332	9.16417	22
8.80596	8.88732	8.96894	9.05080	23
8.70248	8.78482	8.86741	8.95025	24
8.61028	8.69355	8.77708	8.86085	25
8.52793	8.61210	8.69653	8.78121	26
8.45424	8.53928	8.62457	8.71011	27
8.38818	8.47405	8.56017	8.64654	28
8.32887	8.41554	8.50245	8.58960	29
8.27554	8.36297	8.45064	8.53855	30
8.22753	8.31569	8.40408	8.49270	31
8.18426	8.27311	8.36219	8.45150	32
8.14522	8.23473	8.32447	8.41443	33
8.10996	8.20010	8.29046	8.38104	34
8.07809	8.16883	8.25979	8.35095	35

BLENDED MONTHLY PAYMENT FACTORS FOR A LOAN OF $1,000

AMORTIZATION PERIODS 1 TO 35 YEARS

YEARS AMORT	10%	10 1/8%	10 1/4%	10 3/8%	10 1/2%	10 5/8%	10 3/4%	10 7/8%	YEARS AMORT
1	87.82188	87.87766	87.93344	87.98921	88.04496	88.10072	88.15646	88.21219	1
2	46.05166	46.10700	46.16235	46.21770	46.27307	46.32846	46.38385	46.43925	2
3	32.17235	32.22861	32.28491	32.34123	32.39759	32.45398	32.51040	32.56684	3
4	25.26560	25.32313	25.38071	25.43834	25.49602	25.55375	25.61152	25.66935	4
5	21.14770	21.20662	21.26562	21.32468	21.38380	21.44300	21.50226	21.56158	5
6	18.42404	18.48442	18.54487	18.60541	18.66604	18.72675	18.78754	18.84842	6
7	16.49690	16.55875	16.62069	16.68273	16.74488	16.80712	16.86946	16.93191	7
8	15.06739	15.13071	15.19414	15.25769	15.32135	15.38513	15.44903	15.51304	8
9	13.96943	14.03422	14.09913	14.16417	14.22935	14.29465	14.36009	14.42566	9
10	13.10337	13.16960	13.23598	13.30250	13.36917	13.43599	13.50294	13.57004	10
11	12.40575	12.47341	12.54124	12.60922	12.67736	12.74566	12.81412	12.88273	11
12	11.83427	11.90335	11.97259	12.04201	12.11159	12.18135	12.25127	12.32136	12
13	11.35964	11.43009	11.50073	11.57155	11.64255	11.71373	11.78509	11.85662	13
14	10.96090	11.03271	11.10471	11.17690	11.24928	11.32185	11.39460	11.46755	14
15	10.62270	10.69582	10.76915	10.84268	10.91640	10.99033	11.06445	11.13876	15
16	10.33350	10.40791	10.48252	10.55735	10.63239	10.70763	10.78307	10.85871	16
17	10.08447	10.16013	10.23601	10.31210	10.38840	10.46491	10.54164	10.61857	17
18	9.86876	9.94563	10.02272	10.10003	10.17757	10.25531	10.33328	10.41145	18
19	9.68093	9.75897	9.83725	9.91574	9.99446	10.07340	10.15256	10.23193	19
20	9.51664	9.59582	9.67523	9.75487	9.83473	9.91482	9.99513	10.07566	20
21	9.37238	9.45265	9.53316	9.61390	9.69487	9.77606	9.85747	9.93911	21
22	9.24526	9.32659	9.40815	9.48995	9.57198	9.65423	9.73671	9.81940	22
23	9.13290	9.21525	9.29783	9.38064	9.46369	9.54696	9.63045	9.71416	23
24	9.03333	9.11665	9.20021	9.28400	9.36802	9.45226	9.53672	9.62141	24
25	8.94487	9.02913	9.11362	9.19835	9.28330	9.36847	9.45386	9.53947	25
26	8.86612	8.95128	9.03667	9.12228	9.20812	9.29419	9.38046	9.46695	26
27	8.79589	8.88190	8.96814	9.05461	9.14130	9.22821	9.31533	9.40266	27
28	8.73314	8.81997	8.90703	8.99431	9.08181	9.16952	9.25744	9.34556	28
29	8.67699	8.76460	8.85244	8.94049	9.02876	9.11724	9.20592	9.29479	29
30	8.62668	8.71504	8.80361	8.89240	8.98140	9.07060	9.16000	9.24960	30
31	8.58155	8.67062	8.75990	8.84939	8.93908	9.02896	9.11905	9.20931	31
32	8.54103	8.63076	8.72071	8.81086	8.90121	8.99175	9.08247	9.17338	32
33	8.50460	8.59497	8.68555	8.77633	8.86730	8.95845	9.04978	9.14129	33
34	8.47182	8.56281	8.65399	8.74536	8.83691	8.92864	9.02055	9.11262	34
35	8.44231	8.53387	8.62562	8.71755	8.80965	8.90193	8.99438	9.08698	35

BLENDED MONTHLY PAYMENT FACTORS FOR A LOAN OF $1,000

AMORTIZATION PERIODS 1 TO 35 YEARS

YEARS AMORT	11%	11 1/8%	11 1/4%	11 3/8%	11 1/2%	11 5/8%	11 3/4%	11 7/8%	YEARS AMORT
1	88.26792	88.32364	88.37935	88.43505	88.49074	88.54643	88.60211	88.65778	1
2	46.49467	46.55010	46.60554	46.66099	46.71645	46.77193	46.82741	46.88291	2
3	32.62332	32.67983	32.73637	32.79294	32.84954	32.90617	32.96283	33.01952	3
4	25.72722	25.78515	25.84312	25.90114	25.95920	26.01732	26.07548	26.13369	4
5	21.62097	21.68043	21.73995	21.79954	21.85919	21.91889	21.97870	22.03854	5
6	18.90938	18.97042	19.03154	19.09275	19.15404	19.21540	19.27686	19.33839	6
7	16.99445	17.05709	17.11983	17.18267	17.24560	17.30864	17.37177	17.43499	7
8	15.57716	15.64140	15.70575	15.77022	15.83480	15.89949	15.96429	16.02920	8
9	14.49135	14.55717	14.62312	14.68920	14.75540	14.82173	14.88819	14.95477	9
10	13.63729	13.70467	13.77220	13.83986	13.90767	13.97561	14.04369	14.11191	10
11	12.95149	13.02041	13.08948	13.15870	13.22808	13.29760	13.36728	13.43710	11
12	12.39162	12.46204	12.53262	12.60337	12.67428	12.74535	12.81658	12.88797	12
13	11.92833	12.00022	12.07228	12.14451	12.21692	12.28949	12.36224	12.43515	13
14	11.54068	11.61399	11.68749	11.76117	11.83502	11.90906	11.98327	12.05766	14
15	11.21327	11.28797	11.36286	11.43794	11.51320	11.58865	11.66428	11.74010	15
16	10.93456	11.01060	11.08684	11.16327	11.23990	11.31671	11.39372	11.47091	16
17	10.69570	10.77304	10.85059	10.92833	11.00626	11.08440	11.16272	11.24124	17
18	10.48984	10.56843	10.64722	10.72622	10.80542	10.88482	10.96442	11.04420	18
19	10.31152	10.39131	10.47132	10.55152	10.63194	10.71255	10.79336	10.87437	19
20	10.15640	10.23735	10.31851	10.39988	10.48146	10.56323	10.64521	10.72738	20
21	10.02096	10.10302	10.18529	10.26777	10.35046	10.43334	10.51643	10.59971	21
22	9.90231	9.98544	10.06877	10.15231	10.23606	10.32000	10.40415	10.48848	22
23	9.79809	9.88223	9.96658	10.05113	10.13588	10.22084	10.30599	10.39133	23
24	9.70630	9.79141	9.87672	9.96224	10.04795	10.13386	10.21997	10.30626	24
25	9.62529	9.71132	9.79755	9.88398	9.97061	10.05742	10.14443	10.23162	25
26	9.55365	9.64055	9.72766	9.81495	9.90244	9.99012	10.07798	10.16602	26
27	9.49019	9.57792	9.66585	9.75397	9.84228	9.93077	10.01943	10.10828	27
28	9.43389	9.52241	9.61112	9.70001	9.78909	9.87834	9.96777	10.05737	28
29	9.38387	9.47313	9.56258	9.65221	9.74201	9.83199	9.92214	10.01244	29
30	9.33938	9.42935	9.51949	9.60981	9.70030	9.79096	9.88177	9.97275	30
31	9.29977	9.39039	9.48120	9.57217	9.66330	9.75459	9.84604	9.93764	31
32	9.26446	9.35571	9.44713	9.53872	9.63046	9.72235	9.81438	9.90657	32
33	9.23297	9.32481	9.41681	9.50897	9.60127	9.69372	9.78631	9.87904	33
34	9.20486	9.29725	9.38980	9.48249	9.57533	9.66830	9.76141	9.85464	34
35	9.17974	9.27266	9.36571	9.45891	9.55224	9.64570	9.73929	9.83300	35

AMORTIZATION PERIODS 1 TO 35 YEARS

YEARS AMORT	12 7/8%	12 3/4%	12 5/8%	12 1/2%
1	89.10285	89.04724	88.99163	88.93601
2	47.32729	47.27170	47.21612	47.16056
3	33.47409	33.41716	33.36027	33.30340
4	26.60106	26.54247	26.48393	26.42544
5	22.51964	22.45928	22.39898	22.33875
6	19.83353	19.77136	19.70927	19.64725
7	17.94425	17.88026	17.81636	17.75256
8	16.55246	16.48668	16.42100	16.35542
9	15.49184	15.42428	15.35685	15.28953
10	14.66254	14.59324	14.52408	14.45505
11	14.00096	13.92997	13.85913	13.78843
12	13.46469	13.39206	13.31959	13.24727
13	13.02435	12.95014	12.87608	12.80219
14	12.65892	12.58318	12.50760	12.43219
15	12.35299	12.27577	12.19873	12.12185
16	12.09497	12.01635	11.93790	11.85962
17	11.87602	11.79604	11.71624	11.63662
18	11.68923	11.60797	11.52689	11.44598
19	11.52917	11.44669	11.36438	11.28225
20	11.39149	11.30784	11.22437	11.14108
21	11.27266	11.18791	11.10334	11.01895
22	11.16981	11.08402	10.99841	10.91297
23	11.08057	10.99381	10.90721	10.82079
24	11.00297	10.91529	10.82778	10.74043
25	10.93538	10.84684	10.75845	10.67023
26	10.87640	10.78705	10.69785	10.60881
27	10.82487	10.73476	10.64480	10.55499
28	10.77978	10.68897	10.59830	10.50777
29	10.74030	10.64883	10.55749	10.46629
30	10.70568	10.61360	10.52165	10.42982
31	10.67531	10.58267	10.49014	10.39773
32	10.64865	10.55548	10.46242	10.36947
33	10.62523	10.53157	10.43801	10.34456
34	10.60463	10.51052	10.41651	10.32259
35	10.58652	10.49200	10.39756	10.30322

BLENDED MONTHLY PAYMENT FACTORS FOR A LOAN OF $1,000

YEARS AMORT	12%	12 1/8%	12 1/4%	12 3/8%
1	88.71344	88.76909	88.82474	88.88038
2	46.93842	46.99394	47.04947	47.10501
3	33.07623	33.13298	33.18976	33.24657
4	26.19194	26.25025	26.30860	26.36700
5	22.09846	22.15843	22.21848	22.27858
6	19.40000	19.46169	19.52347	19.58532
7	17.49832	17.56174	17.62525	17.68886
8	16.09423	16.15936	16.22461	16.28996
9	15.02147	15.08830	15.15526	15.22233
10	14.18027	14.24876	14.31739	14.38615
11	13.50708	13.57720	13.64746	13.71787
12	12.95952	13.03122	13.10308	13.17510
13	12.50823	12.58147	12.65488	12.72845
14	12.13222	12.20696	12.28186	12.35694
15	11.81610	11.89227	11.96862	12.04515
16	11.54829	11.62585	11.70359	11.78152
17	11.31995	11.39884	11.47792	11.55718
18	11.12419	11.20436	11.28471	11.36526
19	10.95557	11.03696	11.11854	11.20030
20	10.80974	10.89230	10.97504	11.05797
21	10.68318	10.76685	10.85070	10.93473
22	10.57301	10.65771	10.74263	10.82771
23	10.47685	10.56257	10.64847	10.73454
24	10.39273	10.47939	10.56623	10.65324
25	10.31900	10.40655	10.49427	10.58217
26	10.25424	10.34263	10.43119	10.51992
27	10.19729	10.28647	10.37582	10.46533
28	10.14714	10.23706	10.32714	10.41738
29	10.10291	10.19353	10.28431	10.37523
30	10.06387	10.15515	10.24657	10.33813
31	10.02938	10.12127	10.21329	10.30545
32	9.99889	10.09134	10.18392	10.27663
33	9.97190	10.06488	10.15799	10.25122
34	9.94800	10.04148	10.13507	10.22878
35	9.92683	10.02077	10.11481	10.20897

BLENDED MONTHLY PAYMENT FACTORS FOR A LOAN OF $1,000

AMORTIZATION PERIODS 1 TO 35 YEARS

YEARS AMORT	13%	13 1/8%	13 1/4%	13 3/8%	13 1/2%	13 5/8%	13 3/4%	13 7/8%
1	89.15844	89.21403	89.26961	89.32518	89.38075	89.43630	89.49185	89.54739
2	47.38288	47.43849	47.49411	47.54974	47.60538	47.66103	47.71670	47.77237
3	33.53104	33.58802	33.64503	33.70207	33.75914	33.81624	33.87336	33.93052
4	26.65969	26.71837	26.77709	26.83586	26.89468	26.95354	27.01245	27.07140
5	22.58006	22.64054	22.70109	22.76170	22.82238	22.88311	22.94391	23.00476
6	19.89578	19.95811	20.02052	20.08300	20.14557	20.20821	20.27092	20.33372
7	18.00833	18.07250	18.13677	18.20113	18.26558	18.33012	18.39476	18.45949
8	16.61836	16.68436	16.75047	16.81668	16.88301	16.94943	17.01596	17.08259
9	15.55952	15.62732	15.69524	15.76328	15.83143	15.89970	15.96809	16.03659
10	14.73196	14.80152	14.87120	14.94102	15.01096	15.08103	15.15123	15.22155
11	14.07208	14.14335	14.21475	14.28630	14.35798	14.42980	14.50176	14.57385
12	13.53747	13.61039	13.68346	13.75668	13.83005	13.90356	13.97721	14.05101
13	13.09872	13.17325	13.24793	13.32276	13.39775	13.47289	13.54818	13.62362
14	12.73483	12.81090	12.88713	12.96352	13.04006	13.11677	13.19362	13.27063
15	12.43037	12.50792	12.58564	12.66351	12.74155	12.81975	12.89811	12.97663
16	12.17377	12.25274	12.33187	12.41117	12.49064	12.57027	12.65005	12.73000
17	11.95617	12.03649	12.11698	12.19763	12.27846	12.35944	12.44059	12.52190
18	11.77067	11.85228	11.93405	12.01600	12.09811	12.18038	12.26282	12.34541
19	11.61183	11.69466	11.77766	11.86083	11.94416	12.02765	12.11130	12.19511
20	11.47530	11.55929	11.64345	11.72777	11.81225	11.89689	11.98169	12.06665
21	11.35757	11.44265	11.52790	11.61331	11.69888	11.78460	11.87048	11.95651
22	11.25575	11.34187	11.42814	11.51457	11.60116	11.68790	11.77480	11.86184
23	11.16749	11.25457	11.34181	11.42921	11.51675	11.60444	11.69228	11.78027
24	11.09081	11.17880	11.26695	11.35524	11.44368	11.53227	11.62099	11.70985
25	11.02407	11.11292	11.20191	11.29105	11.38032	11.46974	11.55928	11.64896
26	10.96590	11.05554	11.14532	11.23524	11.32530	11.41548	11.50579	11.59623
27	10.91511	11.00550	11.09602	11.18667	11.27745	11.36835	11.45937	11.55051
28	10.87073	10.96181	11.05301	11.14434	11.23579	11.32735	11.41903	11.51083
29	10.83189	10.92361	11.01545	11.10741	11.19948	11.29167	11.38395	11.47634
30	10.79788	10.89020	10.98263	11.07517	11.16782	11.26057	11.35342	11.44636
31	10.76808	10.86095	10.95392	11.04700	11.14018	11.23345	11.32682	11.42027
32	10.74193	10.83531	10.92879	11.02237	11.11604	11.20979	11.30363	11.39755
33	10.71899	10.81284	10.90678	11.00082	11.09493	11.18913	11.28341	11.37776
34	10.69884	10.79313	10.88750	10.98195	11.07648	11.17109	11.26577	11.36051
35	10.68113	10.77582	10.87059	10.96543	11.06034	11.15532	11.25036	11.34547

AMORTIZATION PERIODS 1 TO 35 YEARS

YEARS AMORT	14 1/2%	14 5/8%	14 3/4%	14 7/8%	YEARS AMORT
1	89.82497	89.88046	89.93595	89.99142	1
2	48.05089	48.10663	48.16238	48.21814	2
3	34.21671	34.27404	34.33139	34.38877	3
4	27.36685	27.42607	27.48534	27.54465	4
5	23.30998	23.37120	23.43249	23.49383	5
6	20.64884	20.71209	20.77542	20.83882	6
7	18.78448	18.84974	18.91510	18.98054	7
8	17.41731	17.48456	17.55191	17.61936	8
9	16.38083	16.45001	16.51931	16.58872	9
10	15.57505	15.64611	15.71730	15.78861	10
11	14.93630	15.00918	15.08220	15.15534	11
12	14.42210	14.49673	14.57150	14.64640	12
13	14.00300	14.07930	14.15575	14.23234	13
14	13.65795	13.73585	13.81390	13.89210	14
15	13.37150	13.45093	13.53050	13.61021	15
16	13.13206	13.21293	13.29394	13.37510	16
17	12.93076	13.01299	13.09536	13.17788	17
18	12.76070	12.84421	12.92786	13.01166	18
19	12.61646	12.70117	12.78602	12.87101	19
20	12.49367	12.57951	12.66549	12.75160	20
21	12.38886	12.47575	12.56277	12.64992	21
22	12.29915	12.38702	12.47502	12.56314	22
23	12.22221	12.31099	12.39989	12.48891	23
24	12.15610	12.24572	12.33546	12.42531	24
25	12.09921	12.18961	12.28012	12.37073	25
26	12.05017	12.14129	12.23251	12.32384	26
27	12.00787	12.09965	12.19152	12.28349	27
28	11.97133	12.06372	12.15619	12.24876	28
29	11.93974	12.03269	12.12571	12.21882	29
30	11.91242	12.00587	12.09940	12.19301	30
31	11.88876	11.98268	12.07667	12.17073	31
32	11.86828	11.96262	12.05703	12.15149	32
33	11.85052	11.94525	12.04004	12.13488	33
34	11.83513	11.93021	12.02535	12.12052	34
35	11.82178	11.91718	12.01263	12.10811	35

BLENDED MONTHLY PAYMENT FACTORS FOR A LOAN OF $1,000

YEARS AMORT	14%	14 1/8%	14 1/4%	14 3/8%
1	89.60292	89.65845	89.71396	89.76947
2	47.82805	47.88375	47.93945	47.99517
3	33.98770	34.04491	34.10215	34.15942
4	27.13040	27.18944	27.24853	27.30767
5	23.06568	23.12667	23.18771	23.24881
6	20.39659	20.45954	20.52256	20.58566
7	18.52430	18.58921	18.65421	18.71930
8	17.14933	17.21617	17.28312	17.35016
9	16.10521	16.17394	16.24279	16.31175
10	15.29200	15.36258	15.43328	15.50410
11	14.64607	14.71843	14.79092	14.86354
12	14.12495	14.19902	14.27324	14.34760
13	13.69920	13.77493	13.85081	13.92683
14	13.34780	13.42511	13.50258	13.58019
15	13.05530	13.13412	13.21310	13.29223
16	12.81011	12.89037	12.97078	13.05135
17	12.60336	12.68498	12.76676	12.84868
18	12.42817	12.51107	12.59413	12.67734
19	12.27908	12.36320	12.44747	12.53189
20	12.15176	12.23702	12.32243	12.40798
21	12.04269	12.12902	12.21549	12.30211
22	11.94902	12.03635	12.12381	12.21141
23	11.86839	11.95664	12.04504	12.13356
24	11.79884	11.88797	11.97722	12.06660
25	11.73876	11.82870	11.91875	12.00892
26	11.68679	11.77746	11.86826	11.95916
27	11.64177	11.73313	11.82461	11.91618
28	11.60272	11.69473	11.78683	11.87903
29	11.56884	11.66142	11.75411	11.84688
30	11.53940	11.63253	11.72574	11.81904
31	11.51381	11.60743	11.70113	11.79491
32	11.49155	11.58563	11.67978	11.77399
33	11.47218	11.56667	11.66123	11.75584
34	11.45532	11.55019	11.64511	11.74009
35	11.44063	11.53584	11.63111	11.72642

BLENDED MONTHLY PAYMENT FACTORS FOR A LOAN OF $1,000

AMORTIZATION PERIODS 1 TO 35 YEARS

YEARS AMORT	15%	15 1/8%	15 1/4%	15 3/8%	15 1/2%	15 5/8%	15 3/4%	15 7/8%	YEARS AMORT
1	90.04689	90.10235	90.15780	90.21324	90.26867	90.32410	90.37952	90.43493	1
2	48.27390	48.32968	48.38547	48.44127	48.49708	48.55290	48.60873	48.66457	2
3	34.44617	34.50361	34.56107	34.61856	34.67608	34.73363	34.79120	34.84880	3
4	27.60401	27.66341	27.72286	27.78235	27.84188	27.90146	27.96108	28.02074	4
5	23.55524	23.61670	23.67823	23.73981	23.80146	23.86316	23.92492	23.98674	5
6	20.90229	20.96584	21.02947	21.09317	21.15694	21.22078	21.28470	21.34869	6
7	19.04607	19.11169	19.17740	19.24319	19.30908	19.37504	19.44109	19.50723	7
8	17.68692	17.75457	17.82232	17.89017	17.95811	18.02616	18.09430	18.16254	8
9	16.65824	16.72787	16.79761	16.86746	16.93742	17.00749	17.07766	17.14794	9
10	15.86004	15.93159	16.00326	16.07504	16.14694	16.21896	16.29110	16.36335	10
11	15.22861	15.30201	15.37553	15.44918	15.52295	15.59684	15.67086	15.74500	11
12	14.72144	14.79661	14.87191	14.94734	15.02290	15.09859	15.17441	15.25035	12
13	14.30906	14.38593	14.46293	14.54006	14.61733	14.69473	14.77226	14.84992	13
14	13.97043	14.04890	14.12752	14.20627	14.28515	14.36417	14.44333	14.52262	14
15	13.69007	13.77007	13.85022	13.93050	14.01091	14.09147	14.17215	14.25297	15
16	13.45640	13.53784	13.61943	13.70115	13.78301	13.86500	13.94713	14.02939	16
17	13.26054	13.34334	13.42628	13.50935	13.59257	13.67591	13.75939	13.84300	17
18	13.09559	13.17967	13.26388	13.34823	13.43271	13.51732	13.60206	13.68693	18
19	12.95614	13.04141	13.12681	13.21234	13.29800	13.38379	13.46970	13.55574	19
20	12.83784	12.92422	13.01073	13.09736	13.18412	13.27100	13.35801	13.44513	20
21	12.73721	12.82462	12.91215	12.99981	13.08759	13.17548	13.26349	13.35161	21
22	12.65139	12.73976	12.82824	12.91685	13.00557	13.09440	13.18334	13.27238	22
23	12.57805	12.66731	12.75667	12.84615	12.93574	13.02543	13.11522	13.20512	23
24	12.51528	12.60535	12.69553	12.78581	12.87619	12.96668	13.05725	13.14793	24
25	12.46146	12.55228	12.64321	12.73423	12.82534	12.91655	13.00785	13.09923	25
26	12.41526	12.50677	12.59838	12.69008	12.78187	12.87374	12.96569	13.05772	26
27	12.37556	12.46771	12.55994	12.65226	12.74465	12.83713	12.92968	13.02230	27
28	12.34140	12.43413	12.52694	12.61982	12.71278	12.80580	12.89889	12.99205	28
29	12.31200	12.40526	12.49859	12.59198	12.68545	12.77897	12.87255	12.96620	29
30	12.28668	12.38041	12.47422	12.56808	12.66200	12.75598	12.85001	12.94409	30
31	12.26484	12.35902	12.45325	12.54754	12.64187	12.73626	12.83070	12.92517	31
32	12.24601	12.34058	12.43521	12.52988	12.62459	12.71935	12.81415	12.90898	32
33	12.22976	12.32470	12.41967	12.51469	12.60974	12.70483	12.79996	12.89512	33
34	12.21574	12.31100	12.40629	12.50162	12.59698	12.69237	12.78779	12.88324	34
35	12.20363	12.29918	12.39476	12.49037	12.58601	12.68167	12.77736	12.87306	35

BLENDED MONTHLY PAYMENT FACTORS FOR A LOAN OF $1,000 — AMORTIZATION PERIODS 1 TO 35 YEARS

YEARS AMORT	16%	16 1/8%	16 1/4%	16 3/8%	16 1/2%	16 5/8%	16 3/4%	16 7/8%	YEARS AMORT
1	90.49033	90.54572	90.60111	90.65548	90.71185	90.76721	90.82257	90.87791	1
2	48.72042	48.77628	48.83215	48.88803	48.94392	48.99982	49.05573	49.11165	2
3	34.90643	34.96408	35.02176	35.07947	35.13721	35.19497	35.25276	35.31057	3
4	28.08045	28.14020	28.20000	28.25983	28.31972	28.37964	28.43960	28.49961	4
5	24.04862	24.11056	24.17256	24.23461	24.29672	24.35889	24.42112	24.48340	5
6	21.41276	21.47689	21.54110	21.60538	21.66973	21.73416	21.79865	21.86321	6
7	19.57346	19.63976	19.70616	19.77263	19.83920	19.90584	19.97257	20.03938	7
8	18.23088	18.29931	18.36784	18.43646	18.50517	18.57399	18.64289	18.71189	8
9	17.21833	17.28882	17.35941	17.43012	17.50092	17.57183	17.64284	17.71395	9
10	16.43571	16.50819	16.58078	16.65348	16.72629	16.79922	16.87225	16.94539	10
11	15.81926	15.89364	15.96814	16.04276	16.11749	16.19234	16.26731	16.34239	11
12	15.32642	15.40262	15.47894	15.55538	15.63194	15.70863	15.78543	15.86235	12
13	14.92771	15.00563	15.08367	15.16184	15.24014	15.31856	15.39710	15.47576	13
14	14.60203	14.68158	14.76126	14.84106	14.92099	15.00104	15.08122	15.16151	14
15	14.33392	14.41501	14.49622	14.57755	14.65901	14.74060	14.82231	14.90414	15
16	14.11178	14.19430	14.27695	14.35972	14.44262	14.52564	14.60878	14.69204	16
17	13.92674	14.01060	14.09459	14.17871	14.26294	14.34729	14.43176	14.51635	17
18	13.77192	13.85703	13.94227	14.02763	14.11310	14.19869	14.28440	14.37021	18
19	13.64190	13.72817	13.81457	13.90108	13.98770	14.07444	14.16128	14.24823	19
20	13.53236	13.61972	13.70718	13.79475	13.88244	13.97022	14.05811	14.14611	20
21	13.43985	13.52819	13.61664	13.70519	13.79385	13.88260	13.97146	14.06041	21
22	13.36153	13.45079	13.54014	13.62959	13.71914	13.80878	13.89851	13.98833	22
23	13.29511	13.38520	13.47538	13.56566	13.65602	13.74647	13.83700	13.92762	23
24	13.23869	13.32954	13.42048	13.51151	13.60261	13.69380	13.78506	13.87640	24
25	13.19070	13.28225	13.37388	13.46558	13.55737	13.64922	13.74114	13.83314	25
26	13.14983	13.24201	13.33427	13.42660	13.51899	13.61145	13.70397	13.79655	26
27	13.11499	13.20775	13.30058	13.39346	13.48641	13.57942	13.67248	13.76560	27
28	13.08527	13.17855	13.27189	13.36529	13.45873	13.55223	13.64578	13.73938	28
29	13.05990	13.15365	13.24745	13.34130	13.43520	13.52915	13.62313	13.71716	29
30	13.03822	13.13240	13.22662	13.32088	13.41519	13.50953	13.60391	13.69832	30
31	13.01969	13.11425	13.20885	13.30349	13.39815	13.49285	13.58758	13.68234	31
32	13.00385	13.09876	13.19369	13.28866	13.38365	13.47867	13.57371	13.66878	32
33	12.99030	13.08552	13.18075	13.27602	13.37130	13.46661	13.56193	13.65727	33
34	12.97871	13.07420	13.16971	13.26524	13.36078	13.45634	13.55191	13.64749	34
35	12.96878	13.06452	13.16027	13.25604	13.35181	13.44760	13.54339	13.63919	35

BLENDED MONTHLY PAYMENT FACTORS FOR A LOAN OF $1,000

YEARS AMORT	17%	17 1/8%	17 1/4%	17 3/8%
1	90.93325	90.98857	91.04389	91.09921
2	49.16758	49.22352	49.27947	49.33543
3	35.36842	35.42629	35.48418	35.54210
4	28.55966	28.61976	28.67989	28.74007
5	24.54574	24.60814	24.67060	24.73311
6	21.92785	21.99255	22.05733	22.12217
7	20.10627	20.17326	20.24030	20.30744
8	18.78098	18.85016	18.91944	18.98881
9	17.78517	17.85648	17.92790	17.99942
10	17.01865	17.09201	17.16547	17.23905
11	16.41759	16.49290	16.56832	16.64385
12	15.93939	16.01655	16.09382	16.17121
13	15.55454	15.63344	15.71246	15.79160
14	15.24193	15.32247	15.40313	15.48390
15	14.98609	15.06816	15.15034	15.23265
16	14.77542	14.85891	14.94252	15.02624
17	14.60105	14.68587	14.77080	14.85583
18	14.45614	14.54218	14.62832	14.71457
19	14.33529	14.42245	14.50971	14.59707
20	14.23420	14.32239	14.41068	14.49906
21	14.14945	14.23858	14.32781	14.41712
22	14.07824	14.16824	14.25831	14.34847
23	14.01832	14.10909	14.19994	14.29087
24	13.96781	14.05929	14.15085	14.24247
25	13.92519	14.01732	14.10950	14.20175
26	13.88920	13.98190	14.07465	14.16746
27	13.85877	13.95198	14.04525	14.13856
28	13.83302	13.92670	14.02043	14.11419
29	13.81122	13.90533	13.99946	14.09363
30	13.79276	13.88724	13.98174	14.07627
31	13.77712	13.87193	13.96676	14.06160
32	13.76386	13.85896	13.95408	14.04922
33	13.75262	13.84798	13.94336	14.03875
34	13.74308	13.83868	13.93428	14.02989
35	13.73499	13.83080	13.92660	14.02241

AMORTIZATION PERIODS 1 TO 35 YEARS

17 1/2%	17 5/8%	17 3/4%	17 7/8%	YEARS AMORT
91.15451	91.20980	91.26509	91.32037	1
49.39140	49.44738	49.50337	49.55937	2
35.60005	35.65803	35.71603	35.77405	3
28.80029	28.86055	28.92085	28.98120	4
24.79568	24.85830	24.92098	24.98372	5
22.18709	22.25207	22.31712	22.38225	6
20.37466	20.44196	20.50934	20.57680	7
19.05826	19.12781	19.19745	19.26718	8
18.07103	18.14275	18.21456	18.28647	9
17.31273	17.38651	17.46040	17.53439	10
16.71949	16.79525	16.87111	16.94708	11
16.24871	16.32633	16.40405	16.48189	12
15.87085	15.95021	16.02969	16.10928	13
15.56479	15.64579	15.72690	15.80813	14
15.31506	15.39759	15.48023	15.56298	15
15.11007	15.19402	15.27807	15.36223	16
14.94098	15.02623	15.11158	15.19704	17
14.80092	14.88738	14.97393	15.06058	18
14.68453	14.77209	14.85974	14.94749	19
14.58754	14.67610	14.76476	14.85349	20
14.50652	14.59600	14.68556	14.77521	21
14.43871	14.52902	14.61941	14.70987	22
14.38187	14.47293	14.56407	14.65527	23
14.33415	14.42590	14.51770	14.60957	24
14.29405	14.38641	14.47882	14.57128	25
14.26032	14.35322	14.44618	14.53918	26
14.23192	14.32532	14.41876	14.51223	27
14.20799	14.30183	14.39570	14.48960	28
14.18783	14.28206	14.37631	14.47059	29
14.17082	14.26540	14.35999	14.45461	30
14.15647	14.25136	14.34626	14.44117	31
14.14436	14.23952	14.33469	14.42986	32
14.13414	14.22954	14.32494	14.42035	33
14.12551	14.22112	14.31673	14.41234	34
14.11821	14.21402	14.30981	14.40561	35

BLENDED MONTHLY PAYMENT FACTORS FOR A LOAN OF $1,000

AMORTIZATION PERIODS 1 TO 35 YEARS

YEARS AMORT	18%	18 1/8%	18 1/4%	18 3/8%	18 1/2%	18 5/8%	18 3/4%	18 7/8%	YEARS AMORT
1	91.37564	91.43090	91.48616	91.54140	91.59664	91.65187	91.70709	91.76231	1
2	49.61537	49.67139	49.72742	49.78345	49.83950	49.89555	49.95162	50.00769	2
3	35.83211	35.89019	35.94829	36.00642	36.06458	36.12276	36.18097	36.23920	3
4	29.04158	29.10201	29.16248	29.22299	29.28354	29.34413	29.40476	29.46543	4
5	25.04651	25.10935	25.17226	25.23521	25.29823	25.36129	25.42441	25.48759	5
6	22.44743	22.51269	22.57802	22.64341	22.70887	22.77440	22.83999	22.90565	6
7	20.64434	20.71196	20.77965	20.84743	20.91528	20.98322	21.05123	21.11931	7
8	19.33700	19.40690	19.47690	19.54698	19.61715	19.68740	19.75775	19.82818	8
9	18.35847	18.43058	18.50278	18.57507	18.64746	18.71994	18.79252	18.86519	9
10	17.60849	17.68269	17.75699	17.83139	17.90589	17.98049	18.05519	18.12999	10
11	17.02316	17.09934	17.17563	17.25203	17.32853	17.40513	17.48184	17.55864	11
12	16.55984	16.63789	16.71606	16.79433	16.87217	16.95119	17.02978	17.10847	12
13	16.18898	16.26879	16.34871	16.42874	16.50887	16.58911	16.66945	16.74990	13
14	15.88947	15.97092	16.05247	16.13413	16.21590	16.29777	16.37975	16.46182	14
15	15.64584	15.72880	15.81187	15.89505	15.97833	16.06171	16.14519	16.22878	15
16	15.44649	15.53086	15.61533	15.69991	15.78458	15.86935	15.95422	16.03918	16
17	15.28260	15.36826	15.45402	15.53988	15.62583	15.71188	15.79801	15.88424	17
18	15.14733	15.23418	15.32112	15.40814	15.49526	15.58247	15.66977	15.75715	18
19	15.03532	15.12325	15.21126	15.29936	15.38754	15.47580	15.56415	15.65258	19
20	14.94232	15.03123	15.12022	15.20928	15.29843	15.38735	15.47695	15.56632	20
21	14.86493	14.95473	15.04460	15.13455	15.22456	15.31465	15.40480	15.49502	21
22	14.80041	14.89101	14.98168	15.07242	15.16322	15.25408	15.34501	15.43599	22
23	14.74654	14.83786	14.92925	15.02070	15.11221	15.20377	15.29538	15.38704	23
24	14.70150	14.79348	14.88551	14.97759	15.06973	15.16191	15.25414	15.34641	24
25	14.66380	14.75636	14.84897	14.94162	15.03432	15.12706	15.21984	15.31265	25
26	14.63222	14.72530	14.81843	14.91159	15.00478	15.09802	15.19128	15.28458	26
27	14.60575	14.69929	14.79287	14.88649	14.98013	15.07380	15.16749	15.26121	27
28	14.58354	14.67750	14.77148	14.86550	14.95953	15.05359	15.14766	15.24176	28
29	14.56490	14.65922	14.75357	14.84793	14.94232	15.03672	15.13113	15.22556	29
30	14.54924	14.64389	14.73856	14.83324	14.92793	15.02263	15.11734	15.21205	30
31	14.53610	14.63103	14.72598	14.82093	14.91589	15.01086	15.10582	15.20080	31
32	14.52505	14.62024	14.71543	14.81062	14.90582	15.00102	15.09622	15.19141	32
33	14.51576	14.61117	14.70658	14.80199	14.89740	14.99280	15.08819	15.18358	33
34	14.50795	14.60356	14.69916	14.79476	14.89034	14.98592	15.08149	15.17705	34
35	14.50139	14.59717	14.69294	14.78869	14.88444	14.98017	15.07590	15.17160	35

BLENDED MONTHLY PAYMENT FACTORS FOR A LOAN OF $1,000

YEARS AMORT	19%	19 1/8%	19 1/4%	19 3/8%
1	91.81751	91.87271	91.92790	91.98308
2	50.06377	50.11987	50.17597	50.23208
3	36.29746	36.35574	36.41405	36.47238
4	29.52615	29.58690	29.64769	29.70853
5	25.55082	25.61410	25.67744	25.74083
6	22.97138	23.03717	23.10303	23.16895
7	21.18748	21.25572	21.32403	21.39242
8	19.89869	19.96929	20.03997	20.11074
9	18.93795	19.01080	19.08375	19.15679
10	18.20489	18.27988	18.35497	18.43015
11	17.63555	17.71256	17.78966	17.86687
12	17.18726	17.26615	17.34515	17.42424
13	16.83045	16.91110	16.99185	17.07270
14	16.54400	16.62628	16.70866	16.79113
15	16.31246	16.39623	16.48010	16.56407
16	16.12424	16.20939	16.29464	16.37997
17	15.97056	16.05697	16.14346	16.23004
18	15.84461	15.93216	16.01978	16.10749
19	15.74108	15.82966	15.91831	16.00703
20	15.65576	15.74527	15.83485	15.92449
21	15.58531	15.67565	15.76606	15.85652
22	15.52703	15.61813	15.70927	15.80048
23	15.47876	15.57052	15.66233	15.75419
24	15.43873	15.53109	15.62349	15.71592
25	15.40550	15.49839	15.59131	15.68426
26	15.37790	15.45126	15.56464	15.65804
27	15.35496	15.44872	15.54251	15.63631
28	15.33587	15.43000	15.52415	15.61830
29	15.31999	15.41444	15.50890	15.60336
30	15.30677	15.40150	15.49623	15.59097
31	15.29577	15.39074	15.48571	15.58068
32	15.28660	15.38179	15.47697	15.57214
33	15.27896	15.37433	15.46970	15.56505
34	15.27260	15.36813	15.46365	15.55916
35	15.26729	15.36297	15.45863	15.55427

AMORTIZATION PERIODS 1 TO 35 YEARS

19 1/2%	19 5/8%	19 3/4%	19 7/8%	YEARS AMORT
92.03825	92.09341	92.14857	92.20372	1
50.28820	50.34433	50.40047	50.45661	2
36.53074	36.58913	36.64754	36.70597	3
29.76940	29.83031	29.89126	29.95226	4
25.80427	25.86777	25.93132	25.99492	5
23.23494	23.30100	23.36712	23.43330	6
21.46089	21.52943	21.59805	21.66674	7
20.18159	20.25253	20.32355	20.39465	8
19.22991	19.30313	19.37643	19.44982	9
18.50543	18.58080	18.65627	18.73183	10
17.94417	18.02157	18.09907	18.17666	11
17.50344	17.58273	17.66211	17.74160	12
17.15365	17.23469	17.31584	17.39707	13
16.87370	16.95636	17.03912	17.12197	14
16.64813	16.73228	16.81652	16.90085	15
16.46539	16.55090	16.63649	16.72217	16
16.31670	16.40344	16.49026	16.57716	17
16.19527	16.28313	16.37107	16.45908	18
16.09583	16.18470	16.27363	16.36263	19
16.01420	16.10397	16.19380	16.28369	20
15.94705	16.03763	16.12826	16.21895	21
15.89173	15.98303	16.07438	16.16577	22
15.84609	15.93803	16.03001	16.12203	23
15.80840	15.90091	15.99345	16.08602	24
15.77724	15.87025	15.96329	16.05635	25
15.75147	15.84492	15.93839	16.03188	26
15.73014	15.82398	15.91783	16.01170	27
15.71247	15.80665	15.90084	15.99503	28
15.69783	15.79231	15.88679	15.98127	29
15.68570	15.78044	15.87517	15.96990	30
15.67564	15.77060	15.86556	15.96051	31
15.66730	15.76246	15.85761	15.95274	32
15.66039	15.75571	15.85103	15.94632	33
15.65465	15.75012	15.84558	15.94102	34
15.64989	15.74549	15.84107	15.93663	35

Index